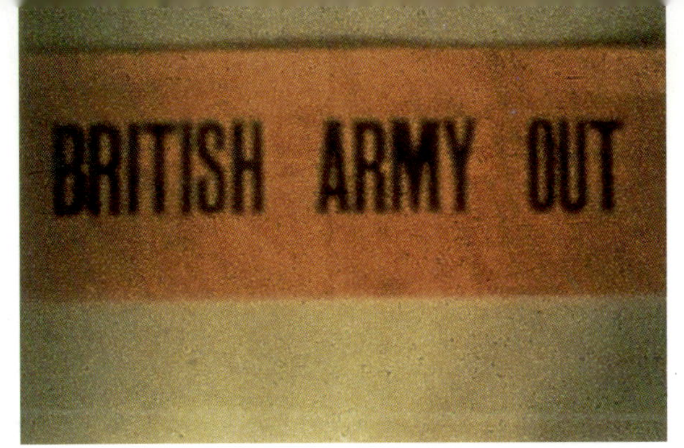

BRITISH ARMY OUT

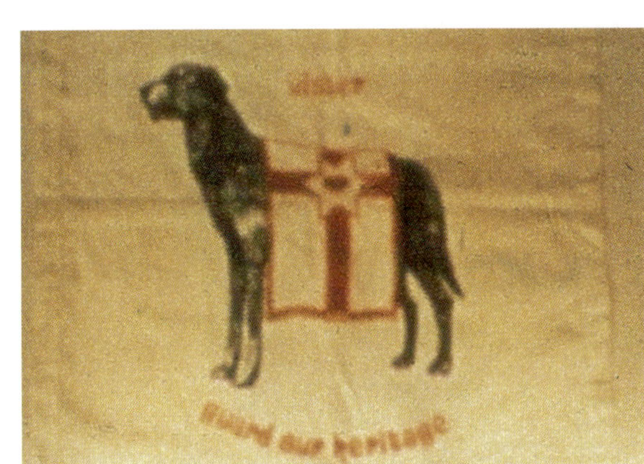

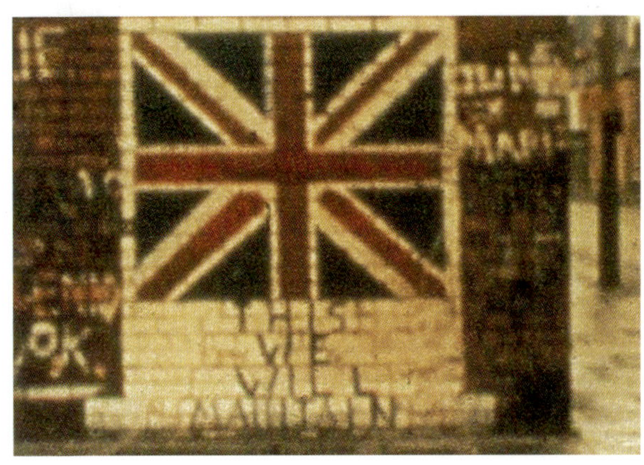

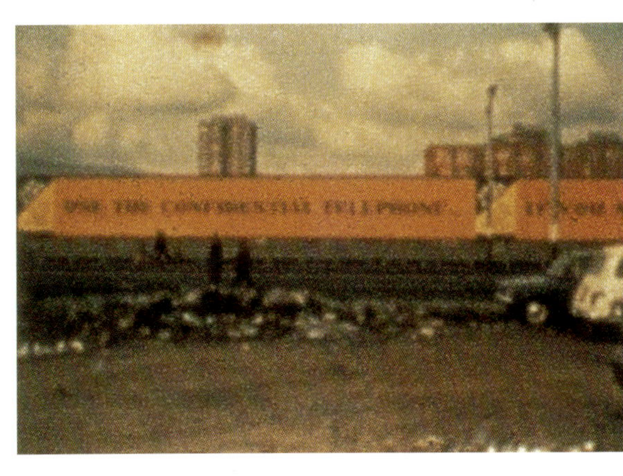

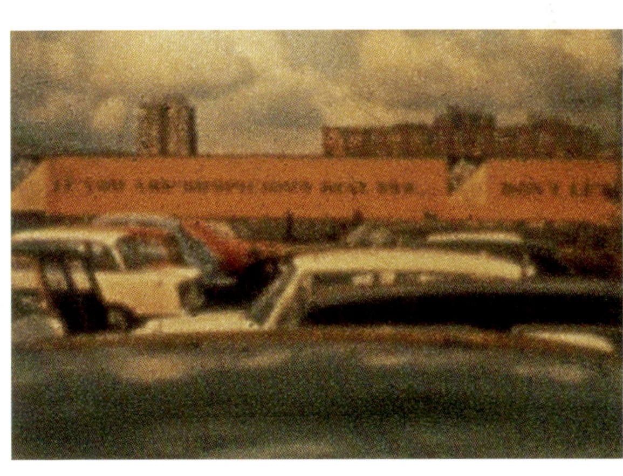

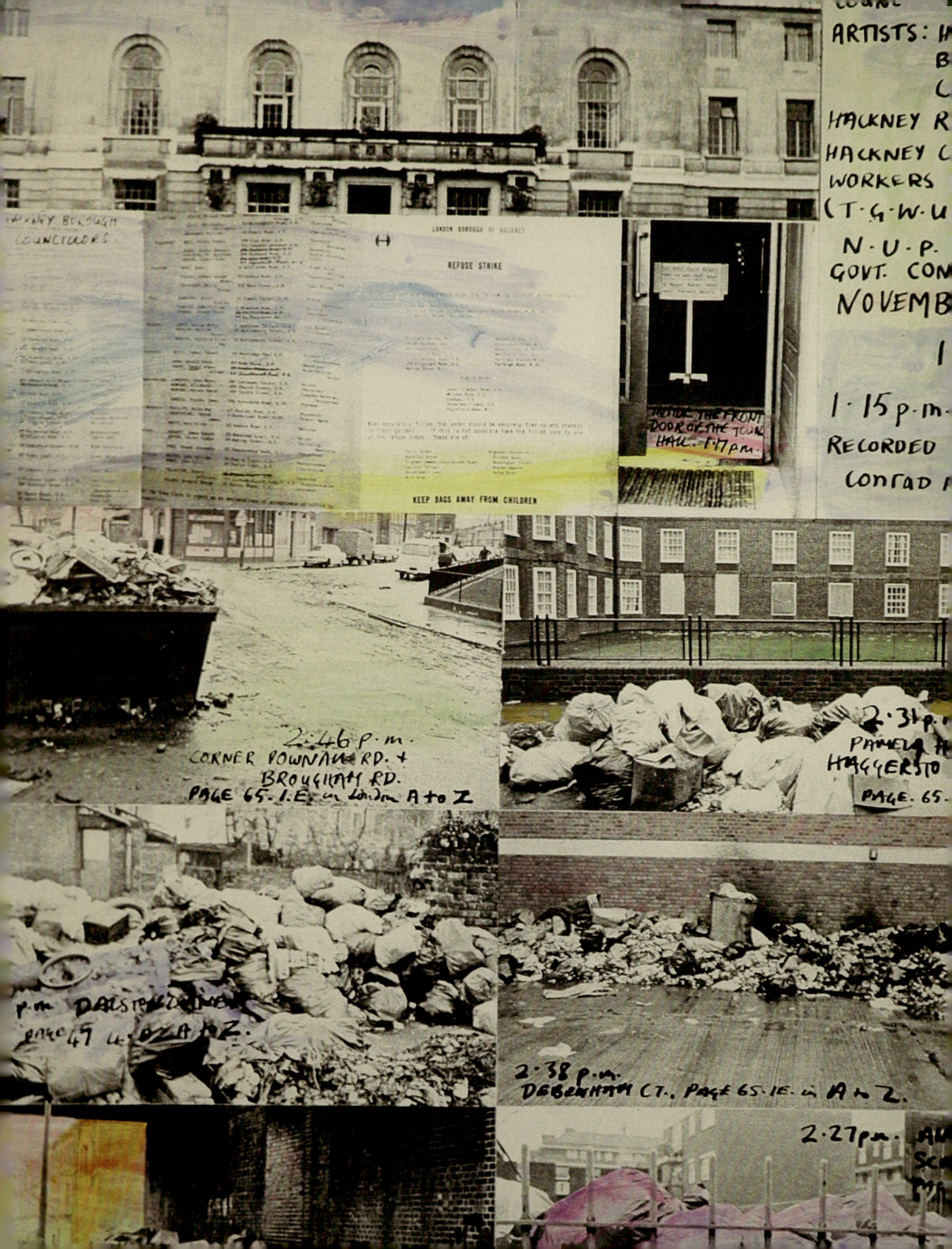
ARTISTS: H
B
C
HACKNEY R
HACKNEY C
WORKERS
(T·G·W·U
N·U·P·
GOVT. CON
NOVEMB
1
1·15 p·m·
RECORDED
Conrad
HACKNEY BOROUGH
COUNCILLORS
INSIDE THE FRONT
DOOR OF THE TOWN
HALL. 1·17 p·m.
2·46 p·m·
CORNER POWNALL RD. +
BROUGHAM RD.
PAGE 65. I.E. in London A to Z
2·31 p·
PAMELA
HAGGERSTO
PAGE. 65.
p·m DALSTON
PAGE 47 4.0Z A to Z.
2·38 p·m.
DEBENHAM CT. PAGE 65. I.E. in A to Z.
2·27p·m. AM
SC
M
LONDON BOROUGH OF HACKNEY
REFUSE STRIKE
KEEP BAGS AWAY FROM CHILDREN

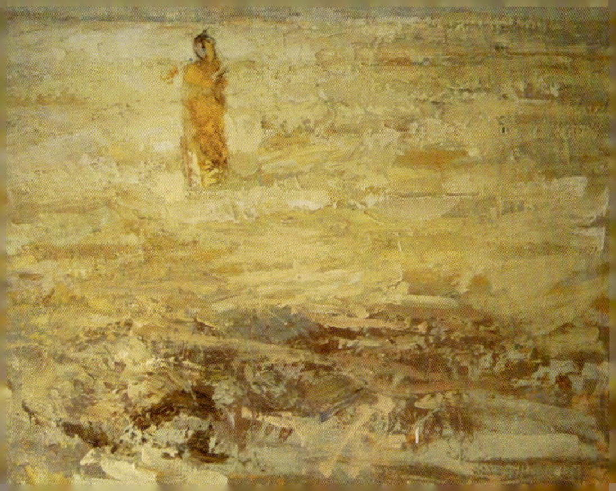

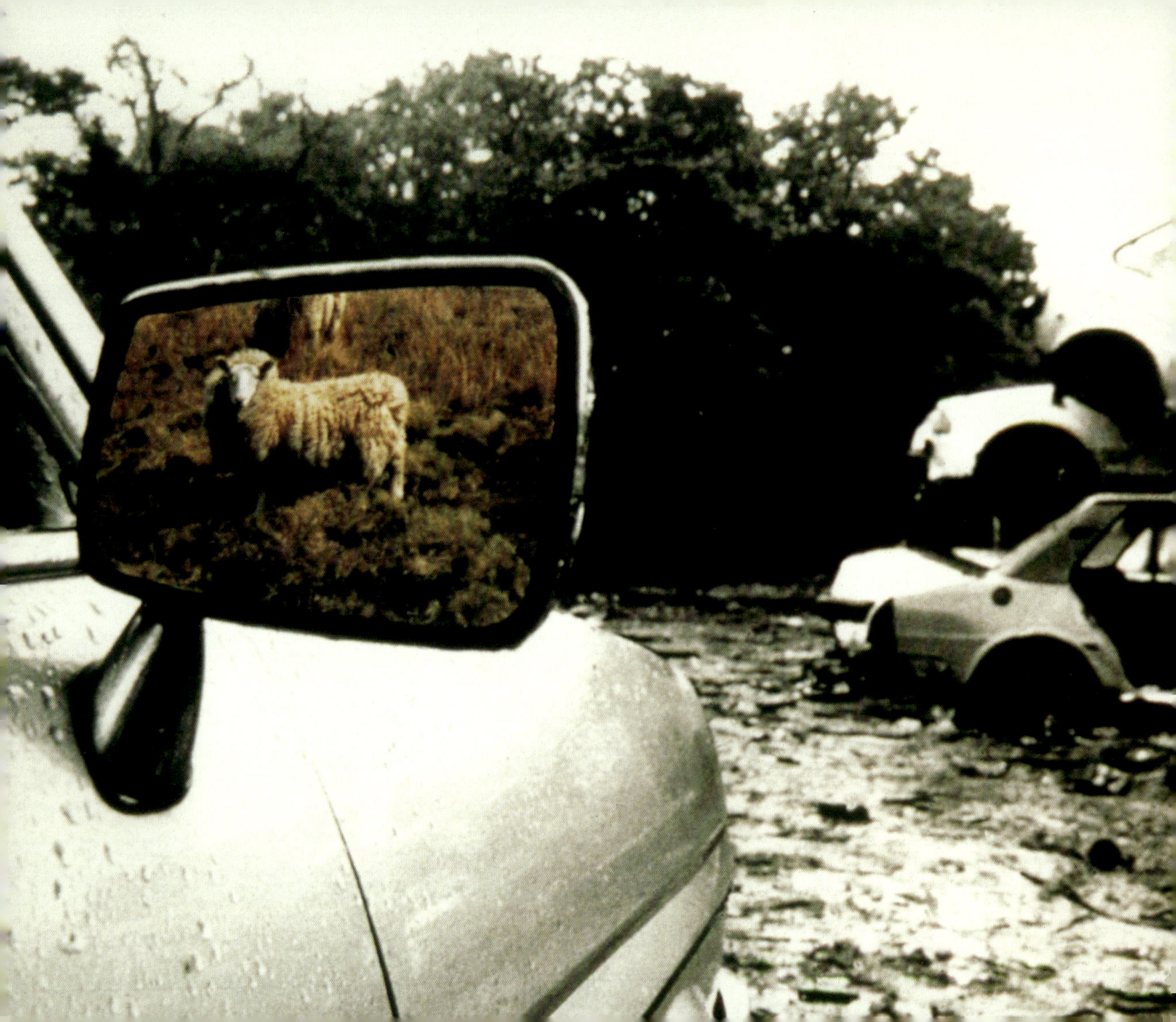

CONRAD ATKINSON LANDESCAPES

DESIGN BY JOHN ISAACS
PRINTED IN USA BY CAPITAL OFFSET, CONCORD NH

     JY 07 '08

THE PUBLICATION OF THIS BOOK HAS BEEN MADE POSSIBLE
BY THE KIND COOPERATION AND GENEROUS SUPPORT OF
RONALD FELDMAN FINE ARTS.

PUBLISHED BY
JOHN ISAACS BOOKS
WILLOWDALE FARM CLAVERACK NY 12513 USA
518-851-5905

DISTRIBUTED BY
TURNAROUND PUBLISHER SERVICES LTD. www.turnaround-psl.com

ISBN 0-9772971-0-1

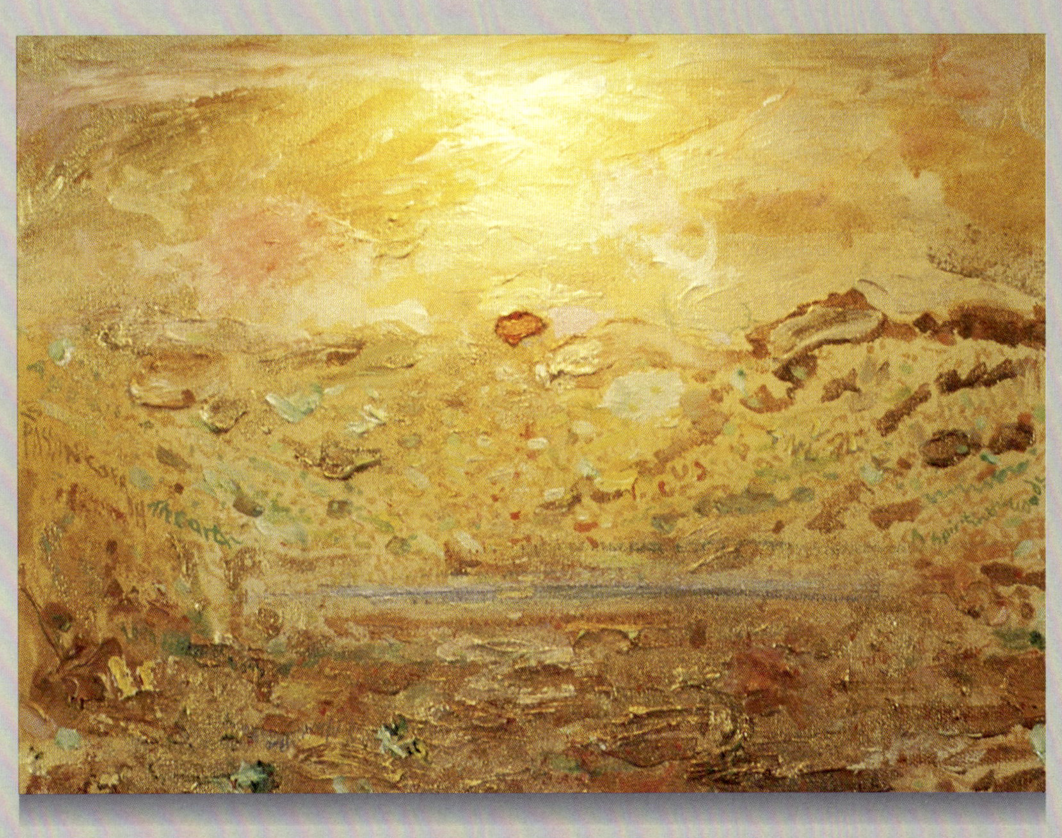

ACKNOWLEDGMENTS

In the preparation of this book, I wish to acknowledge with much gratitude the help, work, and invaluable advice of
Margaret Harrison, Ronald Feldman, and John Isaacs, and the insightful contributions of Richard Cork and Antony Hudek.
I am also naturally indebted to the numerous collectors, galleries, and museums whose support I have received over
the years, and, last but not least, to the unquavering support of my beautiful daughters Sophie and Katie.

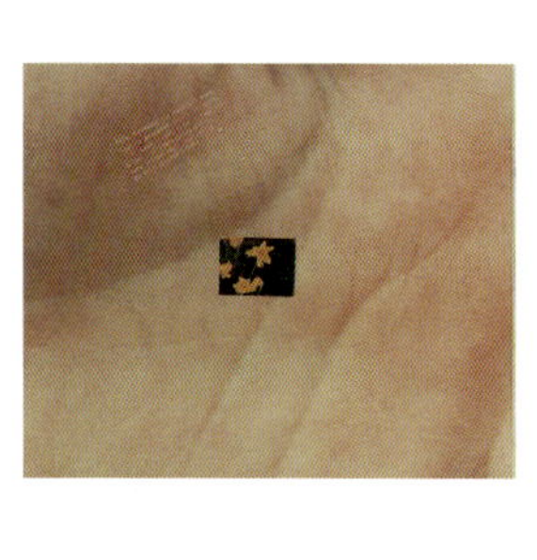
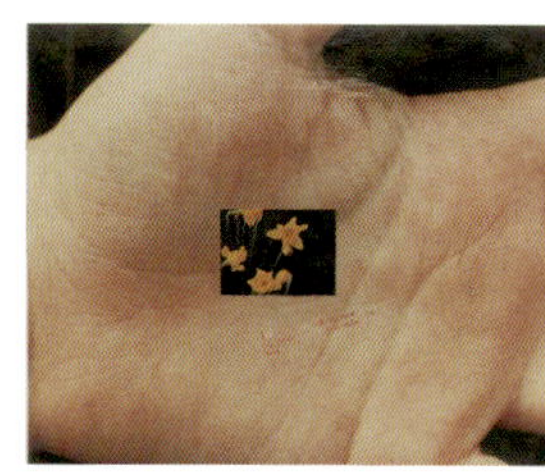
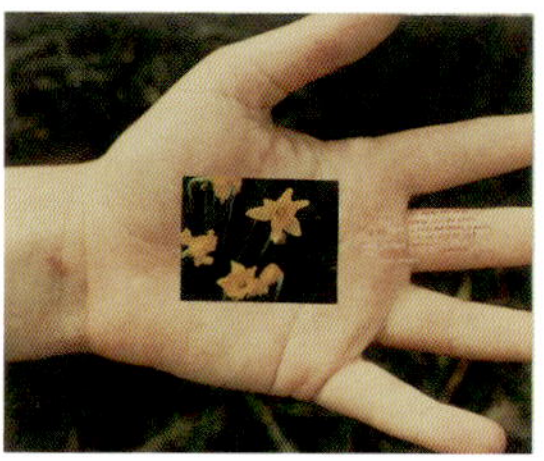
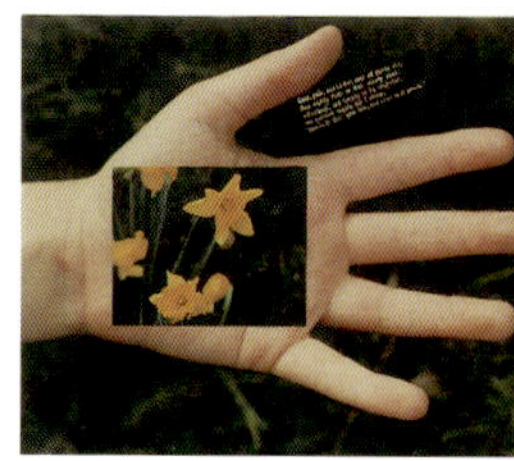
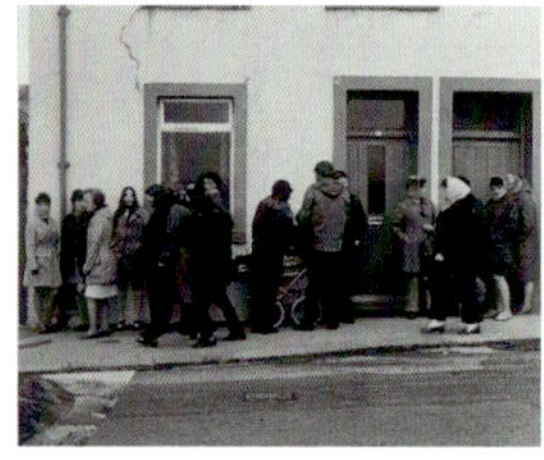
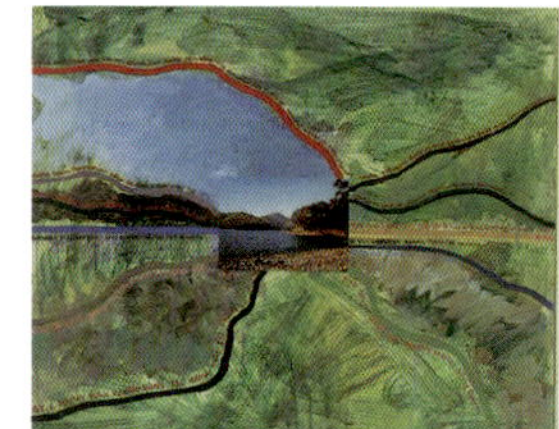

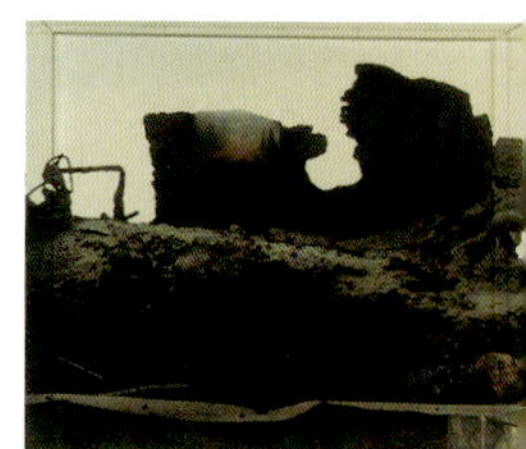

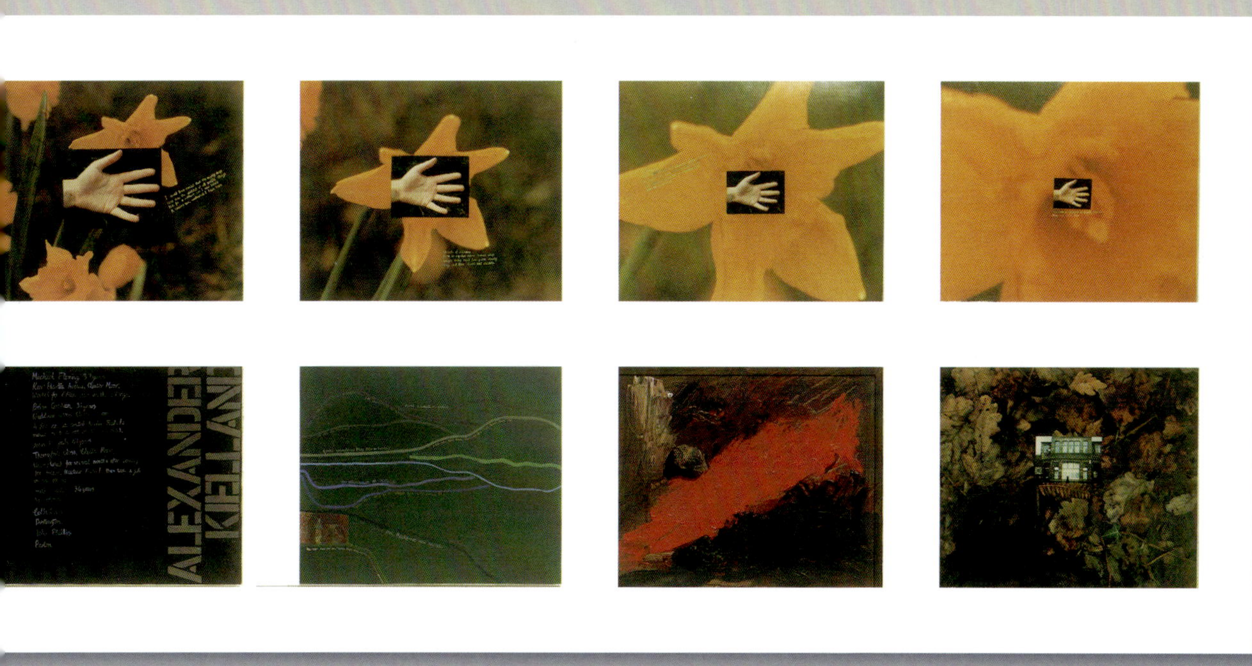

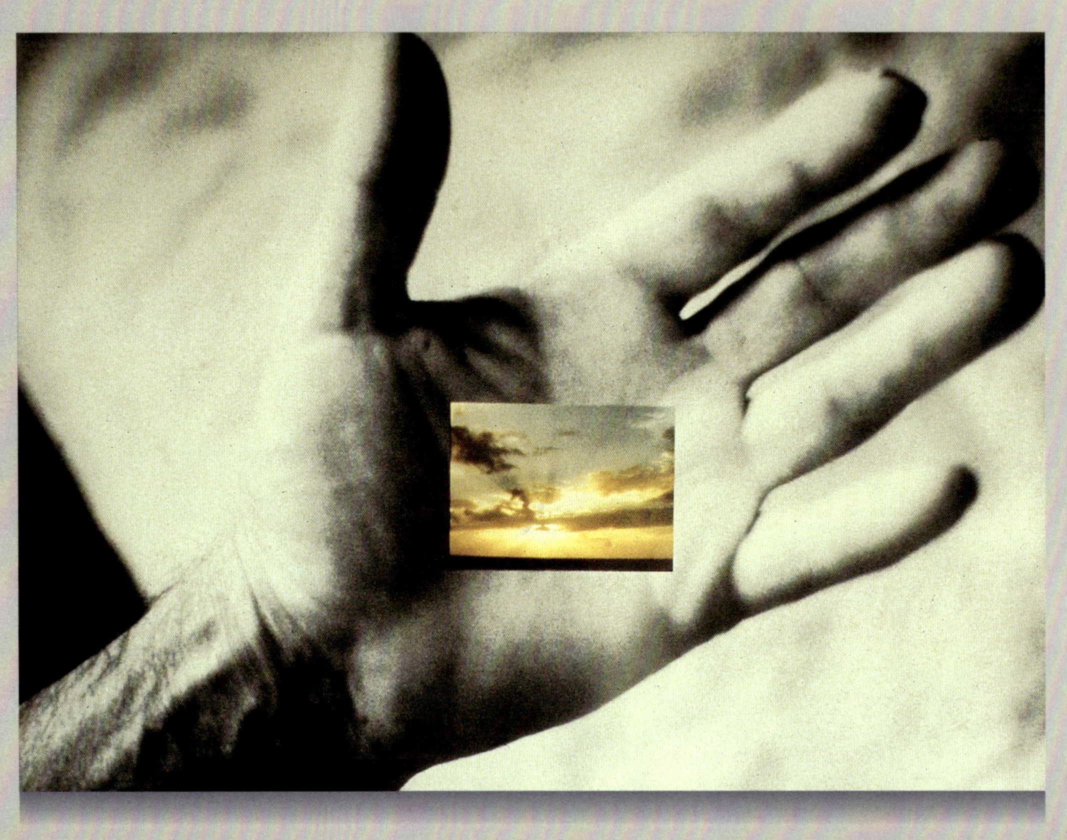

CONRAD ATKINSON: A NEW BEGINNING
BY RICHARD CORK

He intended it as a terminal gesture, concluding his involvement with art once and for all. But when the ICA invited Conrad Atkinson to show at its resplendent metropolitan premises overlooking The Mall, his first London exhibition ended up turning into a new beginning.

The year was 1972, and he had spent most of the previous decade training and then practicing as an artist in the modernist tradition. After studying at his local college of art in Carlisle and then Liverpool, he took his painting degree at the Royal Academy Schools in London. Over that six-year period, Atkinson moved from the austere figurative idiom of his resolute nineteen year-old self-portrait to large abstract canvases. He may have called some of them the *Hiroshima* series, in the hope that his form of abstraction could somehow grapple with the shaping political events of the twentieth century. But he never felt at ease with the alien world of West End dealers and galleries. 'I felt like a working-class astronaut in middle-class space.' Atkinson recalled later, and only a couple of years after graduating he virtually abandoned his commitment to painting.

Having gone to Carlisle College imagining that art was a central activity, he came to the conclusion in the late 1960s that it had become hopelessly marginalized. The work he was encouraged to produce, during his student years, bore no relation to the world he grew up in during and immediately after the Second World War. His childhood had been spent in Cleator Moor, a depressed West Cumbrian area where the closure of coal-mines was creating widespread unemployment. Atkinson's grandfather, who exerted a powerful influence on the boy, had played an active and respected role in the community. As the miners' agent and union man in West Cumberland, he was an outspoken fighter for workers' rights. Most of the people on the housing estate where Atkinson's family lived were Irish Catholics, descended from immigrants who had crossed the sea to find work as miners in the Victorian era.

Towards the end of the Second World War, when Atkinson was around five years old, he helped his grandfather finish a painting of a silver hammer and sickle on a red sheet. They displayed it outside the window of their council house at the heart of the estate, possibly to celebrate a notable Russian victory against Hitler. Atkinson never forgot this formative experience, which involved using a paintbrush to produce an image hung, for everyone to see and understand, in the middle of a tight-knit community. Although he eventually realized that life in West Cumberland was claustrophobic, the values upheld by his family encouraged him to believe in the importance of culture and education. Old Labour supporters knew that colleges could provide the key to a better existence, and Atkinson's parents were impressed when he won a prize for designing a book jacket. They approved of his decision to study art in Carlisle, and his grandfather undoubtedly felt that 'the finer things of life' could enhance everyone's surroundings. In this respect, William Morris's influence still lingered in socialist circles, but it was very far removed from the priorities of an art-school generation for whom Jackson Pollock and the New York avant-garde were supreme. The more Atkinson studied at his successive colleges, the more estranged he felt from the beliefs that had governed his boyhood.

In order to recover his lost sense of an engagement with contemporary issues, Atkinson turned away from painting in 1967 and began producing posters. They were focused, with polemical intent, on political causes of the day, most dramatically the tragic spate of assassinations that destroyed Martin Luther King, Bobby Kennedy, and Malcolm X. But poster-making did not solve the main problem confronting Atkinson at that turbulent time, when the entire activity called 'art' was being challenged and redefined in so many different ways by the emergent generation. He felt increasingly dissatisfied with the level of debate, which often remained at a philosophical level and avoided acknowledging the importance of subject-matter.

That is why Atkinson responded so defiantly to the ICA's invitation. He was only prepared to mount a show there if it took the form of an attack on art. Conceived as a disenchanted farewell rather than an auspicious debut, the exhibition was pitched at the rawest possible level. And Atkinson deliberately turned back to his roots, telling the ICA that there was only one thing he intended to deal with: the current strike in his home town.

A year before, Brannan Thermometers factory in Cleator Moor had become the arena for a major dispute. The management gave certain members of the work-force a privileged status, and the rest of the factory reacted with indignation. In June 1971 they withdrew their labor, announcing that the preferential treatment was at once arbitrary and unjustified. Since the management refused to respond, the dispute focused on the workers' right to be consulted and have a say in their own conditions. Outside help was brought in to keep the factory running, but eighty union members continued to picket Brannan's day and night. Since Atkinson had gone to school with many of the strikers, he felt passionately about their predicament and wanted to help them bring about significant change. So he set to work, amassing a formidable amount of carefully researched evidence from the battleground itself.

All this material was used in the ICA exhibition. Tersely entitled *Strike*, it included letters, written statements, photographs, and interviews constantly transmitted on three video monitors. The show as a whole refused to rely on the impact of a documentary program, where everything is summarized and punched across with an emphasis on dramatic effect. Instead, Atkinson provided the viewer with a mass of data which could only be absorbed fully after prolonged, detailed scrutiny. His own loyalties could be discerned, above all in the emotive contrast between photographs of the factory owners' resplendent houses and the stark hardship so evident in the workers' home surroundings. *Strike* ended up unequivocally condemning the management, but it adopted the tone of an inquiry rather than a polemic.

The gallery was even transformed into an arena for a well-attended meeting of strikers and local MPs. Considerable publicity was generated, drawing national attention to a dispute that had failed, initially, to attract the press coverage it deserved. Women's groups joined in the discussions, reflecting their awareness that the strike had largely been organized by a dedicated women's work-force. Atkinson made prints for sale at the exhibition, to help raise money for the strike fund. And as a result of all these efforts, Brannan's London factory was unionized. It was an remarkable victory, proving that artists can indeed have direct political effect if their focus is defined with sufficient clarity and conviction.

Judged as a work of art, though, *Strike* was considered less successful. Writing in the *Evening Standard*, I agreed that 'the medium of an art exhibition does provide a marvelously free forum for the promotion of such a committed viewpoint.' But I concluded that, compared with a television program on the same subject, 'this gallery-full of data seems undeniably hamfisted.' The final word stung Atkinson into writing a pugnacious letter to the *Evening Standard*. We subsequently exchanged correspondence and met for the first time. The following year, he contributed a work called *Wage Differential* to my *Critic's Choice* exhibition in London. More tightly organized and refined than *Strike* had been, it prophesied the direction Atkinson would take in his 1974 show at the ICA.

Although *Work, Wages and Prices* did not target a solitary example of industrial conflict, it shared *Strike's* belief in taking social injustice as its theme. To this extent, Atkinson still aimed at changing the consciousness of exhibition visitors by inviting them to think in a harder, more concentrated way about his chosen subject. On another level, however, *Work, Wages and Prices* was directed at an art audience rather than the world of strikers, unions, and bosses that he had addressed in his previous ICA show. In *Strike*, one wall was devoted to worker/management while the other concentrated on meetings and fundraising. In *Work, Wages and Prices*, by contrast, the principal argument was put forward in a sequence of printed cards running relentlessly round the room's four walls.

The very first card announced the principal thrust of the exhibition with startling clarity: 'Wealth is considerably more unequally distributed in Britain than in the United States despite all its millionaires and billionaires.' Anyone who doubted the accuracy of that statement was subjected, in the remaining cards, to a barrage of examples. The salaries of the wealthiest were spelled out, and contrasted with the abject take-home pay of the poorest. The burgeoning price of property in the most expensive areas of London was set against the alarming number of homeless families in the same metropolis. And the capricious, self-indulgent eating habits of the rich were placed in the gruesome context of an old woman who had died on Christmas Eve, after desperately struggling to keep alive by devouring cardboard.

While visitors followed the devastating analysis spelled out in the cards, they became aware of the pay-slips running along the walls above. The figures printed there disclosed just how wretched the income of a farm worker, a railway maintenance man, or a student nurse really was. Then, on a visual level, the conditions endured by the work-force in a factory was revealed in a strip of contact prints. And finally, at the very top, Atkinson displayed a ticker-tape reel from the Stock Exchange registering the incessant changes in the price of shares.

There seemed to be no escape from the evidence marshaled there, like exhibits in a particularly damning courtroom prosecution. Elsewhere in the room a trio of screens transmitted images from the streets, where graffiti protesting about rents were filmed alongside posters, advertisements and mass demonstrations. Compared with the crisply edited techniques deployed in a hard-hitting television documentary, Atkinson's approach seemed lacking in immediate, visceral impact. On a formal level, his organization of purged and rectilinear elements owed much to Malevich and Mondrian at their most austere. But after a while, his dogged insistence on piling up the evidence paid dividends. The very lack of showmanship or 'artistic' pyrotechnics ensured that nothing distracted attention from the exhibition's central thrust.

Because everyone knows about the social inequalities he exposed at the ICA, they often prove easy to ignore. But Atkinson did not let the visitor evade them for an instant. They were foregrounded at every turn, and viewers also found themselves encouraged to participate by supplying comments or contributions of their own. To that extent, Atkinson demonstrated how well he understood the conventions of an art exhibition, establishing a forum for debate throughout the duration of his tough, single-minded show.

A year later, the Arts Council of Northern Ireland and the Irish Congress of Trade Unions asked Atkinson to stage an exhibition in Belfast. While expecting him to tackle an Irish subject, they did not specify what his theme should be. But so far as he was concerned, the chronic political unrest in the country could not be avoided. Traveling round Armagh, Belfast and Derry, Atkinson found that the tragedy of a divided country impinged on his consciousness, and his conscience, wherever he looked. Talking to people, taking photographs, writing notes, and collecting found objects, he assembled a profoundly unsettling abundance of material for his exhibition at the Arts Council Gallery in Belfast.

Subsequently shown at Art Net in London, the show was called *A Shade of Green, An Orange Edge*. But if anybody imagined that Atkinson would offer a quiet, pleasing meditation on color, they were swiftly disillusioned. From the start, he set out to explore the aggression, bitterness, despair, and occasional sardonic humor abounding in Northern Irish life. 'No Surrender' cried the slogan painted on a Spar Foodmarket roof. Atkinson's photograph of this resolute graffito set the tone for the rest of the exhibition, riddled as it was with militant defiance on every side. 'This we will maintain' declared the inscription above the Queen's image on a drum, whereas a sticker on a plastic bucket called for 'Troops Out Now'. The heat generated by all these conflicting exhortations was so intense that it did not need any further rhetoric on Atkinson's part. Quite the reverse: the cool, methodical reticence of his marshaling skills threw all the uncompromising hatred into bleak relief. The exhibition gained enormously from the artist's refusal to organize his findings in an emotive way.

Only once did he permit himself to highlight an image with conspicuous drama. Having obtained permission to photograph a bloodsmeared banner that once covered victims of the Bloody Sunday massacre, Atkinson repeated the picture thirteen times in a row. He also included newspaper images of people killed on that terrible day, along with verbal testimonies by eye-witnesses. Written statements played a powerful role in this exhibition, and Atkinson heightened their significance by printing them on green, orange, or white cards. Far from using color in an abstract manner, like so many modernist painters, he let it pinpoint the political sympathies of the statements.

As in *Strike*, Atkinson showed no hesitation in assailing visitors with a daunting profusion of material. But the sheer quantity of visual and verbal information seemed an appropriate way to deal with the avalanche of militant signs and symbols confronting everyone who visits Northern Ireland. Atkinson imprisoned his visitors inside a room packed with explosive comments and equally incendiary images, like the implacable silhouette of a gun daubed on a concrete motorway wall. And he reinforced them with a fusillade of remarks written by people who had reacted strongly to his Belfast installment of the show. 'God Save Ireland! (Nobody else will)' conveyed a sense of desperation echoed by many, and yet one visitor contributed a note of complaint: 'There are beautiful people, beautiful buildings, beautiful scenes in this country. Why aren't they here, please?'

The contents of Atkinson's show provided its own implicit reply to that bewildered and indignant question. Faced with the grueling reality of civil struggle, he could not pretend that it somehow did not exist and concentrate instead on pastoral idylls. Besides, he had written in the exhibition catalogue that the show was 'really pointing to priorities and only when the soil bed of such issues is lain will it be possible for me to plant or paint flowers.' His attitude was entirely understandable. Atkinson aimed at using the exhibition as a catalyst for change, even if Northern Ireland's problems appeared so deep-seated that optimism was difficult to sustain. What possible way forward could there be, at a time when everything seemed mired in hatred, violence, and mistrust?

One answer lay in the campaign for a Bill of Rights. Impressed by such an eminently achievable cause, Atkinson made sure that the video section of his show focused on discussions of this key issue by the Northern Ireland Civil Rights Association and the Ulster Citizens Civil Liberties Centre. Their stubborn, resolute hope offered a reassuring and much-needed contrast to many of the comments recorded elsewhere in the show, ranging from 'Northern Ireland has a problem for every solution' to the British soldier who protested that 'we are here to be targets while the politicians mark time.'

The most inspirational contribution to the video sequences came from Fenner Brockway, who had given a speech opening Atkinson's show in Belfast. He insisted on cutting through the miasma of negation and declaring that 'there is an extraordinary unanimity of opinion in Northern Ireland about the need for a Bill of Civil Rights.' So at the centre of all the visual images displayed in the exhibition, where partisan murals depicting King William riding a white horse were juxtaposed with diehard citizens wearing clothes emblazoned with patterns from the Union Jack, a palpable source of progress was identified. On one card, Atkinson had recorded a slogan on a Ballymurphy wall asking: 'Is there a life before death?' But his decision to concentrate on the Bill of Rights suggested that despair was premature, and that contemporary artists could lend their energies to a thoroughgoing exploration of the tragedy.

After taking on such an enormous and multi-faceted subject, Atkinson decided in 1978 to aim at a tightly defined target. He was invited, as a member of the Slade School of Art's teaching staff, to make a print for presentation to the Queen Mother. The gift commemorated the 150th anniversary of University College London, and the mood was supposed to be celebratory. Atkinson, however, had no intention of producing an image replete with blandness and self-congratulation. He realized that the chosen date, in April 1978, also marked the twentieth anniversary of the introduction to Britain of Thalidomide, the drug that ended up damaging the lives of too many babies and their families. So he made his Anniversary Print in the style of a glossy advertisement for Distillers (Biochemicals), the company that began marketing Thalidomide in April 1958.

For two years, it was sold across the counter under the trade name 'Distaval', and Atkinson placed this disastrous product in the foreground of his image. Ranged round it, in a majestic still life, were many of the bottles produced by Distillers in their alcoholic drinks range, including Haig Whisky and Gordon's Gin. They were shown against a backdrop of the City of London, dominated by the dome of St. Paul's Cathedral. But the most damning part of the print was positioned below this glowing image, where the story of Thalidomide was spelled out in words and statistics. Following its withdrawal in 1961, and the acquisition of Distillers (Biochemicals) by an American company, the parents of children who had been blighted by the drug struggled to obtain compensation. Atkinson charted the history of Distillers' reluctant and evasive negotiations with the families, as well as the inadequacy of their eventual offers. At the same time, he specified the colossal profits made by the company. As a final thrust, he noted that 'pleas to Buckingham Palace to withdraw the Royal Warrant from Distillers products fell on deaf ears.' Hence his determination to call this print *A Children's Story (For Her Majesty)*. The bottles grouped in the resplendent image were shown with the Royal Warrant ringed on their labels.

As a result, the Queen Mother was left in no doubt about her family's connection to the tragedy, and Atkinson's print became notorious when Derek Boshier purchased a copy for the Arts Council's collection. He then chose it for inclusion in an exhibition called *Lives*. Writing an angry and outspoken text for the catalogue, Atkinson condemned the Royal Family for 'lending its name' to the Distillers Company. He declared that 'the Royal Family and their advisors have shown a deplorable lack of taste and compassion'—a frontal attack that was bound to cause alarm within the highest Arts Council circles. Atkinson was duly summoned to the council headquarters in Piccadilly and told, without any explanation, that his print had been 'withdrawn' from the *Lives* exhibition. Moreover, his accompanying text was removed from the catalogue, following 'legal advice' taken by the council. After protesting, Atkinson sued the Arts Council for breach of contract and loss of earnings. Two years later, in 1981, he was finally offered compensation and accepted it.

Not that his scrutiny of multinational companies was exhausted. On the contrary: Atkinson's next ICA exhibition, opening in the same year as his settlement with the Arts Council, widened out from Distillers to embrace the overall balance of economic power across the globe. With supreme irony, he couched his show in the language of love. No less than sixteen red hearts were sprayed on the ICA's white walls. They appeared to be the work of a graffiti artist celebrating Valentine's Day, but there was nothing affectionate about the contents of the first heart encountered by exhibition visitors. Inside a watercolor image of a world map, small white cards were assembled in rows with disturbing facts to convey. One of them disclosed that 'in 1979 nearly one third of all world trade was from sales and transfers within multinational corporations.' Different aspects of this disturbing imbalance were scrutinized by other cards, including South America's subservience to a single megacompany's ultra-assertive ambitions.

But Atkinson did not confine himself solely to dissecting big-business monopolies across the globe. In the second heart, he painted a yellow butterfly whose body and wings were choked with packets and tins of insect killer, vegetable pest duster and bird repellent spray. The user-friendly packaging with its purring texts—'now in ready measured sachets'—failed to disguise the unsettling, lethal power of these horticultural weapons. Nor did Atkinson become any less uncompromising in the other hearts. The danger of everything from radiation leakage to irresponsible slimming advertisements was highlighted with the aid of newspaper cuttings, postcard views of verdant landscapes and an abundance of other, carefully selected material. By cramming each heart with so much alarming evidence, he also implied that the body of the world had become congested to bursting-point.

Even when the images suggested jauntiness, they turned out to reflect a deplorable global malaise. A dog appeared in the seventh heart, assembled with considerable wit and vivacity from pet food packets. But its frisky, outflung limbs and erect tail were made from the delicacies that wealthy owners lavish on their animals. Whether 'Good Boy Choc Drops' or 'complete moist meals in individual airtight packs—seafood flavour', they testified to the money lavished on these cosseted favorites. And the two fragments of paper kicked by the dog's hind legs describe how underdeveloped countries, plagued by famine and malnutrition, export an abundance of quality protein to the West. It is a pernicious waste of resources, for the majority of this precious protein is consumed by livestock and pets. While African children starve, our four-legged friends are heaped with an embarrassment of culinary delicacies.

Nor did Atkinson's indictment stop there. The hearts painted on the other wall were stricken with a whole array of different afflictions, including South African apartheid, the threat posed by nuclear extinction, the legacy of Vietnam, and growth of arms manufacturing. Verbal information was given pictorial vitality by watercolor camouflage designs and other pictorial diversions. But the words carried the most unnerving disclosures, like the admission that 'a recent American Alert signaled world-wide preparing all aircraft for takeoff was a mistake, due to the running of a war-game program on a military computer without switching out the connection to the Alert system.'

Conscious perhaps that he might risk wearying the ICA's visitors with a surfeit of words, Atkinson provided respite on the gallery's floor. For the hour-glass arranged there was largely reliant on its visual power alone. Time appeared to be running out within the glass, where one half was engorged with a superfluity of food, armaments, and media overkill while the other half contained only funereal leaves and empty food-bowls. Here, Atkinson reduced the clamor on the walls to a stark, ruthlessly simplified confrontation between rampant excess and destitution. It was plainly intended to stir the onlooker's conscience, and nothing has happened in the decades since this exhibition to ameliorate the ills he deplored.

Moving incessantly between the particular and the universal, Atkinson has devoted much of his subsequent work to generating an awareness of malevolent aggression on the one hand and acute suffering on the other. The deliberate sobriety of his early work, with its emphasis on marshaled facts and documentary images, gave way to a more oblique and visually seductive approach.

It appeared initially in some work stimulated by Atkinson's revaluation of Shelley and Wordsworth. Searching for an English tradition to which he could relate his own work, he found it in Romantic literature. When studying Wordsworth at school, Atkinson had impatiently concluded that the Laureate of the Lakes had no relevance for the people he grew up with on the coastal industrial strip. Subsequently, however, he realized that the young Wordsworth had been fired by an intense revolutionary fervor. Re-reading *The Ruined Cottage*, Atkinson admired Wordsworth's readiness to write about the dilemma of a couple forced to leave their home and, while it decayed, find work elsewhere. The area where Atkinson spent his childhood was similarly blighted, especially in comparison with the contemporary Lake District where tourism thrived and holiday or 'second' homes abounded. So he devoted a major, sixteen-foot work to a meditation called *For Wordsworth; For West Cumbria*, and its acquisition by the Tate Gallery in 1981 meant that his work was now encountered by a wider audience than before. It also ushered in a desire on his part to replace what he called 'bunches of statistics' with a new emphasis on the personal within the collective.

When Atkinson had explored iron-ore mining, he studied hands clubbed and swollen by pneumoconiosis. It inaugurated his fascination with the metaphor of the human body, and *For Wordsworth; For West Cumbria* is dominated in the top row by the motif of the outstretched hand. At first the palm is enormous, containing at its center a diminutive image of nature. But by the end, the hand has shrunk to a minuscule size in relation to the vastly enlarged nature behind. Quotations from Wordsworth, including a heartfelt passage describing how his brother's death at sea transformed the poet's attitude to nature, accompany these images. And then, on the bottom row, Atkinson's own angry images of industrial West Cumbria offer a stark alternative. The Brannan's strike picket is followed by the plight of a nineteenth-century iron-ore miner, whose life was ruined by dispossession. Leaping between past and present, Atkinson encompasses in succeeding panels the death of West Cumbrian migrants on a North Sea oil rig, and a worker at Windscale nuclear power station killed by leukemia at the age of 36. The whole complex work terminates in a bleak image of the unemployment office at Cleator Moor, ironically juxtaposed with a montaged reference to the Lake District. Taken in its entirety, *For Wordsworth; For West Cumbria* takes an impassioned stand against smug, unquestioning ideas about the English landscape. And it is informed by personal anguish, for Atkinson suspects that his own mother and father both died from their working involvement with Windscale.

At heart, the tragedy of human suffering underpins all the disparate subjects Atkinson has tackled. Just as he revivified our understanding of Wordsworth by placing his poetry in the context of Cumbrian unemployment and death, so he prompted us to look with fresh eyes at the Courtauld Collection's medieval and Renaissance paintings. During his period there as Distinguished Visiting Professor in 2002, he became preoccupied with images of martyrdom. Focusing on the idea of 'beautiful mutilations', he realized that the bloodiest and most tortured Courtauld paintings related to his involvement with the imagery of modem war. He aimed at 'breaking open the collection, like a wound', and visitors found Atkinson's work dramatically intervening in the normal gallery display.

'Aesthetics can be a pretty ugly business' announced a digitized embroidery inscription on a Daniel Hechter wool suit. As if to bear out the truth of this paradoxical assertion, Atkinson extracted the gash in Christ's side from a Fra Angelico predella panel. Transferred to a jacket, the blood-soaked wound made the garment resemble evidence discovered at the location of a murder. He even removed the leaves covering Adam and Eve's genitals in a Cranach painting. They were turned into vine-leaf motifs ornamenting the base of a glazed and gold-luster ceramic. But any suspicion that Atkinson had turned the leaves into decorative devices was allayed by our realization that the seductive, glinting ceramic took the form of a land-mine.

Heavily involved with land-mine campaigns over the last decade, Atkinson returns now to the Lake District even more determined to reveal the most radical strain in Wordsworth's vision of the landscape. Before the Romantic era, travelers passing through the Lakes often shunned the terrain. But in his finest poetry, Wordsworth conveyed the full complexity of his clear-eyed response to his homeland, and he was even prepared to arrive at the desolate admission that 'the things which I have seen I now can see no more.' Atkinson persuades us to look at Wordsworth's vision of nature all over again. And *Common Sights*, his exhibition at the Wordsworth Trust, is not afraid to deal with even the most sacrosanct material in audacious new ways.

Atkinson is at his boldest in the textual pieces, where he has the temerity to allow some of Wordsworth's most celebrated poems to be invaded by provocative song writers and rappers of today. Kurt Cobain's suicidal meditation on emotional numbness and heroin abuse is permitted to penetrate Wordsworth's 'To a Butterfly'. But nothing is more calculated to unsettle traditional devotees of the Laureate than Atkinson's radical version of 'Ode: Intimations of Immortality'. Eminem's unbridled rap greeting, 'Hi there little boys and girls (FUCK YOU!)' is allowed to kick-start Atkinson's alternative version. Only then does he allow Wordsworth's sorrowful first line, 'There was a time when meadow, grove, and stream', to enter the poem. From then on, Eminem and Wordsworth fight it out, line after conflicting line. The urge to 'poison squirrels' clashes with 'the earth and every common sight', while 'celestial light' comes up against retarded Bob who 'sits at home and smokes pot.' Gradually, this bizarre interpolation strategy begins to pay off. By the time Wordsworth arrives at the elegiac admission that his childhood vision of nature has been lost, his despair is envenomed by Eminem's everdarkening story of Bob lurking in the nocturnal parking lot for waitresses he wants to murder.

The most powerful part of the poem intercuts between his killings in the woods and Wordsworth's yearning references to the moon's 'delight' or 'waters on a starry night.' They become unexpectedly sinister, and Eminem monopolizes the final lines now that the overall mood has grown so rancid. Terminating in a cri de coeur about a penis 'the size of a peanut', coupled with warnings about the lethal effect of ecstasy, Atkinson's heretical work nevertheless gives new life to the despair in Wordsworth's grim insistence that 'there hath past away a glory from the earth.' With a shock, we realize how this venerated line could have a bearing on our contemporary afflictions as well, including the corrosive evils that Atkinson has spent his career as an artist striving to pinpoint, expose and, in the end, arraign.

Richard Cork is chief art critic of The Times *of London and author of major books on Claes Oldenburg, David Bomberg, and others.*

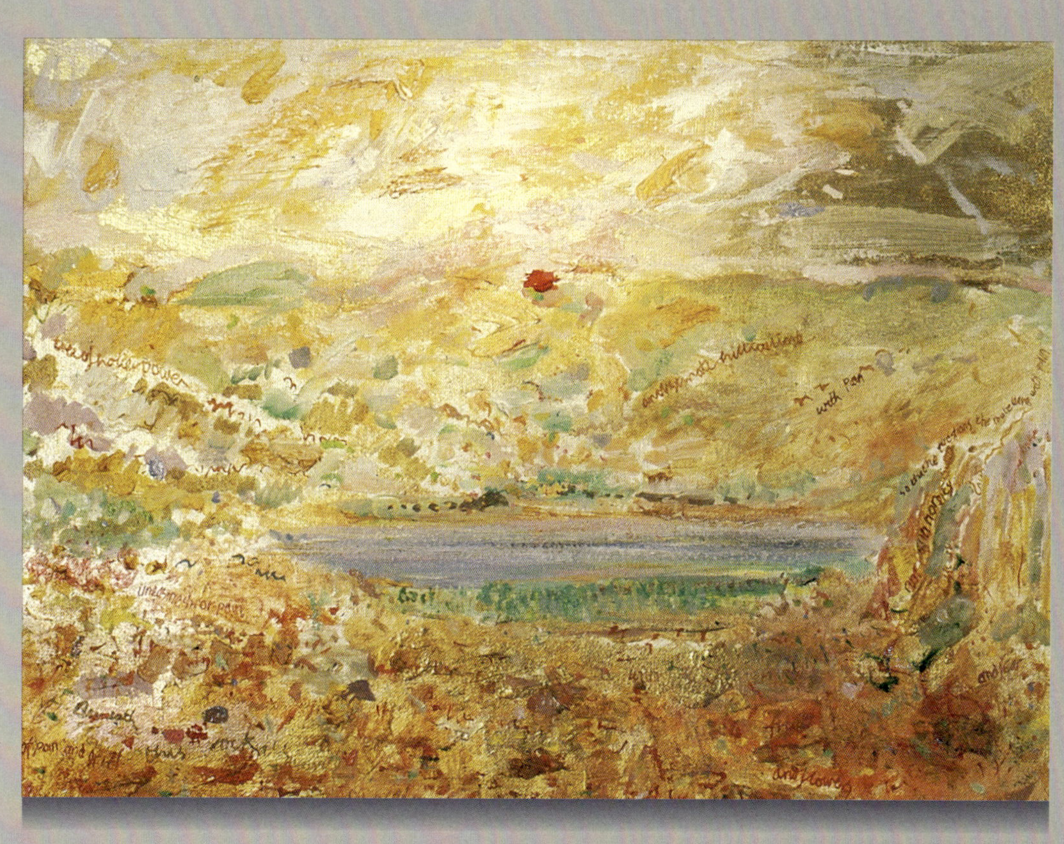

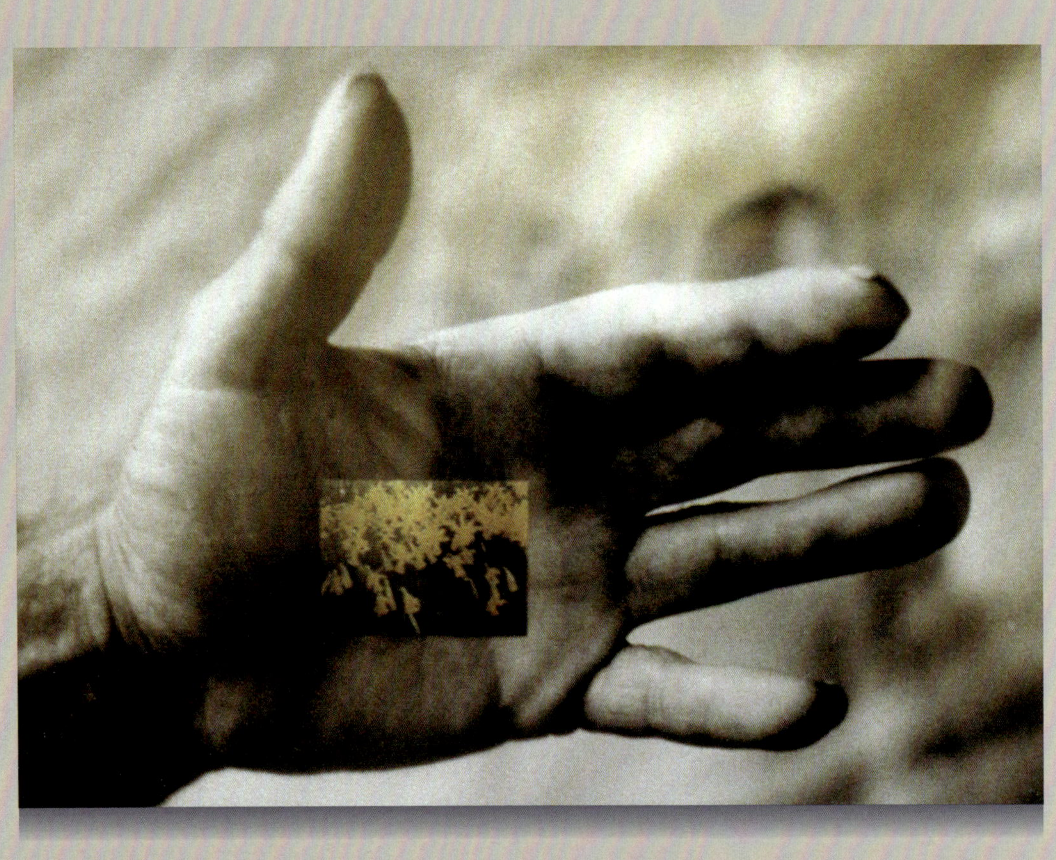

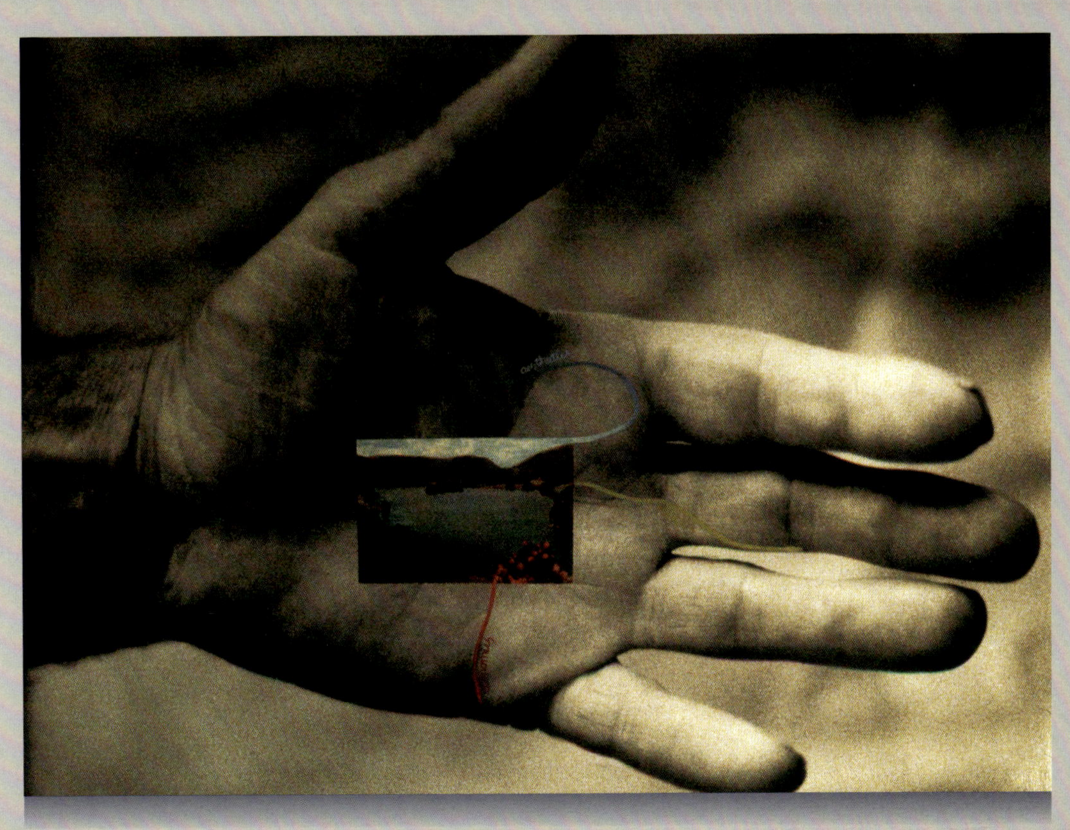

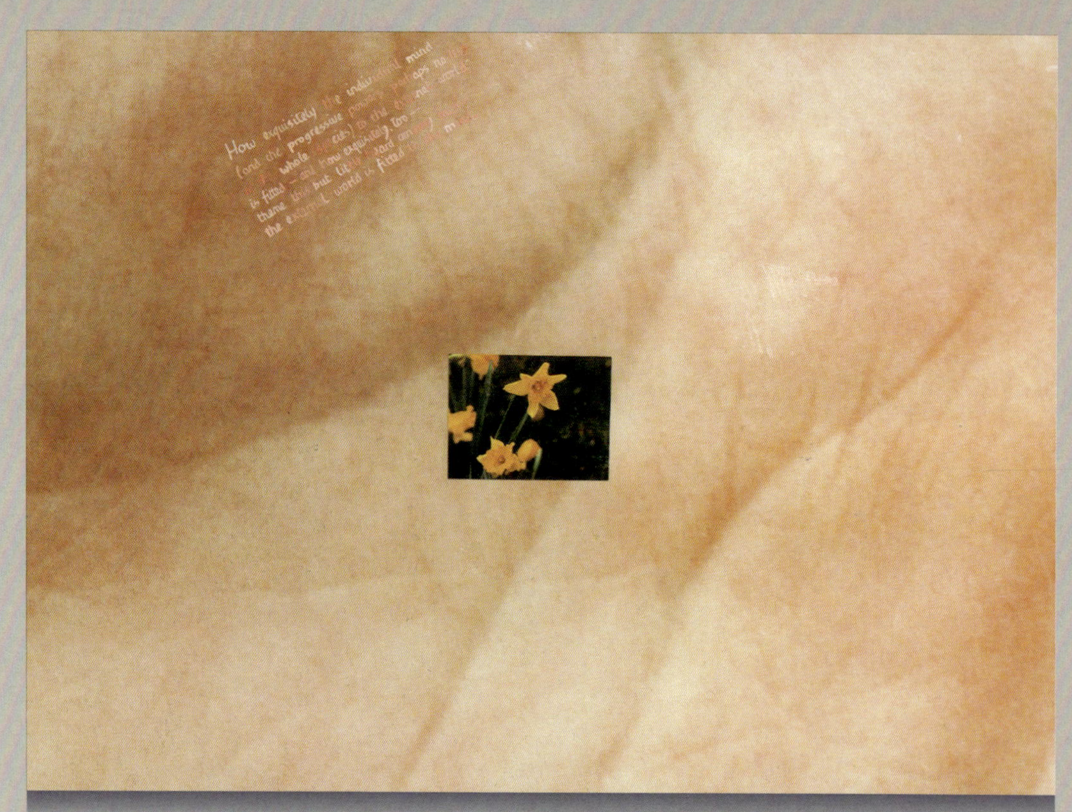

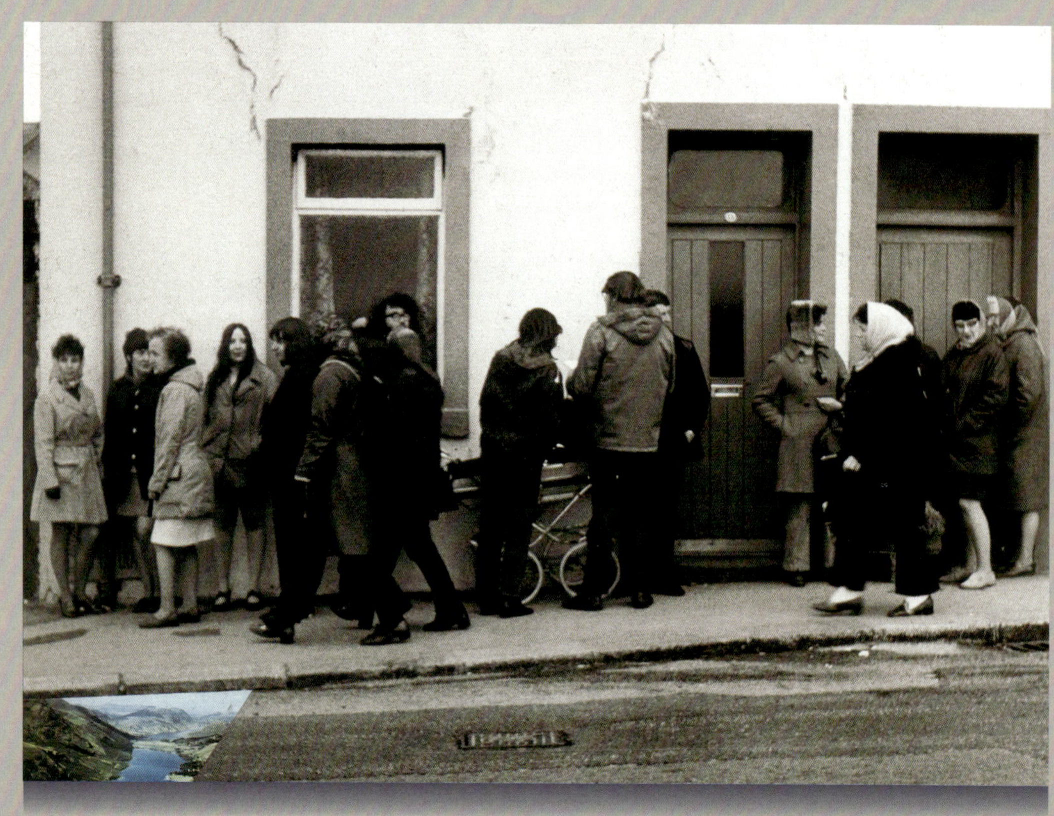

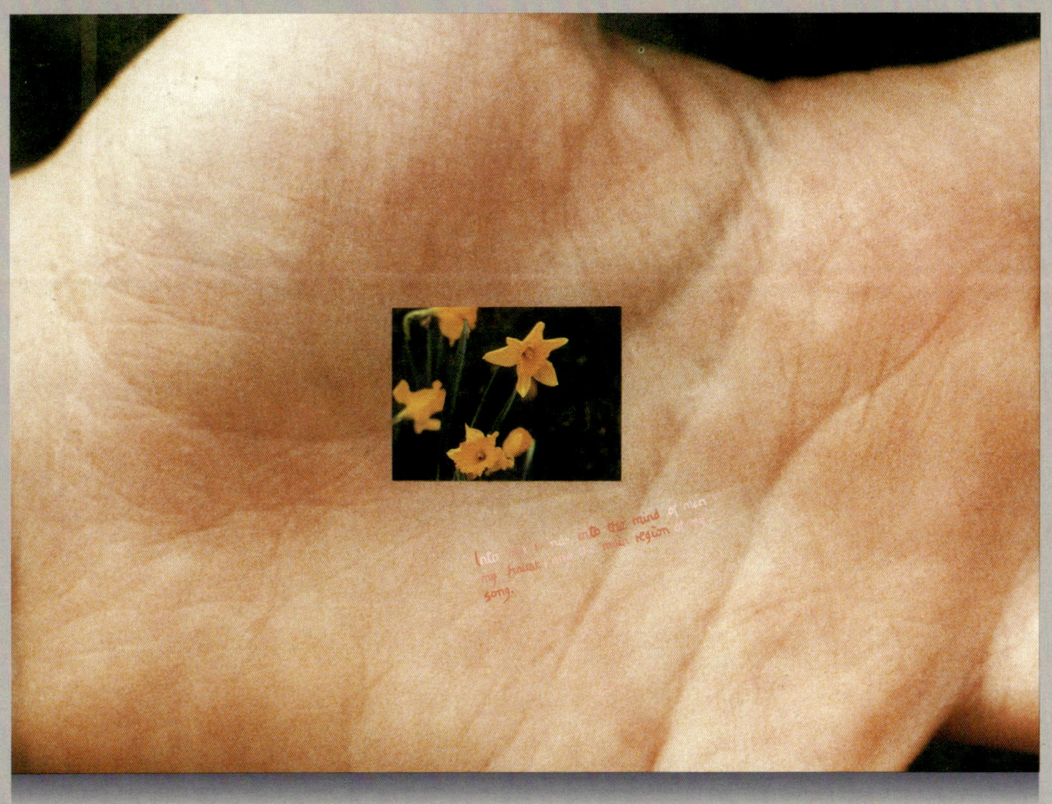

Into ... into the mind of man
my house ... the ... region
song.

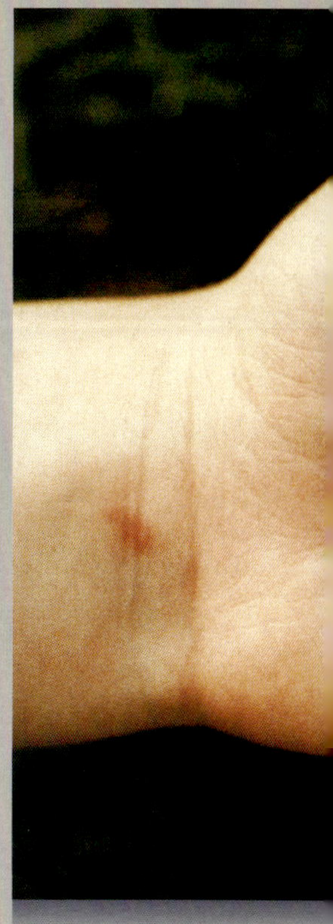

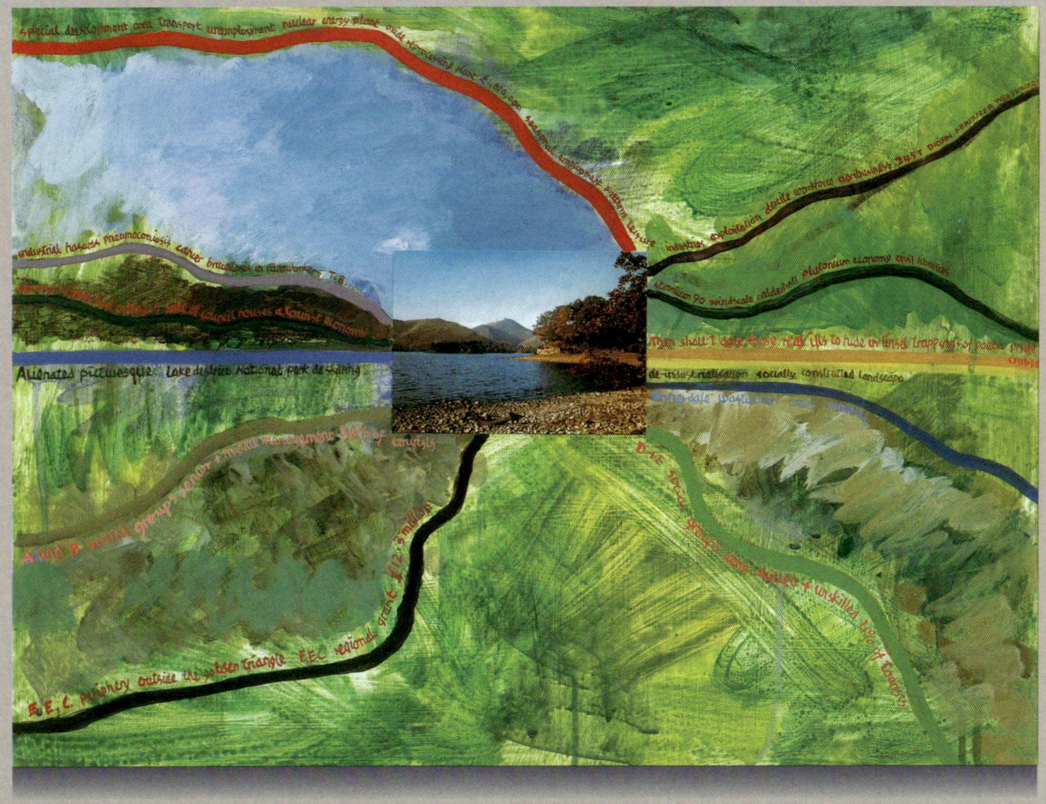

special development area transport unemployment nuclear energy plant
industrial hazard pneumoconiosis cancer
Alienated picturesque. Lake District National Park de-skilling
B.E.C. periphery outside the golden triangle. B.E.C. regional grants

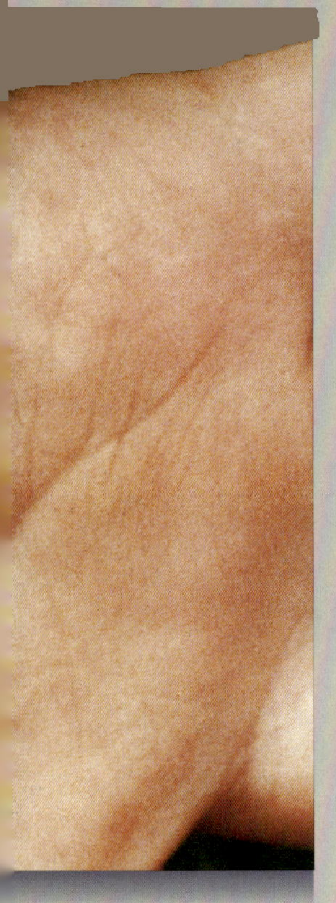

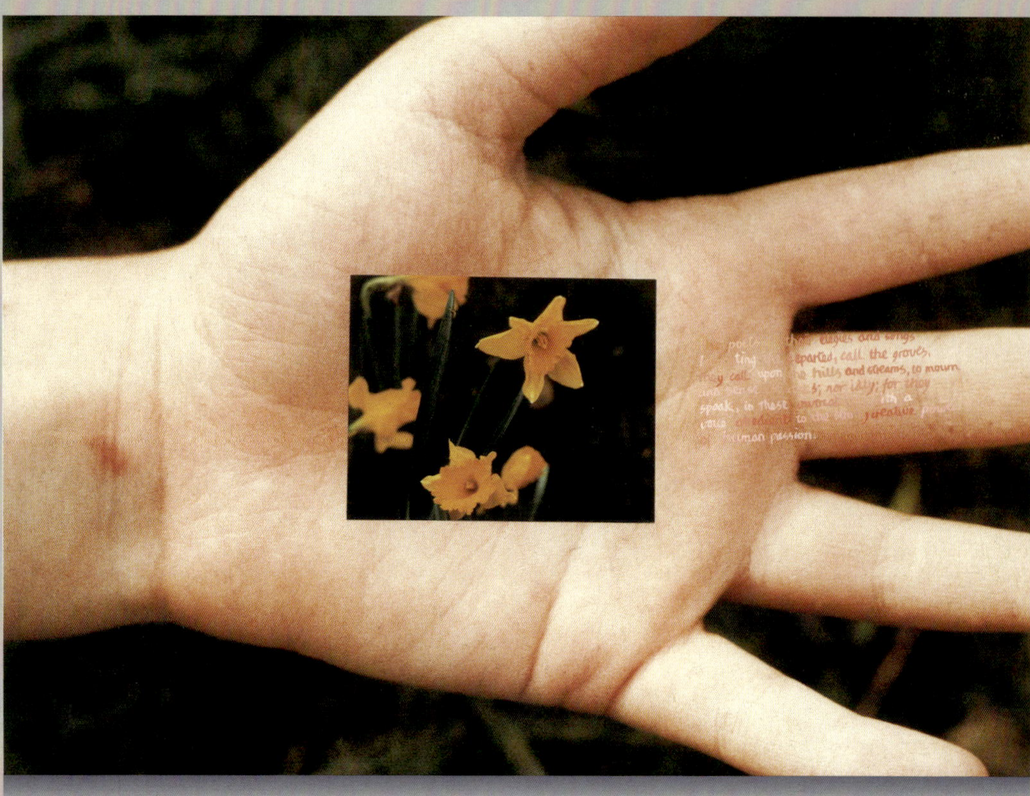

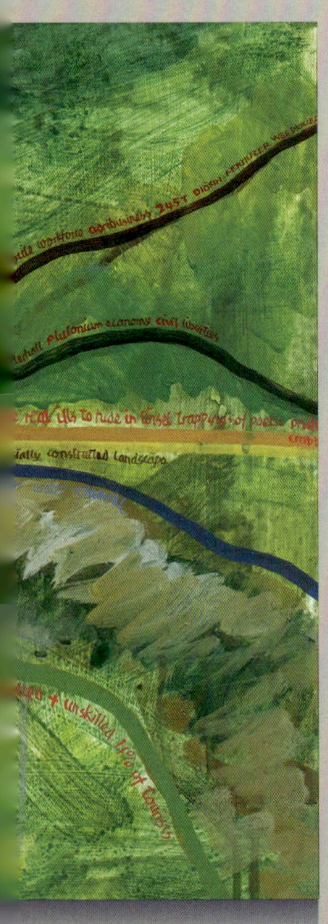

For things are getting worse and worse;
The country's done they say.
The labouring miner now-a-days
Can scarce exist at all;
Provisions are so very dear
And wages are so small.
There's Crowgarth pit is now done up,
The mineral is wrought out,
And Stirlings works have fallen in;
They'll not last long, I doubt.
On Bigrigg Moor and round Pica side
Things are but going slack;
I'll just pack up my clothes at once,
And swing them o'er my back.
Go where you will, on every side
You'll hear men complain;
Numbers of workmen go about,
And cannot work obtain.
You'll all agree, and say with me,
From work 'tis time to stop
When poor men can't earn enough
To pay their tommy shop
No matter what a man may be,
Though he toil like a slave.
If he's not cash to pay his bills,
He's termed a rogue and knave
Men are so weak and vain
Mankind, you'll find, on every side.
Work on a different plan;
A man of sense is term'd a fool,
While money makes the man.

Notice to quit your situation—
I mean your farm and habitation;
The landlord says this must be done
To make those small farms into one
All your persuasion will not do,
Others must quit as well as you
All our remonstrances did fail,
So of our goods we made a sale,
And, with many a heartfelt tear,
We left the home we loved so dear;
'Mong strangers sought work to obtain,
That we a livelihood might gain.
'Twould be in vain for me to show
The hardships we'd to undergo,
For tongue of mine could not express
The full amount of our distress.
My parents succumbed to the blow;
Death soon did ease them of their woe;
We from each other then were squandered,
Like sheep which from the fold have wandered.
Two brothers and two sisters dear
Did o'er the broad Atlantic steer,
And found a home and are at rest,
In the wild prairies of the West;
One brother still in Ireland, and one
Has to Australian gold fields gone,
And I, oppressed and troubled sore,
Resolved to quit my native,
And into England take a tour,
So here I am on Cleator Moor.
Dick Watson an Iron Ore Miner 1888

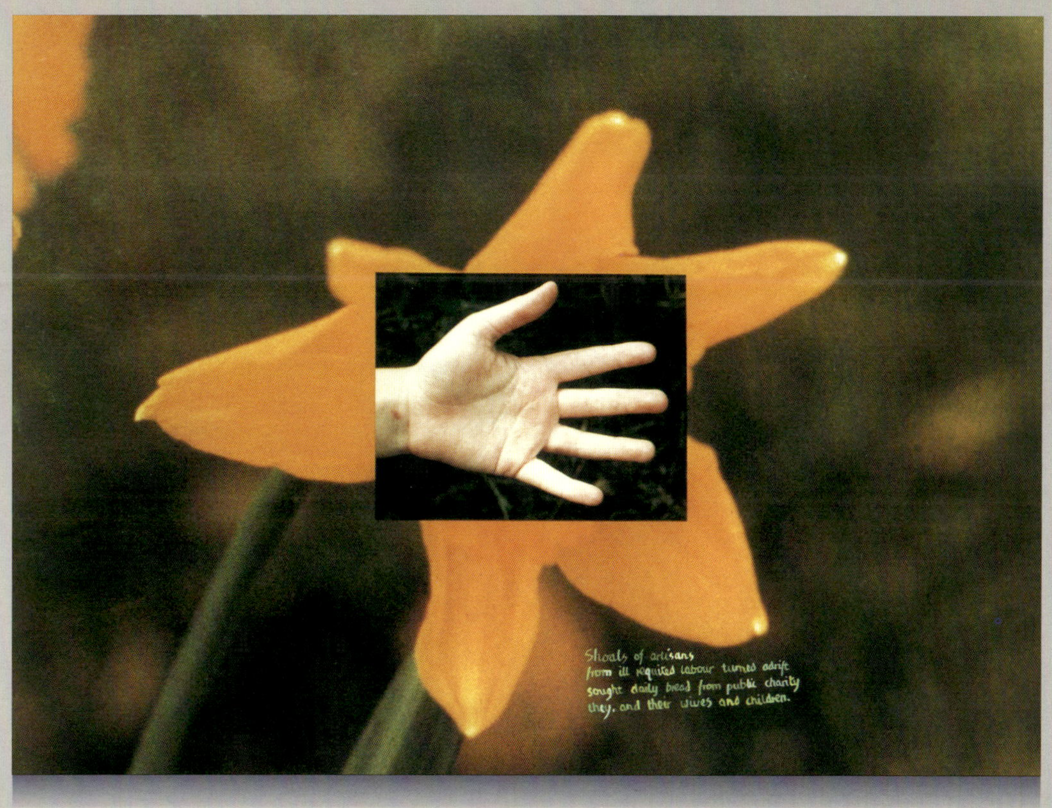

Shoals of artisans
from ill requited labour turned adrift
sought daily bread from public charity
they, and their wives and children.

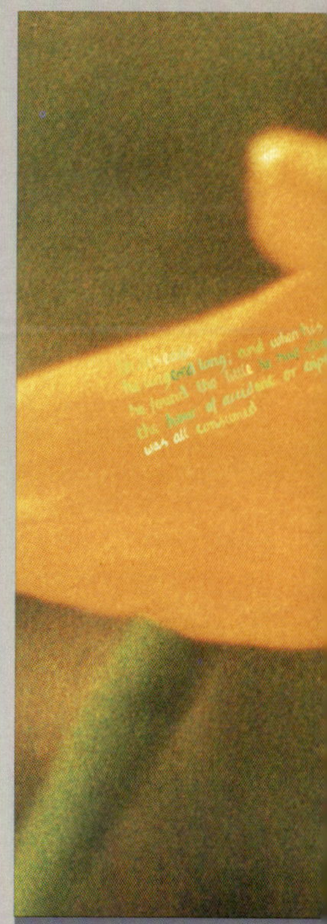

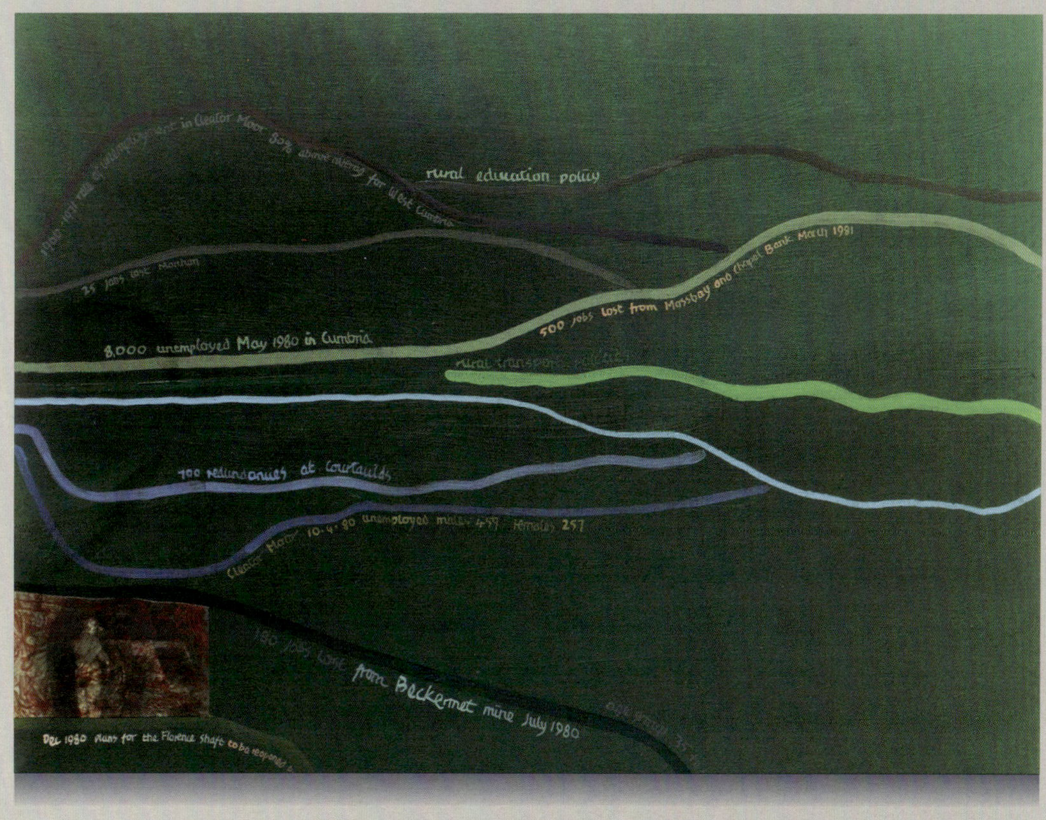

rate of unemployment in Cleator Moor 80% above average for West Cumbria
rural education policy
25 jobs lost Monkton
500 jobs lost from Mossbay and Chapel Bank March 1981
8,000 unemployed May 1980 in Cumbria
rural transport policy
700 redundancies at Courtaulds
Cleator Moor 10.4.80 unemployed males 457 females 257
180 jobs lost from Beckermet mine July 1980
Dec 1980 plans for the Florence shaft to be reopened

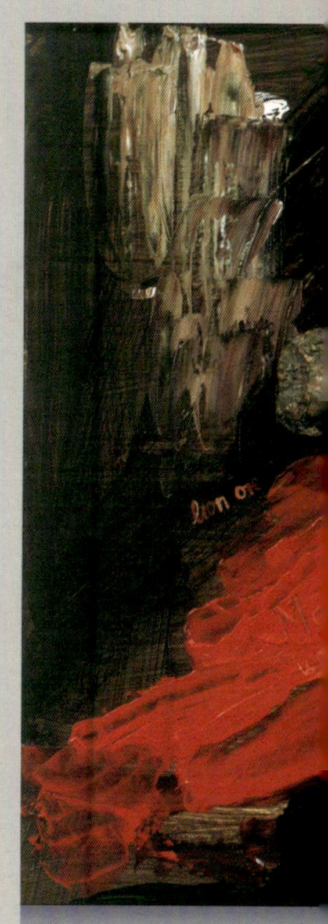

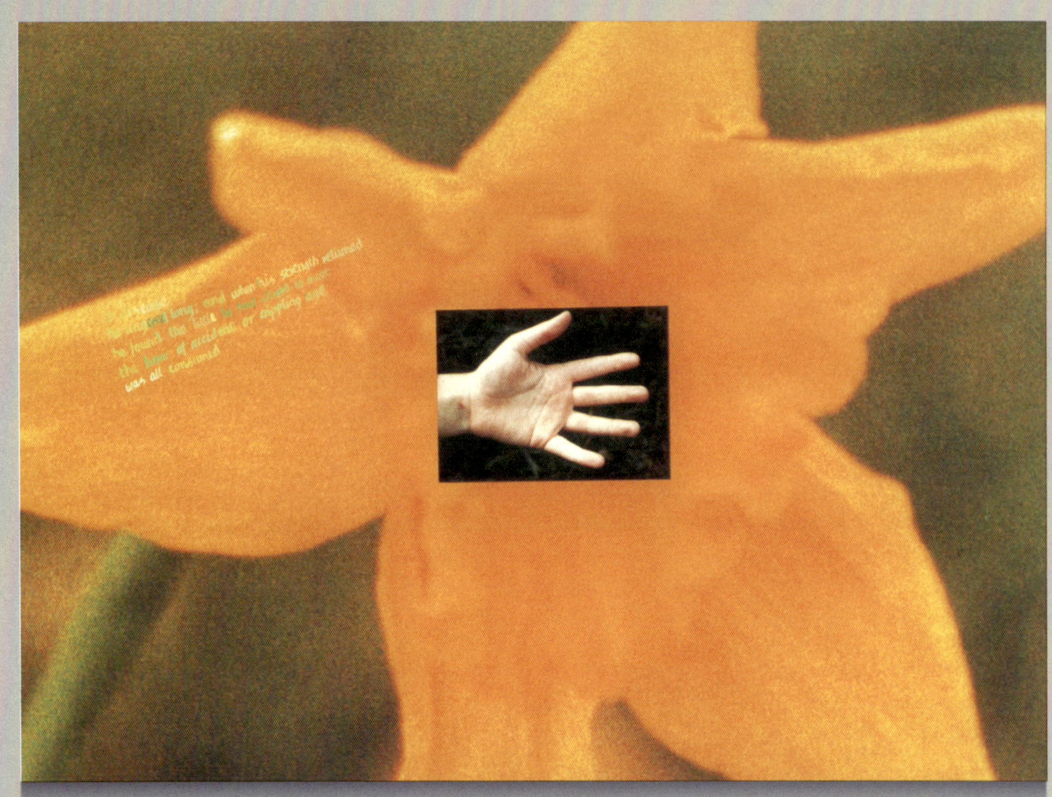
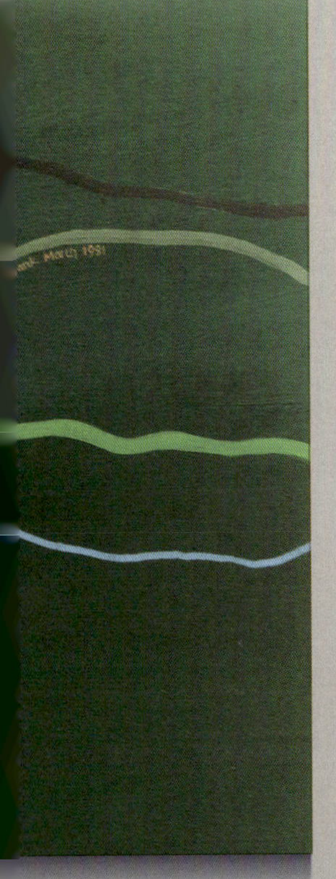
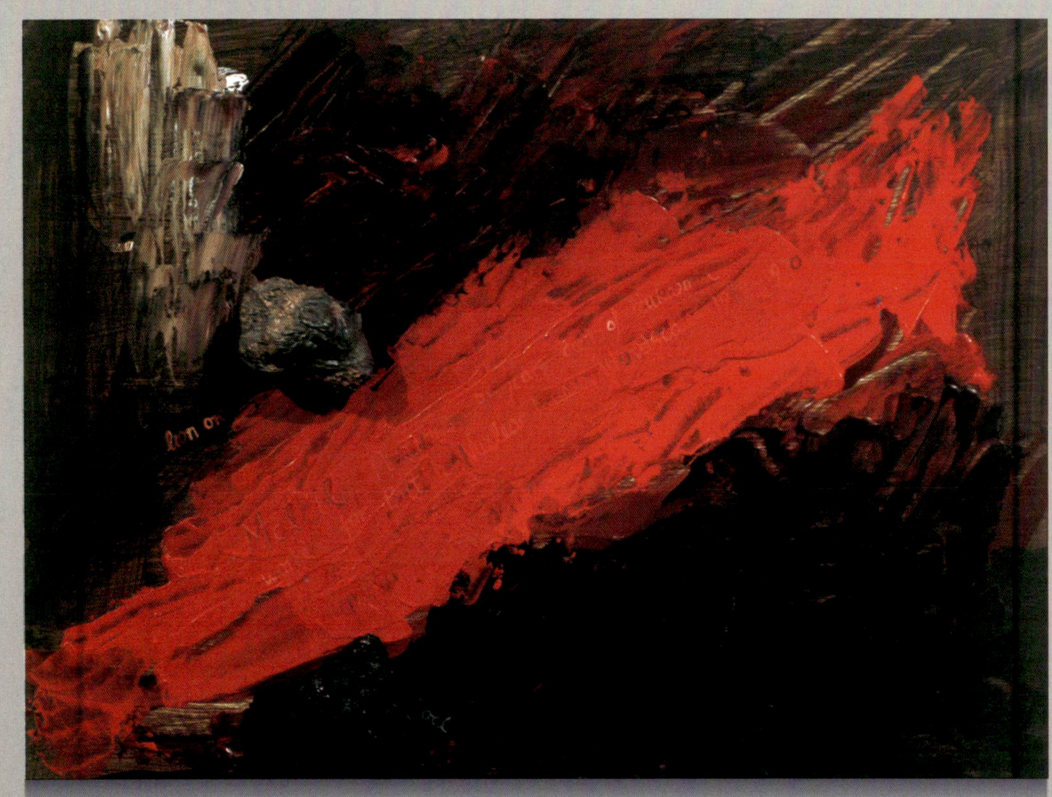

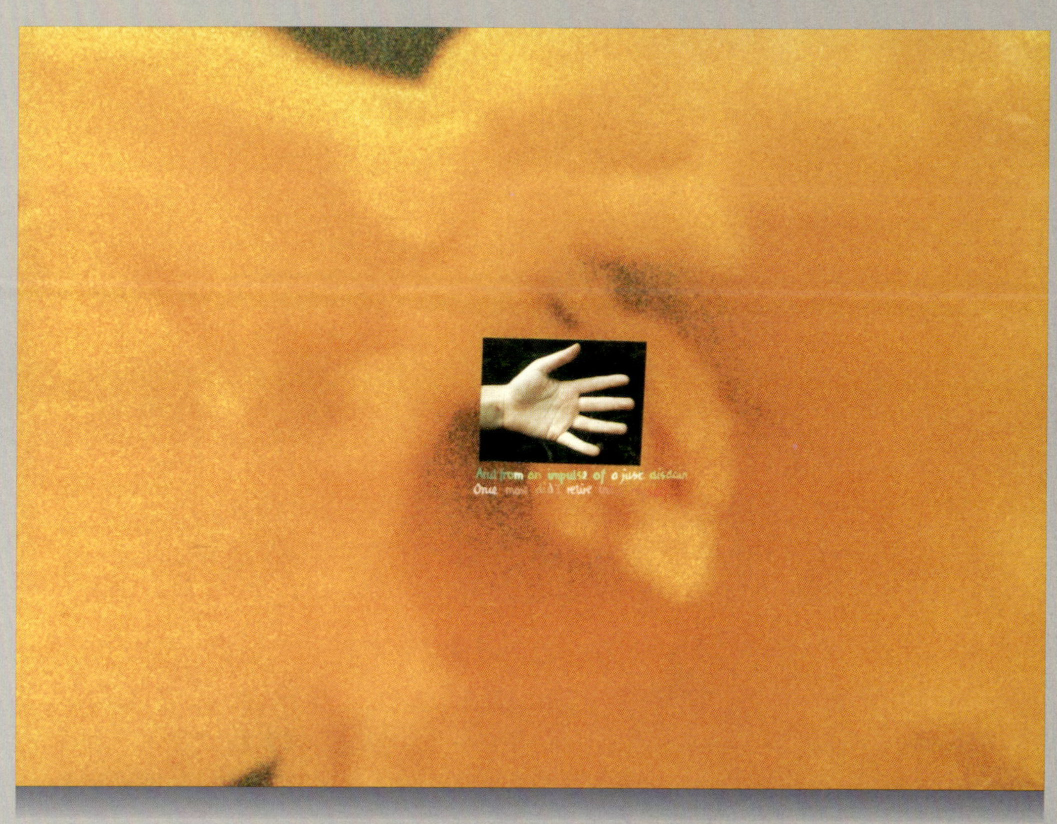
And from an impulse of a just disdain
Once more did't retire

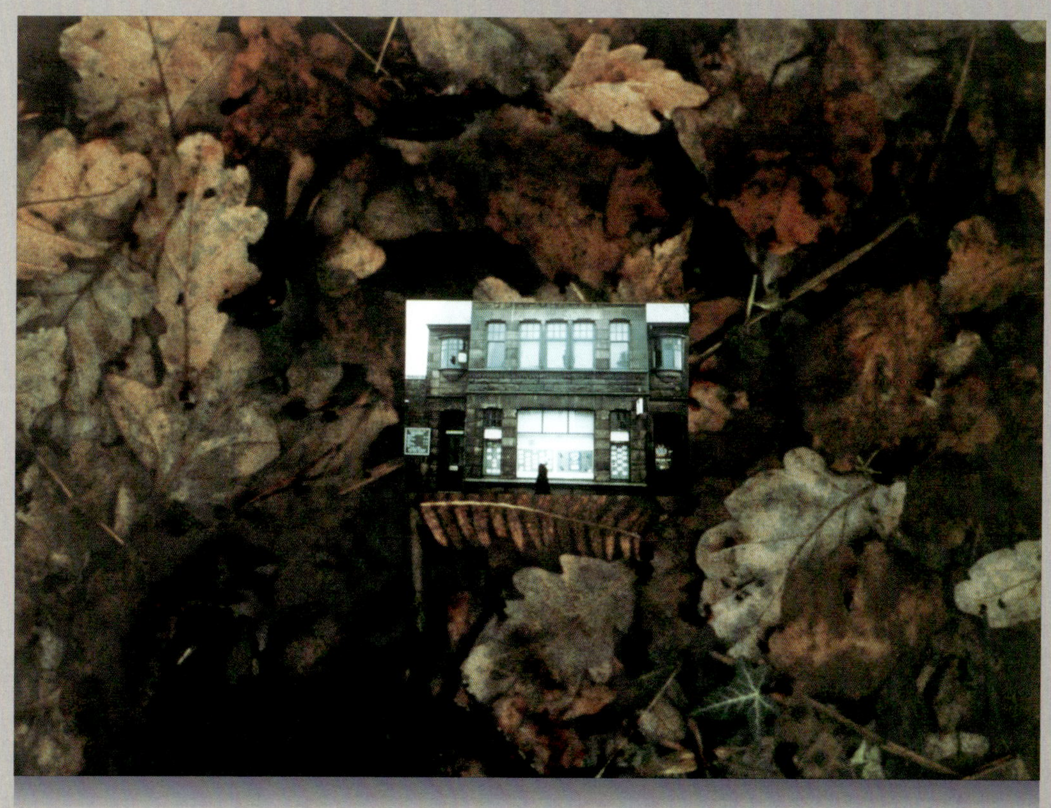

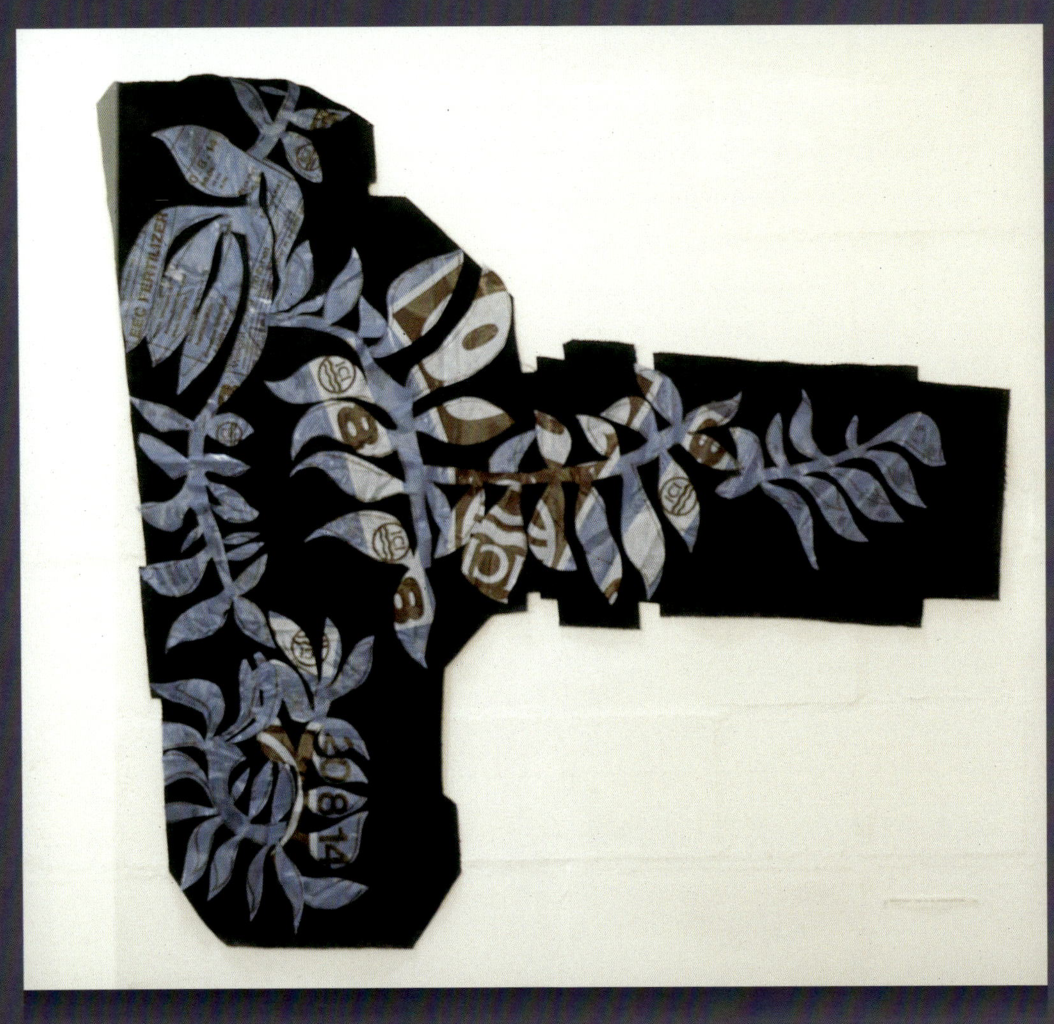

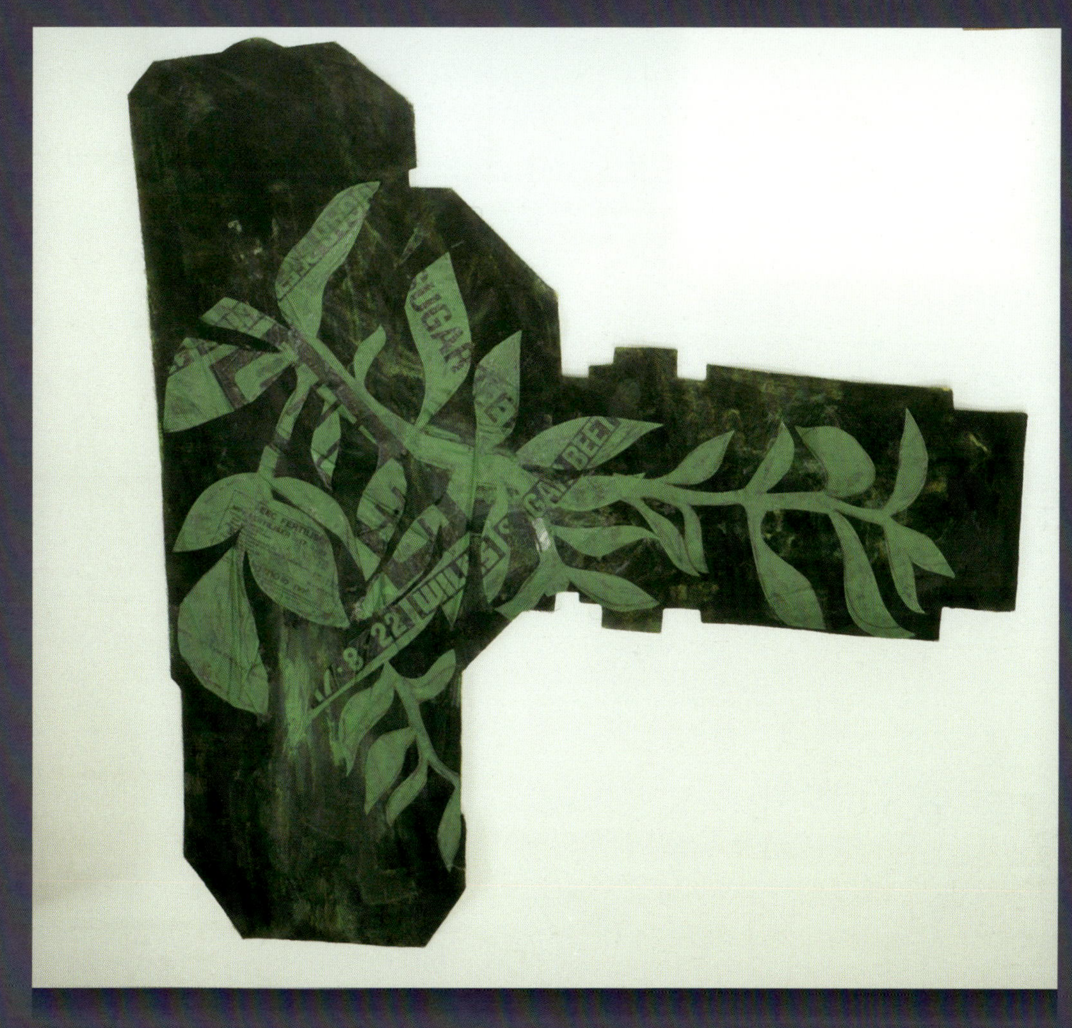
SUGAR
SUGAR BEE
IS CAN BEE
14-8-22

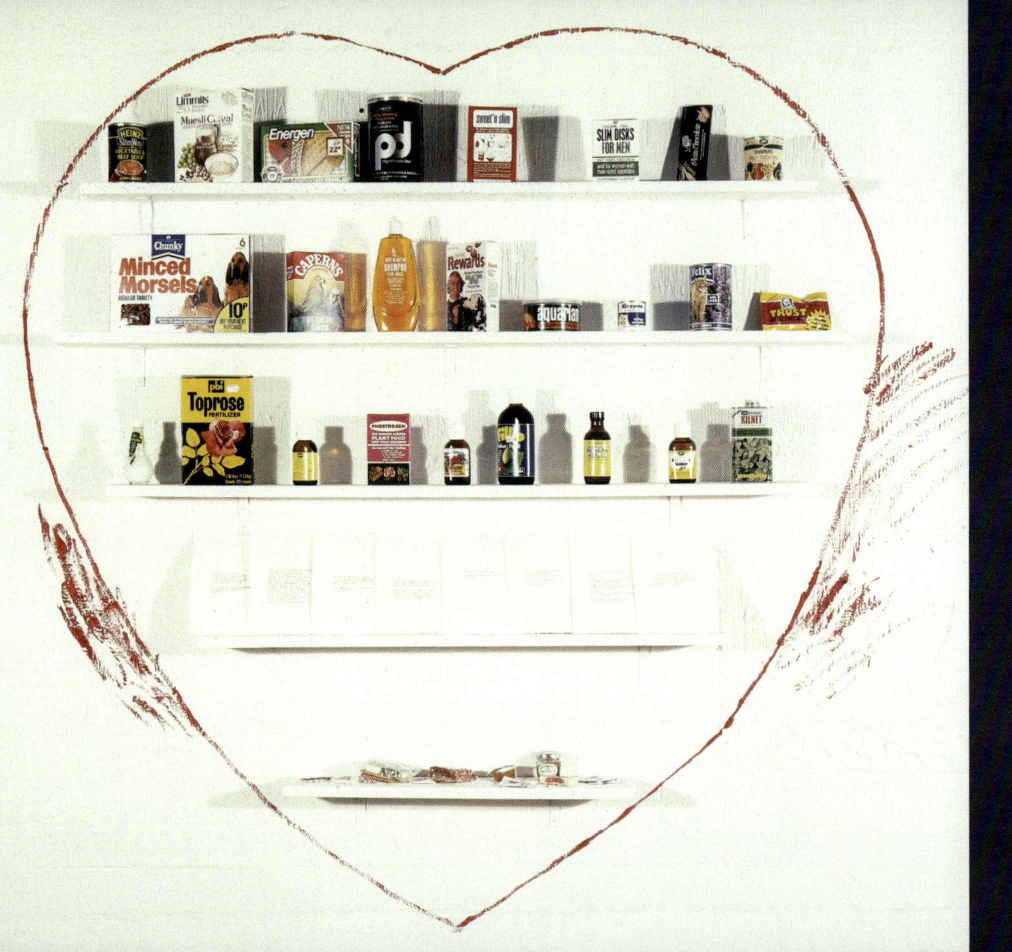

Limmits
Muesli Cereal
HEINZ Slim Way VEGETABLE & BEEF SOUP
Energen
psJ
sweet'n slim
SLIM DISKS FOR MEN
and for women with more sized appetites
Chunky
Minced Morsels
REGULAR VARIETY
10P OFF YOUR NEXT PURCHASE
CAPERNS
SKIPPER SHAMPOO FOR DOGS
Rewards
aquarian
Felix
TRUST
pbi Toprose FERTILIZER
PHOSTROGEN
PLANT FOOD
KILNET

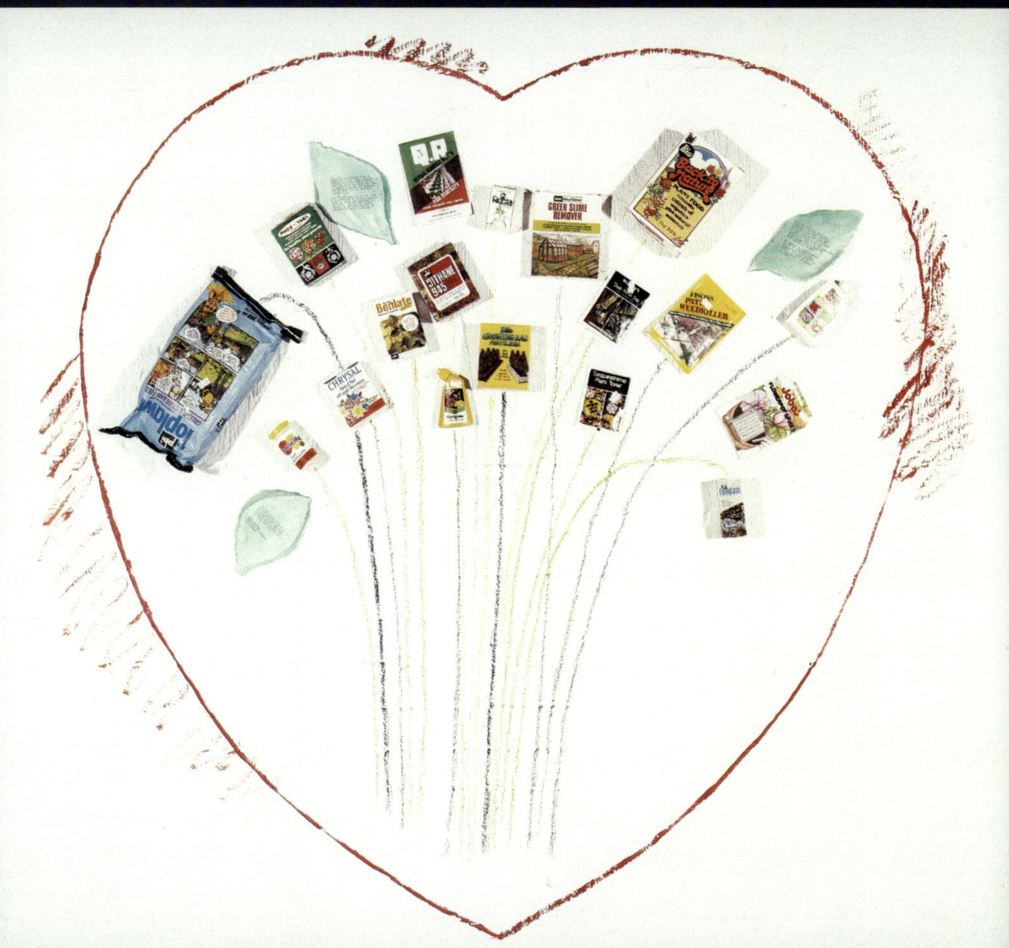

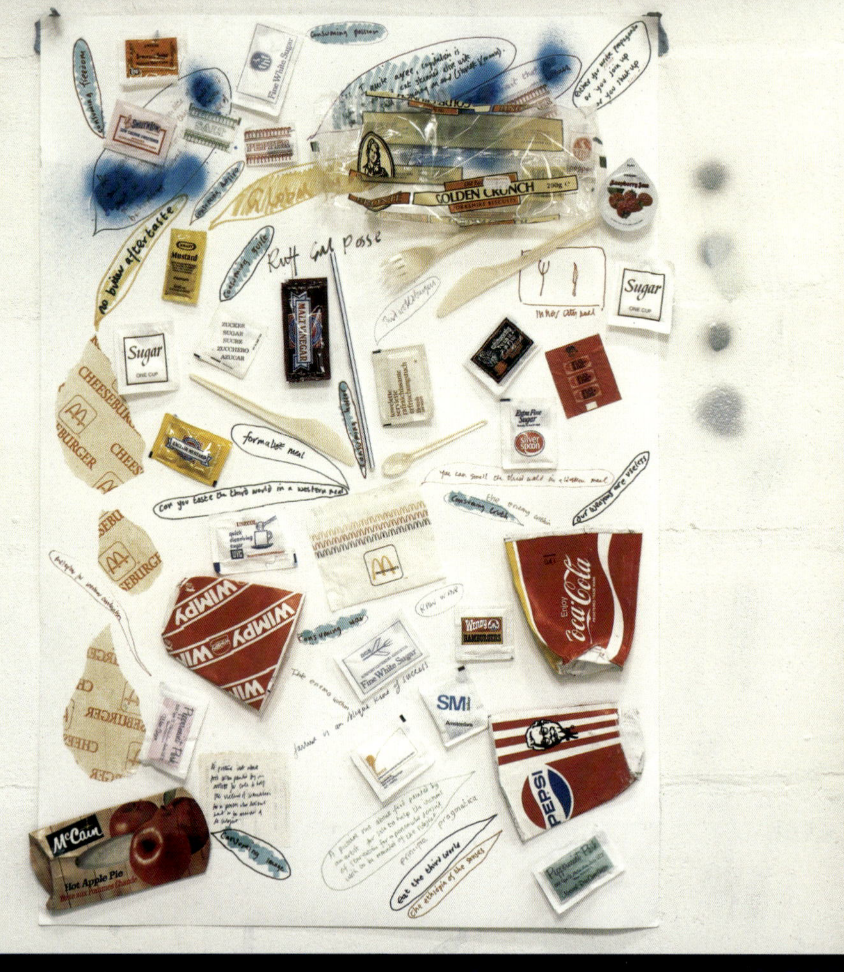

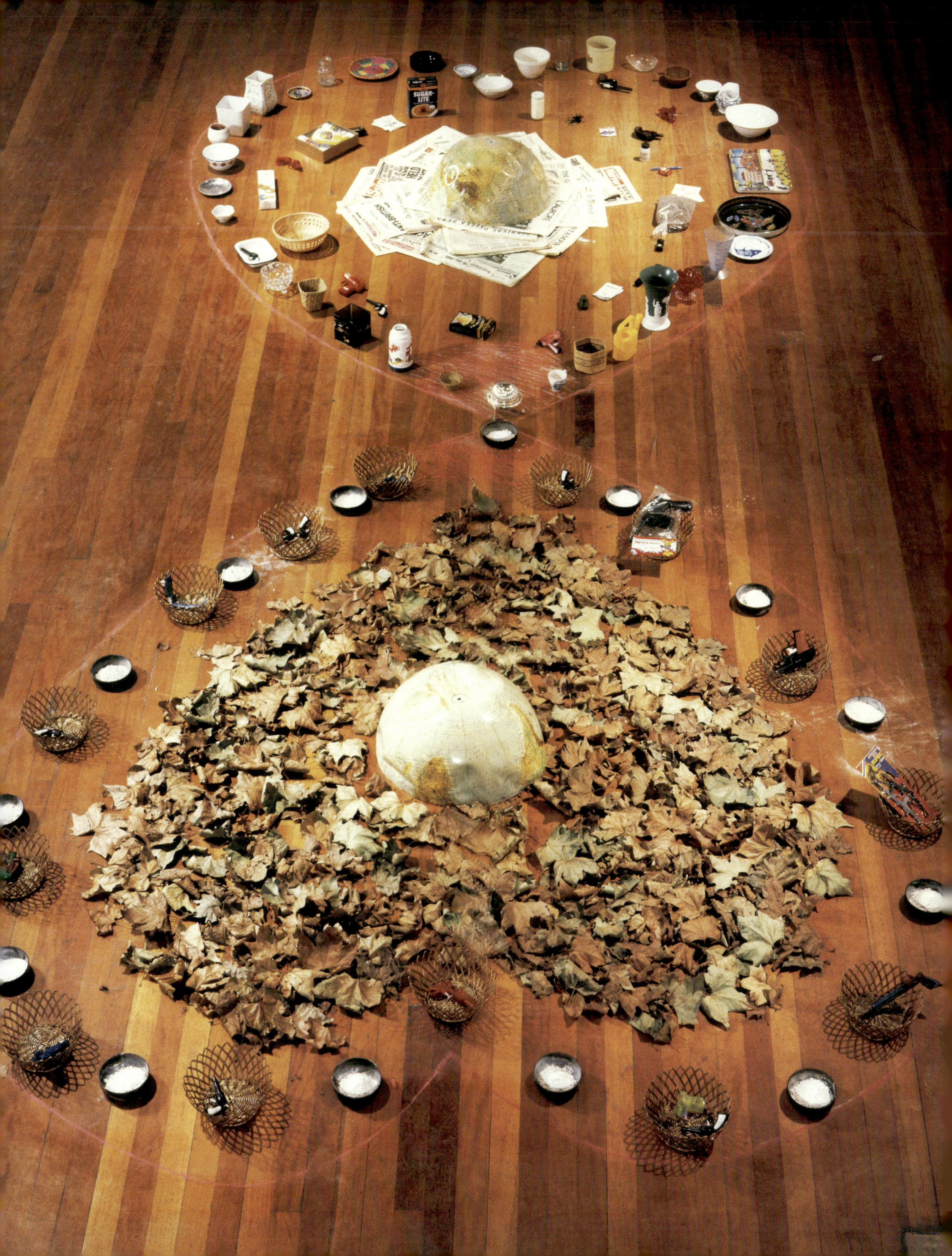

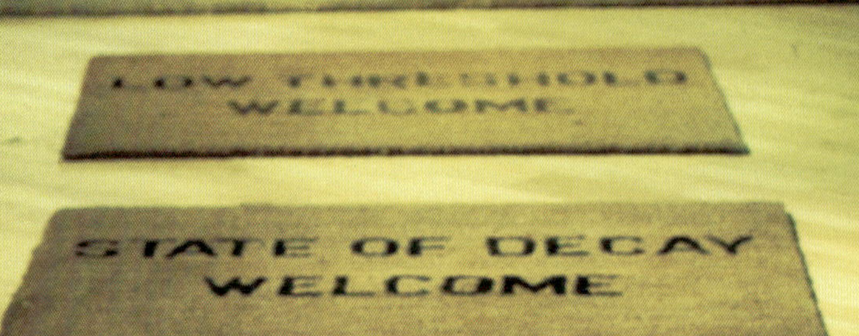
THE SEDUCTIVENESS OF THE
END OF THE WORLD
WELCOME
LOW THRESHOLD
WELCOME
STATE OF DECAY
WELCOME
INVISIBLE DESIRES
WELCOME
RESIDUES OF POWER
WELCOME
STATE OF READINESS
WELCOME

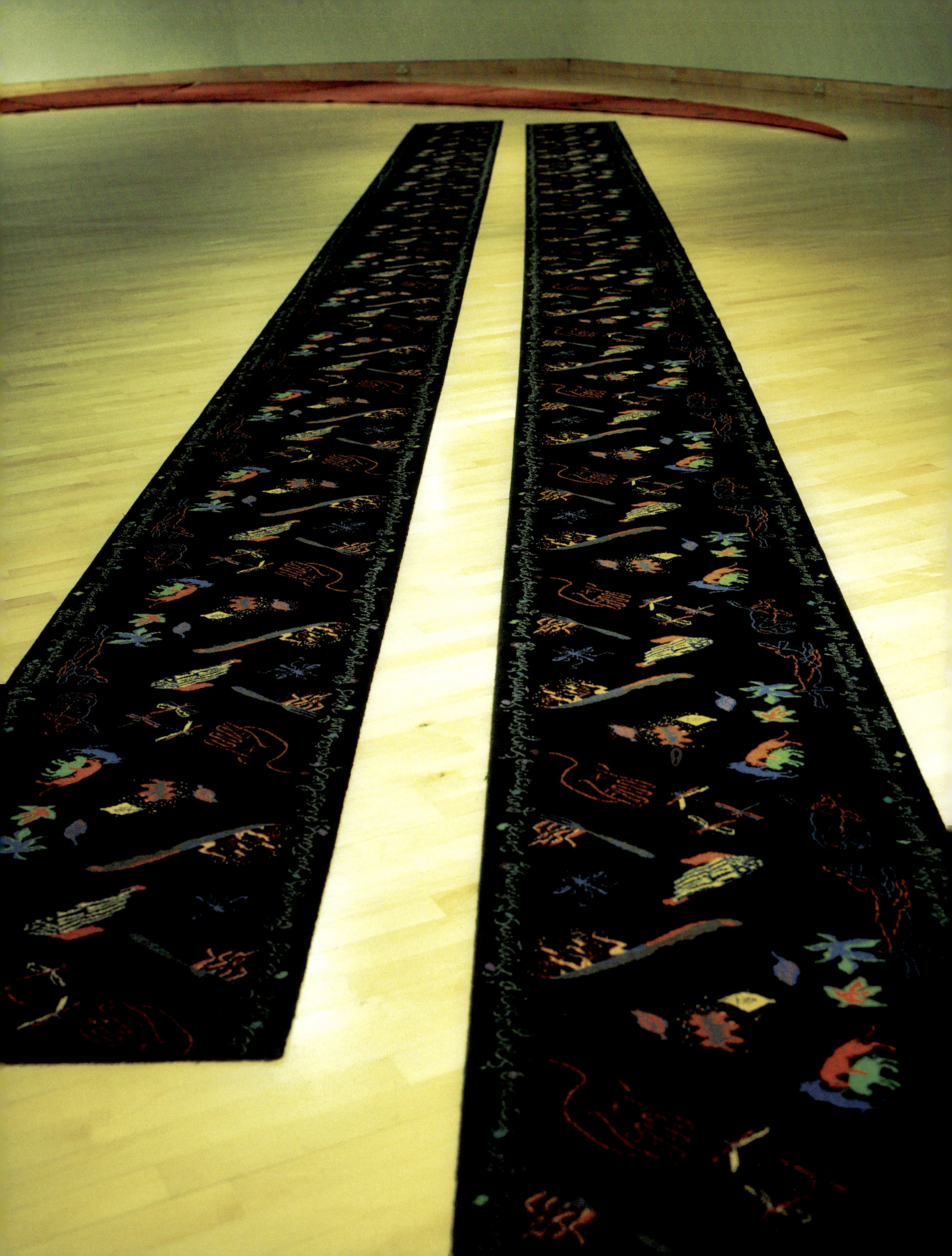

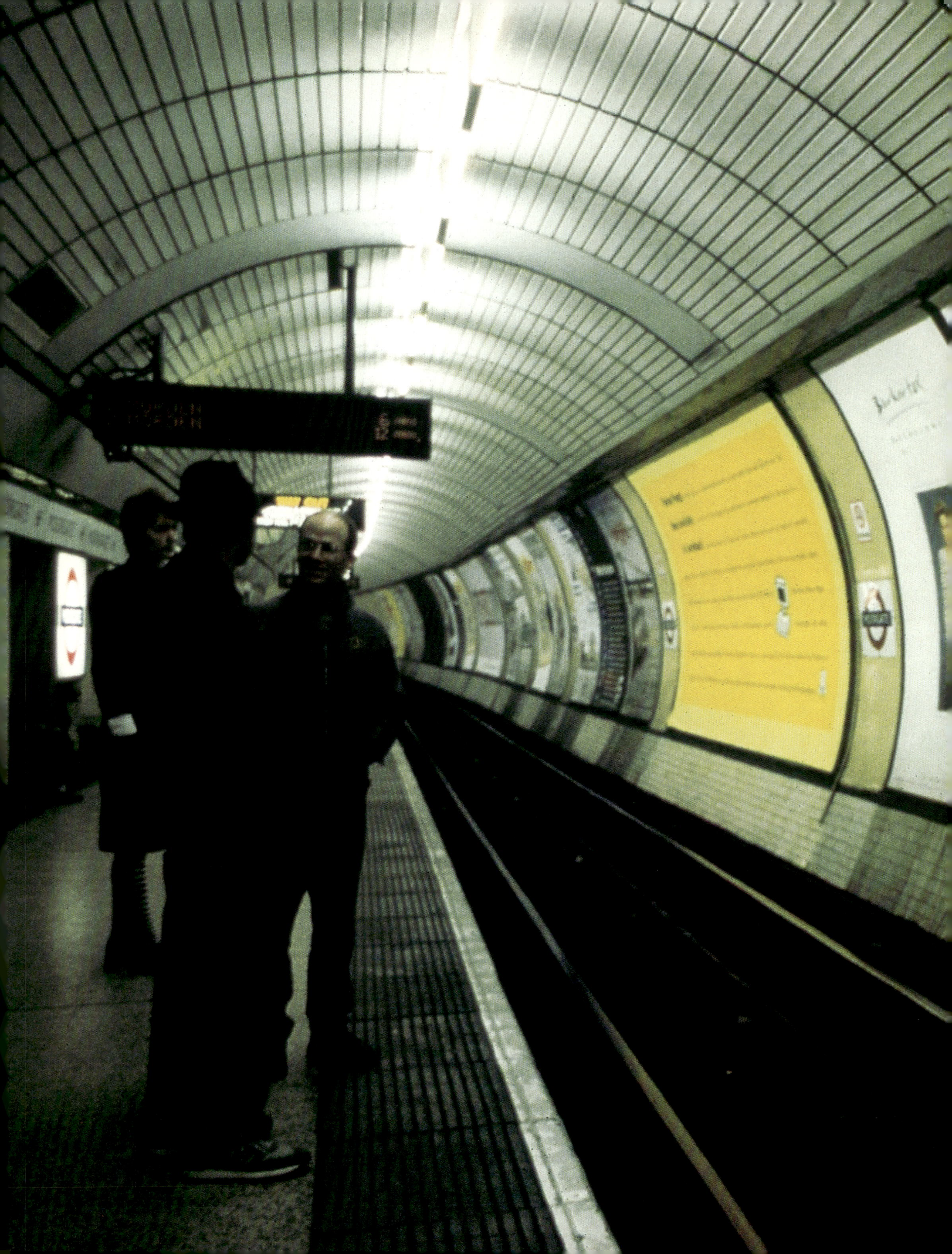

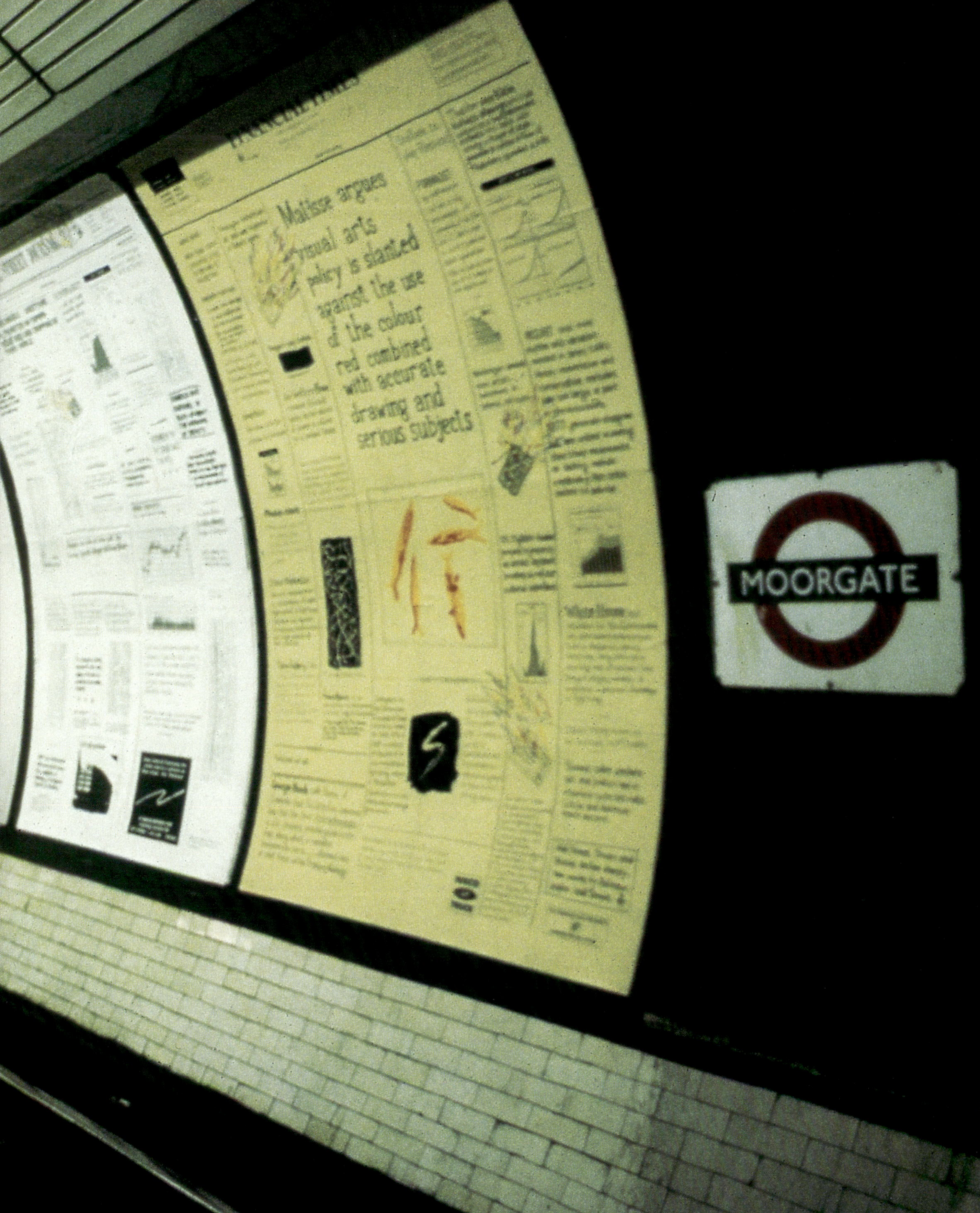

Matisse argues
visual arts
policy is slanted
against the use
of the colour
red combined
with accurate
drawing and
serious subjects
MOORGATE

eagon turns
strategic
ace initiative
Velasquez
Today
DA VINCI HUSTLES
N.A.S.A. on GENERAL
PHILOSOPHICAL
PRINCIPLES
VERM...
ATTE...
TALK...
MARKET STATISTICS
Dow Jones Industrial Average
Reagan tax plan at odds with the
Divine Spirit alleges William Blake
MATTISSE SAYS
THATCHERISM
TO 'RECORD
PLEASU...
Fra Angelico utterly
opposed to star wars
defines the plan as
unethical, unworkable,
ungodly
ART OR CRAFT? —
Let's get personal
s & Company, Inc
u to a seminar
Art Retrieval

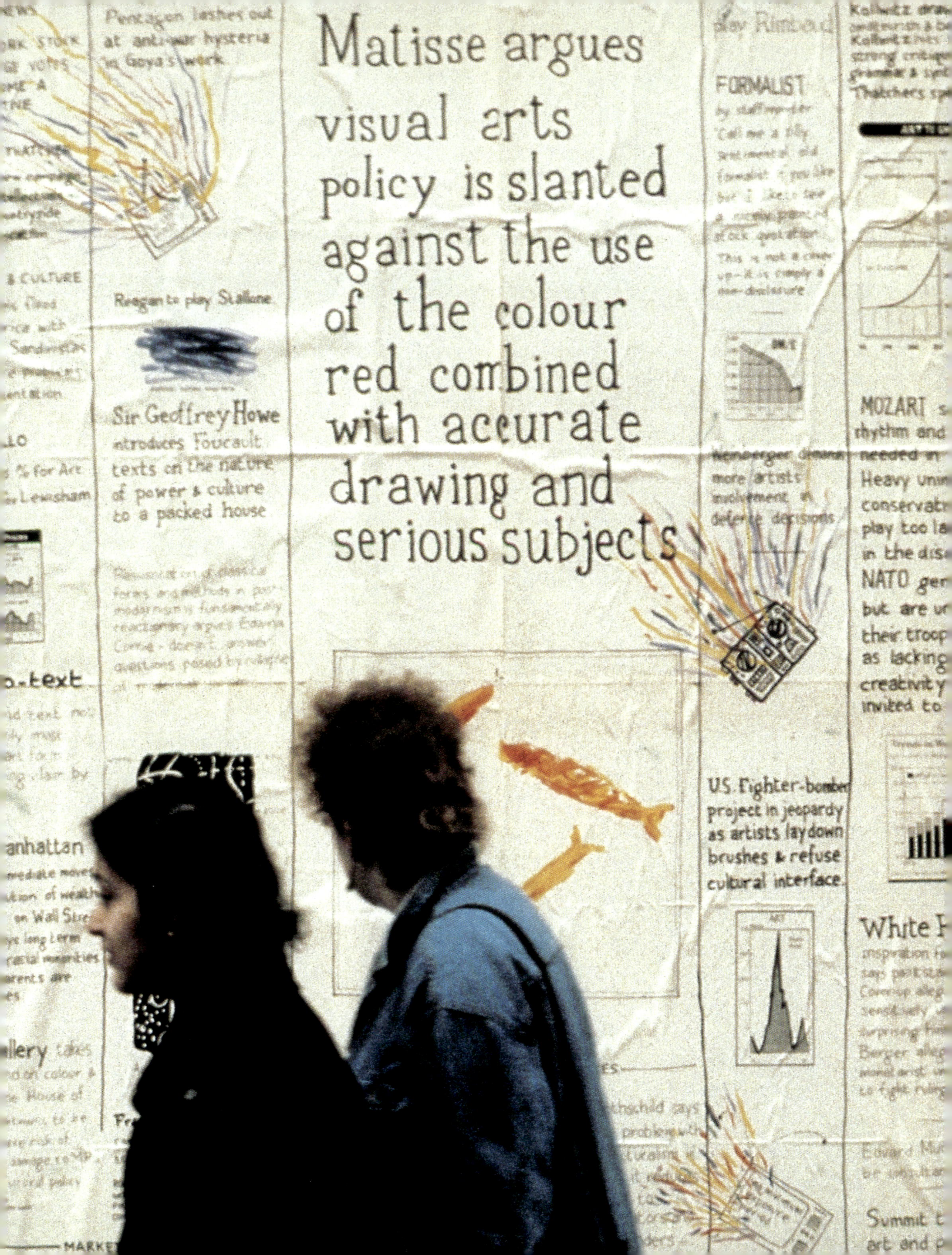

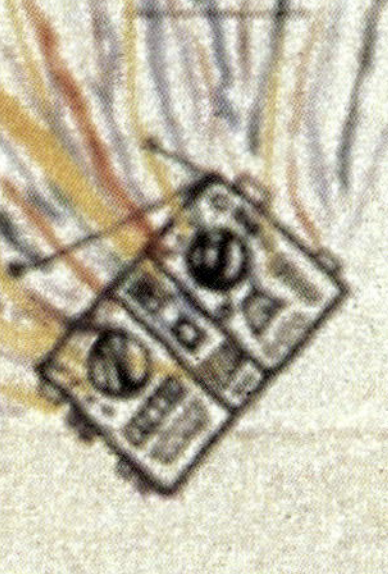
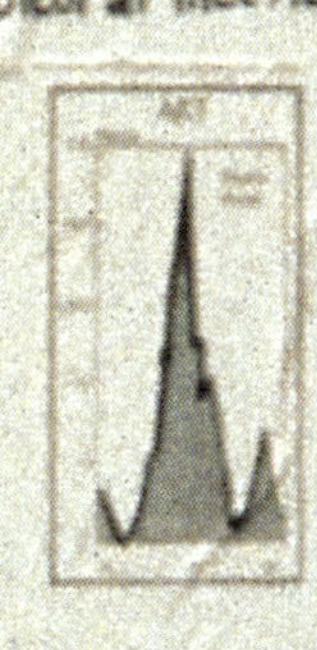
Matisse argues
visual arts
policy is slanted
against the use
of the colour
red combined
with accurate
drawing and
serious subjects
Pentagon lashes out
at anti-war hysteria
in Goya's work.
Reagan to play Stallone.
Sir Geoffrey Howe
introduces Foucault
texts on the nature
of power & culture
to a packed house
& CULTURE
play Rimbaud
FORMALIST
by staff member
Call me a silly
sentimental old
formalist if you like
but I like to see
a nice red spot of
stock quotation.
This is not a cover
up—it is simply a
non-disclosure
more artists
involvement in
defence decisions
MOZART's
rhythm and
needed in
Heavy unin
conservat
play too la
in the disc
NATO gen
but are ur
their troop
as lacking
creativity
invited to
U.S. fighter-bomber
project in jeopardy
as artists laydown
brushes & refuse
cultural interface.
White P
Summit
art and p

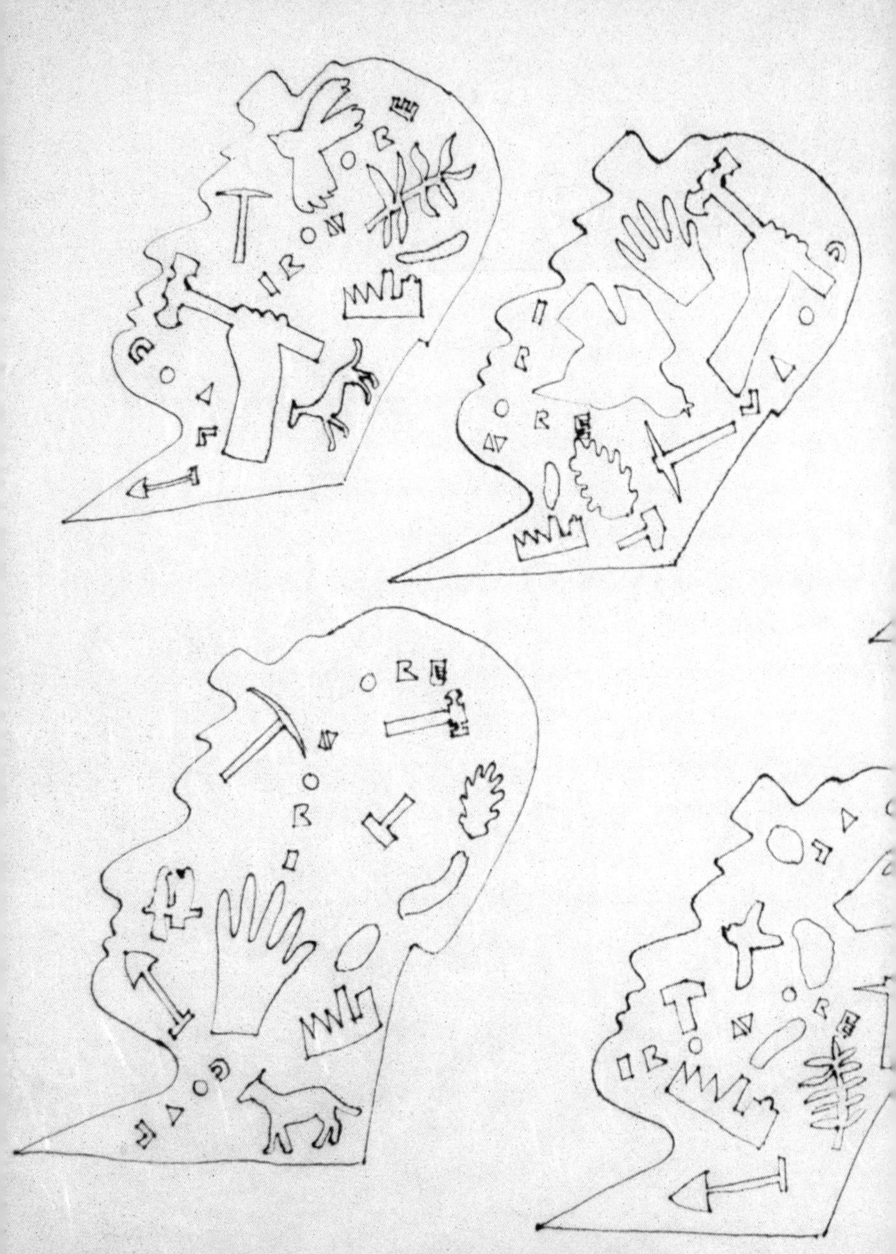

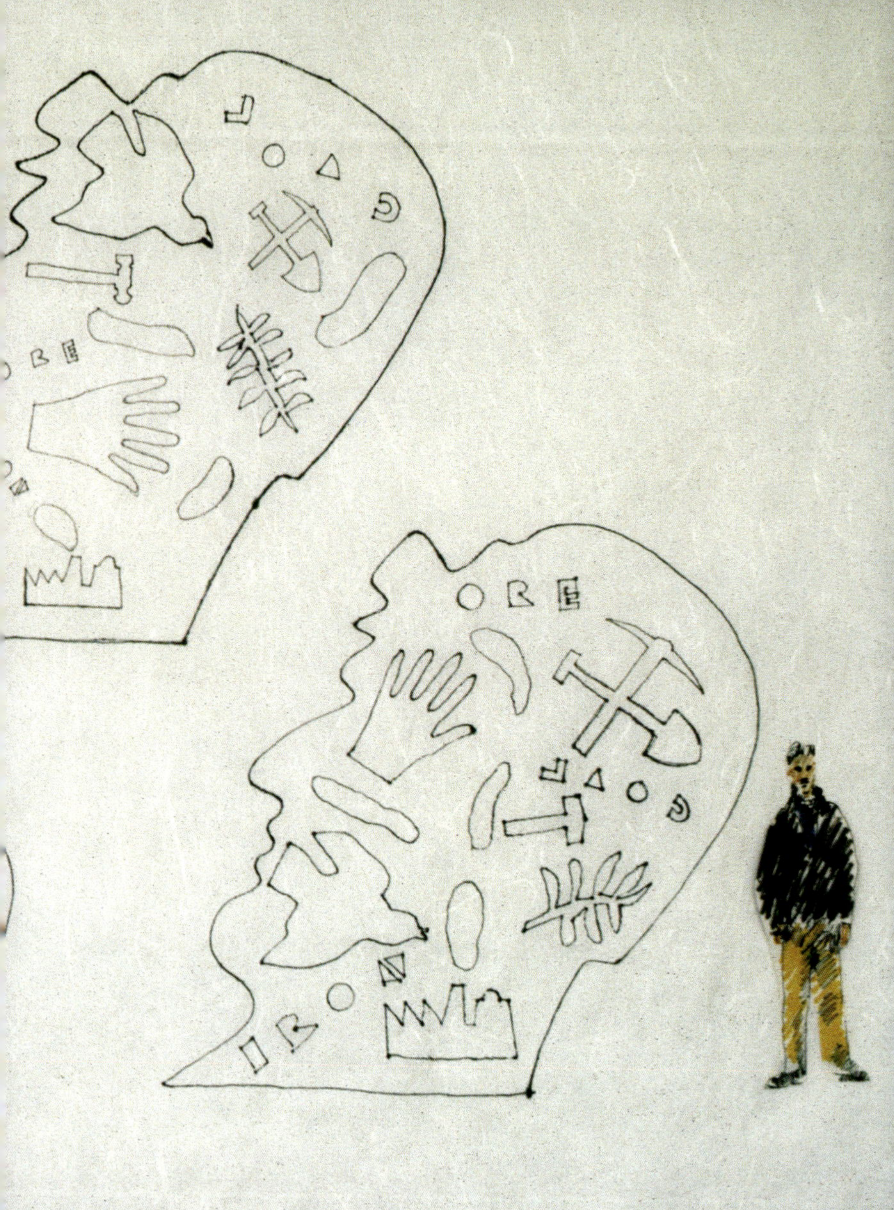
LOAD
ORE
IRON
ORE
LOAD
IRON

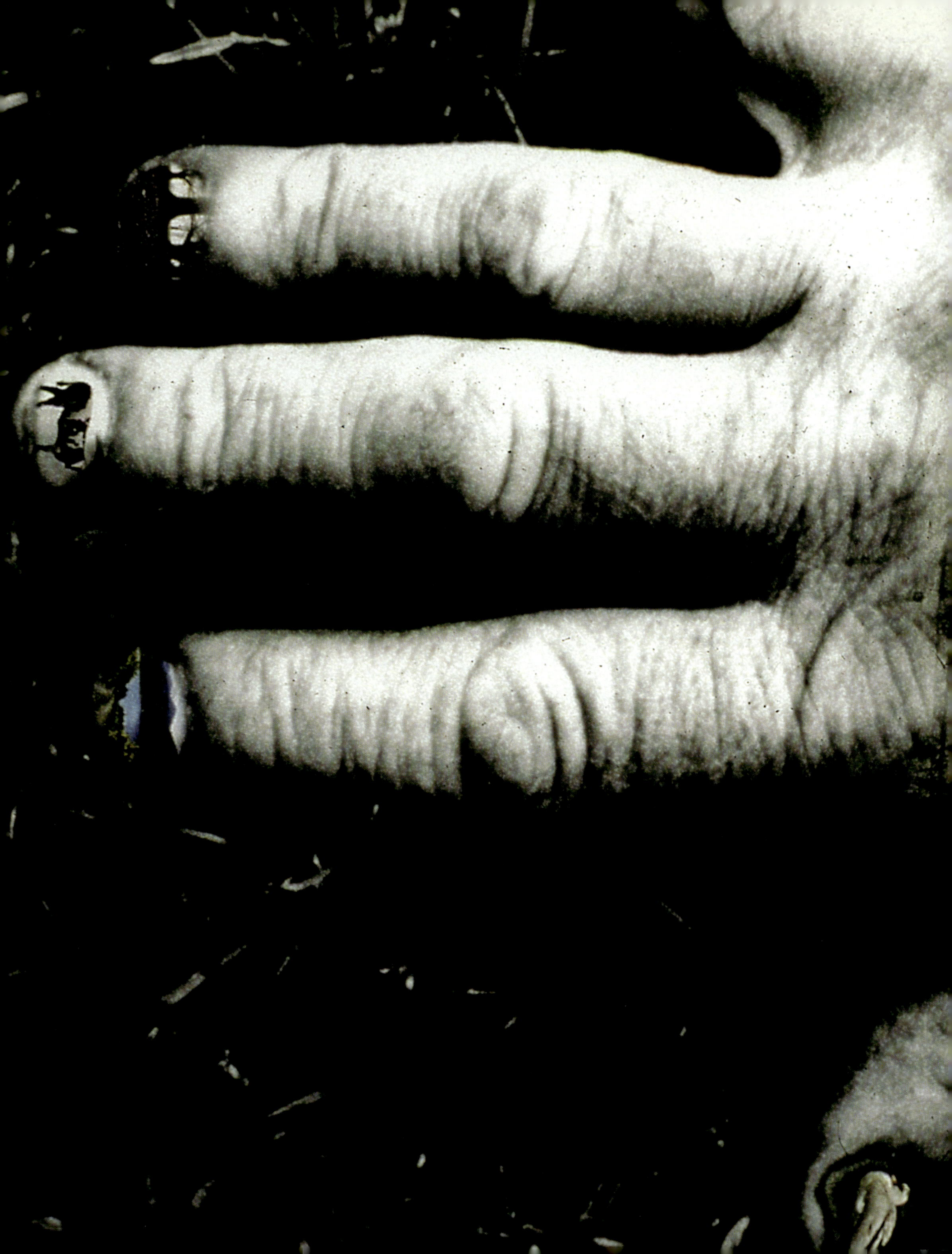

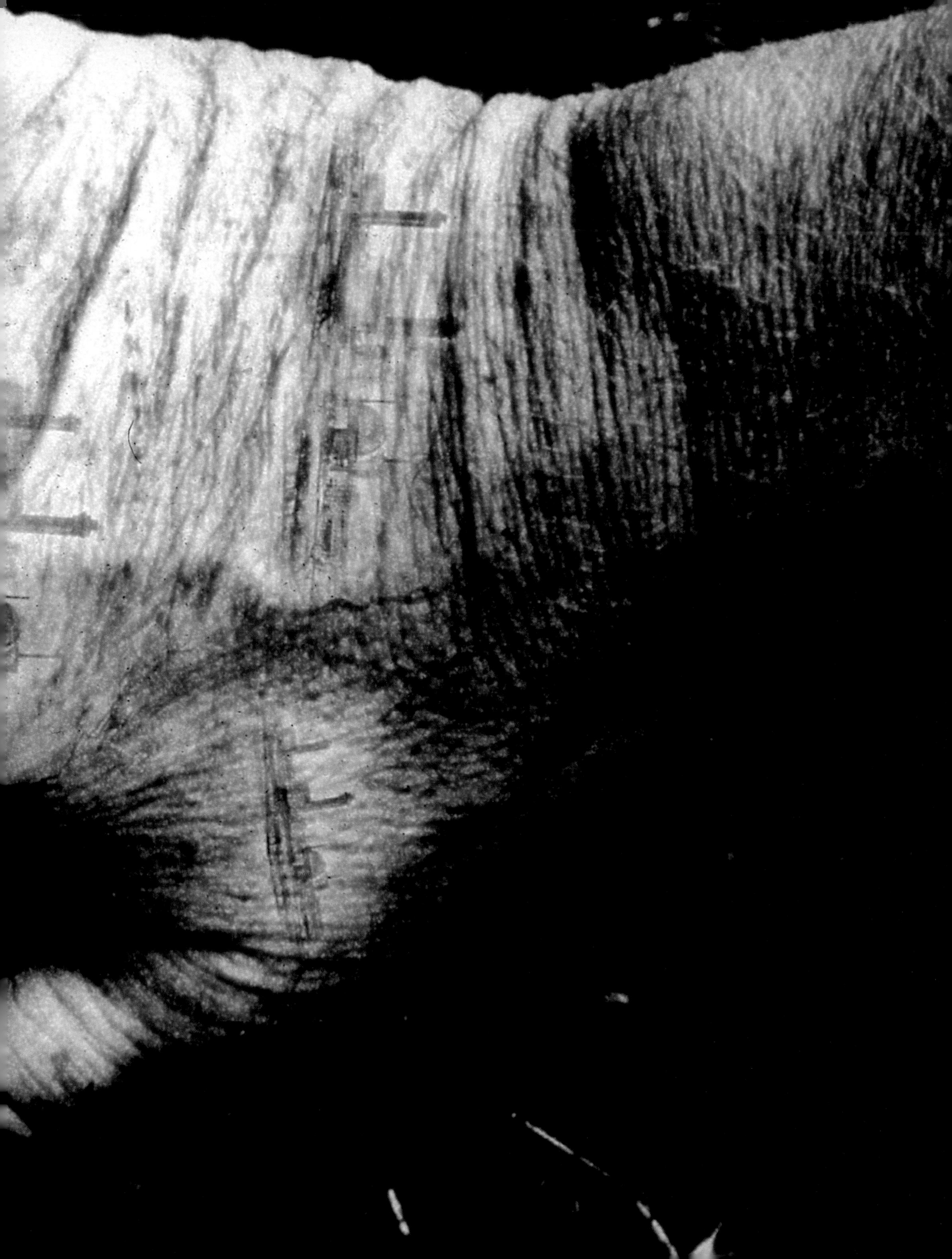

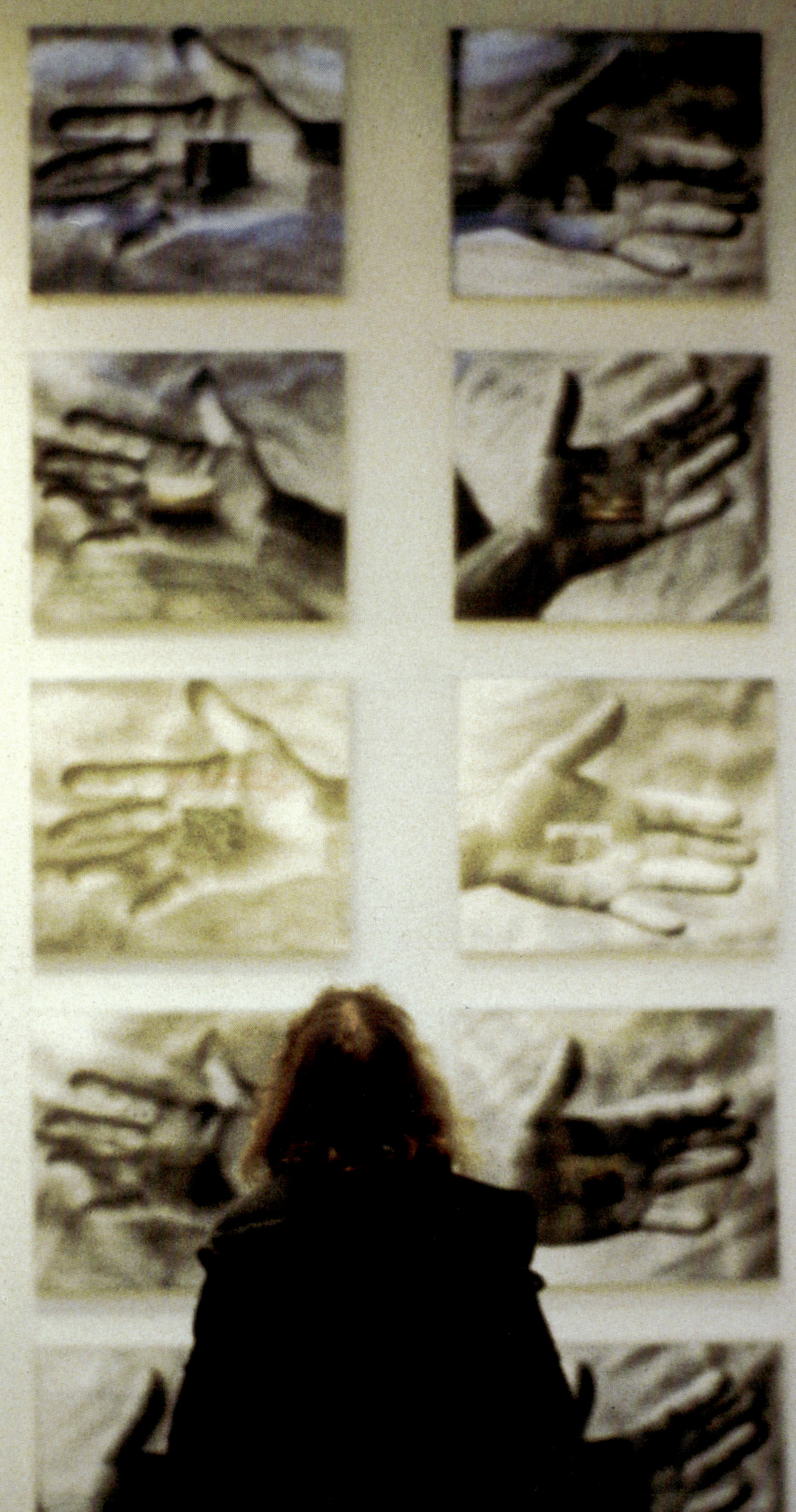

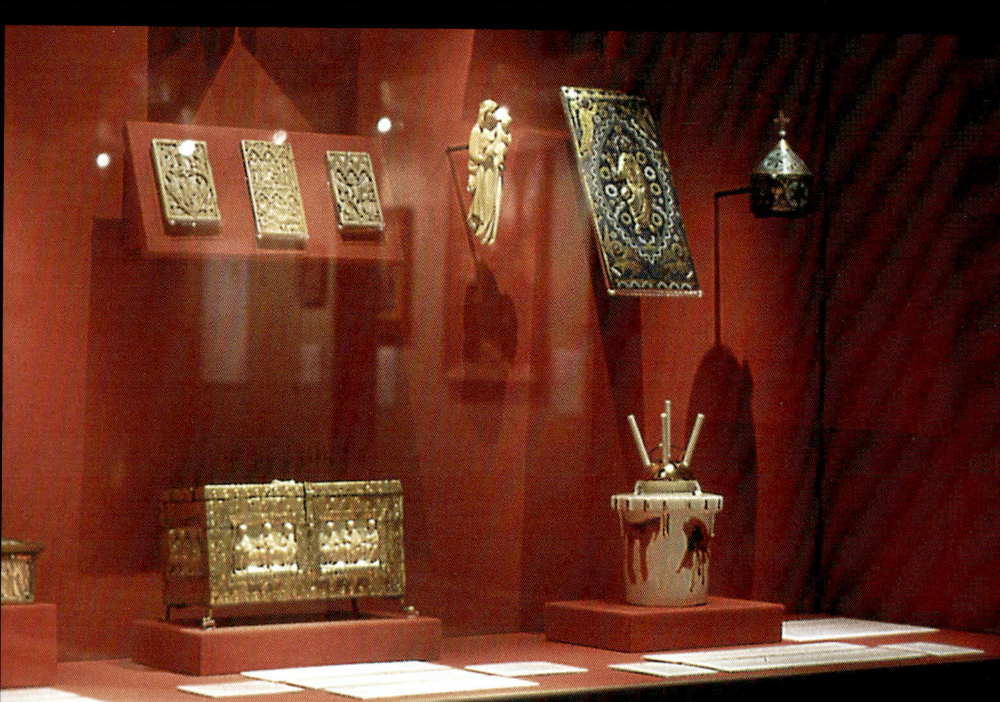

AH: What first strikes me about your showing at the Courtauld is that this gallery is made up of a series of once-private collections and, like all collections of this type, acts as a prestigious accumulation of wealth and display. How does your work, which is built on more or less contrary principles, relate to this collection?

CA: The financial value of the collection doesn't interest me one bit. Looking around, what surprised me was how interested I was in the ground floor and the first floor material, which was all to do with mutilation, torture, and crucifixion. This wasn't from a Foucauldian perspective at all—nowhere near that. What I was interested in was how closely the works themselves were responding to the ideology of their time, which was a religious ideology, and in how the artists situated themselves in relation to major questions without getting their heads chopped off, which was rather difficult if you were Spanish, and Christian, and doing images.

What I wanted to try and do was to see how I could make connections with the serious issues that I am interested in dealing with, and about which I can develop a polemic. I looked at all the scars in the collection, and made some paintings of them just to see how they felt—to know what the motivation was, because some scars were gushing, some were just there, some were painted like a Jackson Pollock. There is a painting by a Spanish master down in the first room (the Seilern Master) if you look at the way the blood describes the body and how loose it is—it's like a Jackson Pollock. The blood is more real than Marc Quinn's blood ever is, and it's more terrifying than anything Damien Hirst has done. That is what interested me. One of the great questions of our time is AIDS –and the blood, its symbol—and how we relate to it. In Africa, but also everywhere else, it's one of those universal symbols which goes through things. It's part of that tacky notion of a 'shared symbolic order'.

AH: What other issues are you dealing with in this exhibition?

CA: The notion of corruption interests me right now, and the notion of metaphor. My early work you could say was kind of interventionist, it was activist, it was to an extent documentary, and I knew what all the problems were then —people have often rehearsed them. Half way through the '70s I realized that we weren't producing any stunning visual imagery, that it was quite boring. The visual was everywhere around us in popular culture, so that I then gradually began to look for and create strong images.

The other theme which is running through some of these works is the notion of not being able to see anything. It's X-Files stuff in a way, it's like: you just can't believe anything. Just last week with Edwina Currie and John Major, you simply cannot believe it. Like the erased de Kooning drawing, and like Man Ray's covered objects, I was obliterating text in newspapers. In this collection, I notice that van Gogh had covered his ear up, when it would have been much more like him to have painted it without the covering on. So part of what I was doing was uncovering his ear.

AH: You have always been concerned with dialogue, listening to people in the first instance, then trying to communicate the results efficiently. But your use of metaphor might alter that relationship, render dialogue more indirect. Are the ceramic tongues, one of the pieces at the Courtauld, a departure into a more fully metaphorical realm?

CA: They are metaphorical. They have partly to do, again, with that obliteration of text. The Bruegel painting which I had in mind was the 'Tower of Babel', with its overload. This blizzard of information between people, but equally between organizations, corporations, multinationals, and George Bush, all trying to pull the meaning to their side. The piece was actually to pull the meaning out of things, to the other side. The tongues came out of a piece that I did in 1993 which had real tongues in a freezer, with golden books inside—it was about *Wuthering Heights*, Emily Brontë, children, and speechlessness. I couldn't think of how to use casts of these tongues. I couldn't make them work. Then I found a way which I think does work, as a metaphor for the way in which we're all rendered speechless and meaningless. It sounds slightly pretentious, but that's the notion: that we're rendered speechless by the amount of speech and information around us, and this despite all of the facilities to be able to speak, like mobile phones.

AH: How would you like the visitor to respond to your interventions?

CA: In one way it's going to be the shock of the familiar. It's going to be like: I've seen that. I recognize that. The familiar will shock us. One of the labels on one of the suits says 'Aesthetics can be a pretty ugly business.' You look at all the torture, the wounds, the crucifixions going on in the first room, and the ladies and gentlemen can look at that saying: 'That's very beautiful.' You can imagine people sitting in Tehran or in California looking at the Anthrax germ and saying 'That's very beautiful.' The work is not meant to shock. I don't want to shock the English middle classes, because actually, this is one of my more selfish exhibitions. It has a lot to do with my understanding of this collection, so in that sense I'm not saying 'Look, there's blood everywhere and there will be more blood soon.' I'm just saying that this is what artists have always been interested in, and artists are embedded in society, they're not outside of society. Important things interest me. My dealer Ronald Feldman has just sent me an e-mail saying: 'For God's sake, Conrad, lighten up.' I wrote back—again, slightly pretentiously—'You wouldn't tell Goya to lighten up.' (laughs) My background with my dad and all my family working in coal mines, having pneumoconiosis, then working in Sellafield and dying of cancer: that's where I'm coming from. Although I do have a sense of humor, I think. What I don't like is the notion of the artist as an anarchist, because I don't think that works, and I don't particularly like the idea of shocking people. Nor do I like the notion of there being no such thing as society, which is what a lot of contemporary artists believe, I think. A lot of prominent ones act as if there is no such thing as society. I know it's a reaction against gender politics, gay politics, and class politics, yet I still believe that these things structure our existence.

AH: So one could see this exhibition as a way for you to break open the collection. Like a wound?

CA: Yes, hopefully.

AH: In contrast to the retrospective at Wolverhampton City Art Gallery, the Courtauld exhibition appears to be much more centered on a specific time and place.

CA: Who knows what people will think about these works when they're out of this context? Duchamp said that a work of art lasts fifty years before it becomes something else. I'm happy if it lasts the three weeks it's in a show. I've never pretended that there would be anything for posterity in what I do. You obviously hope that there will be, but it's not something you can build in. If you seek to create a timeless, placeless, personless, universal argument, you'll probably produce something like what the Victorians produced when they thought they were producing Roman busts, which is time-specific provincial work. Basically I'm trying to find serious subjects that fit in with my ideology and view of the world, in the same way as those artists who were doing crucifixions and tortures.

AH: You frequently refer to your traditional education as a painter, and one may be tempted to see your Courtauld show as a means of reapproaching a terrain that you had given up...

CA: Mellowing? (laughs)

AH: ...yet at the same time you remain critical towards traditional media, especially in your quotations of Duchamp, with the sinks.

CA: Well, wait: if you look at most of the work in the (Courtauld) gallery, Duchamp's methodology is closer to them than it is to Lucien Freud, for example. Now, what I mean by that, is that if you look at Andrea del Sarto's Botti Madonna, and you read about it—if you read that nicely produced catalogue, all the way through it talks about workshop, workshop, workshop. If you look at Lucien Freud's paintings, it's all about the fetish: every single thing about them is about him, basically he wouldn't dream, like Duchamp, or me, or del Sarto, of letting anybody else touch that canvas of his. It's a fetishized brush stroke, and to that extent, it's solipsistic, self-referential. In a different way than mine, where I have a technician who is making some of these ceramic works, or who is making some of these embroidered works. I don't actually do them, in that sense, but I am arguing that I would be closer to the del Sarto model or to the Rubens model, or to most of the artists in this collection, apart from, say, Manet, or Cezanne: I am closer to the former than I am to Freud. I am not making any direct comparisons, because it really is a different attitude to the self, as not being the center of the universe. I am not the hero of my own work, because I think there are more important things out there, than there are in here. That's the notion: that I don't want my work to be particularly about me, although of course it will be to some extent.

AH: You have always enjoyed positively disruptive relationships to institutions such as museums. Can we see the effectiveness or success of your work in this particular case as something, perhaps, to be regretted?

CA: (laughs) We don't know if it's going to be a success yet. No, when I first started off I was just totally angry. I'm still very angry. But about different things. One of the things that artists always start off with doing in art is trying to demolish art. You know. It's something you do when you're very dissatisfied with things. I was very angry when I did *Strike at Brannans* in 1972, and thought it would be my last gesture to the art world, and I would never get any other show. Strangely enough, it hit a nerve and I got many offers after that. So I don't particularly want to disrupt the collection: but I would like people to realize that, as I said, aesthetics is a very ugly, dirty business. You can't look at someone getting tortured and say it's beautiful. You can say that it's nicely painted and ignore the subject matter. You can do that—which I suppose, if you're talking about Lucien Freud, would be appropriate. I'm just trying to look with fresh eyes at these artists, and their motivations, and their subjects.

AH: There's a quote from the catalogue of the *Live in Your Head* show at the Whitechapel where you say that 'British art of the 1970s made the British art of the 1990s possible.' How close do you feel to the contemporary scene, and how important is it to come back to London now?

CA: Well it's very strange. First of all there's Gavin (Wade) with the *Strike* exhibition in Wolverhampton. The other thing that happened was that I was invited to show another work from the 1970s in Belfast this November. Because there is now a Sinn Fein mayor in Belfast, so they wanted to show work from the 1970s. The Courtauld was interested in having me here while I was on my sabbatical from California. At the same time, the Victoria & Albert Museum, for I think it's called 'A Hundred Impressions'—it's a print for each year of the 20th century—selected the thalidomide print for the print of 1978. Now this is a print that was banned, and which Tate refused to buy because they said it was a bad print even though they bought all the other prints (in the original series), and this is a print about which questions were asked in Parliament, and for which I sued the Arts Council of Great Britain, and won. I mean it's a cyclic thing. I've always felt that the '70s was a great period and it was a 'Back to Basics' period for art. It was art for whom, what sort of art, how would you make it, what would the audience be, and what's the role of the artist in contemporary society, a role which hadn't really been questioned in that sense up until 1968. In '68 you know that the cry was 'Out of the studios, into the streets,' and in the '70s it was 'Out of the streets, into the galleries,' and in the '80s: 'Out of the galleries, into the streets.' There was a definite questioning of the basics of it all. And a definite questioning of not only 'What was art for?' but also 'Who was it for?' and 'Who made the art?' It's what we call postmodernism: it's a break-up of that certainty that if you did certain things you were on the cutting-edge, you were the avant-garde. It's the breakdown of that notion.

AH: But this historical return can never be a return to the same. Do you feel that your Courtauld intervention is contemporary? Because you also stressed that it was a personal exhibition.

CA: In one sense, it is personal. Although I understand why you're saying 'intervention.' I don't particularly feel it's an intervention. It's probably a reinforcement. In other words, it's my contention that these artists who made these works were involved in their situation in the same way that the works that I'm showing are involved in our situation. And I think they're important. Those works downstairs are not about those specific artists, they're about other things. It's a reinforcement, not an intervention. I've done interventions, as you probably know, the most dangerous being an intervention in Northern Ireland in 1975, and the most personal was the intervention in the strike in 1972 in my own village. No. This is actually in solidarity.

Antony Hudek is a Ph.D. student at the Courtauld Institute of Art.

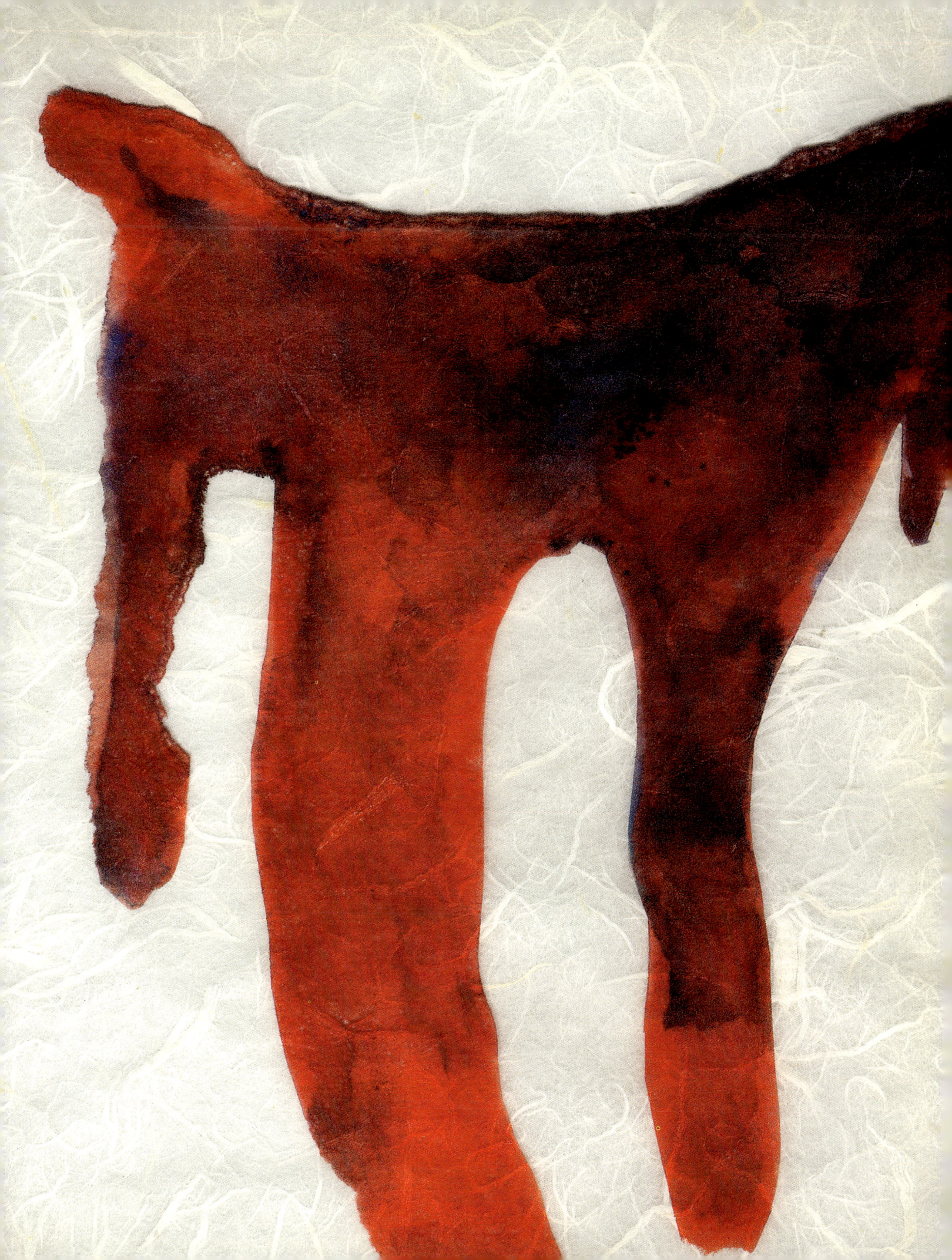

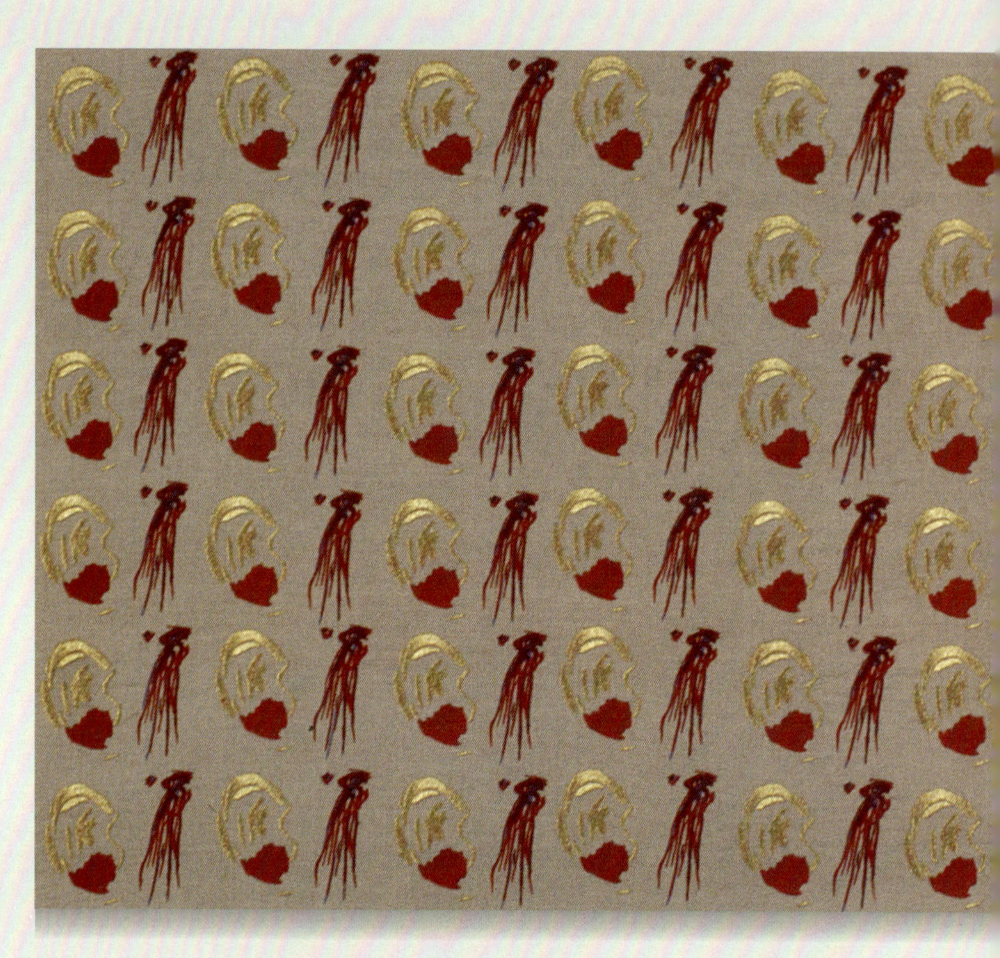

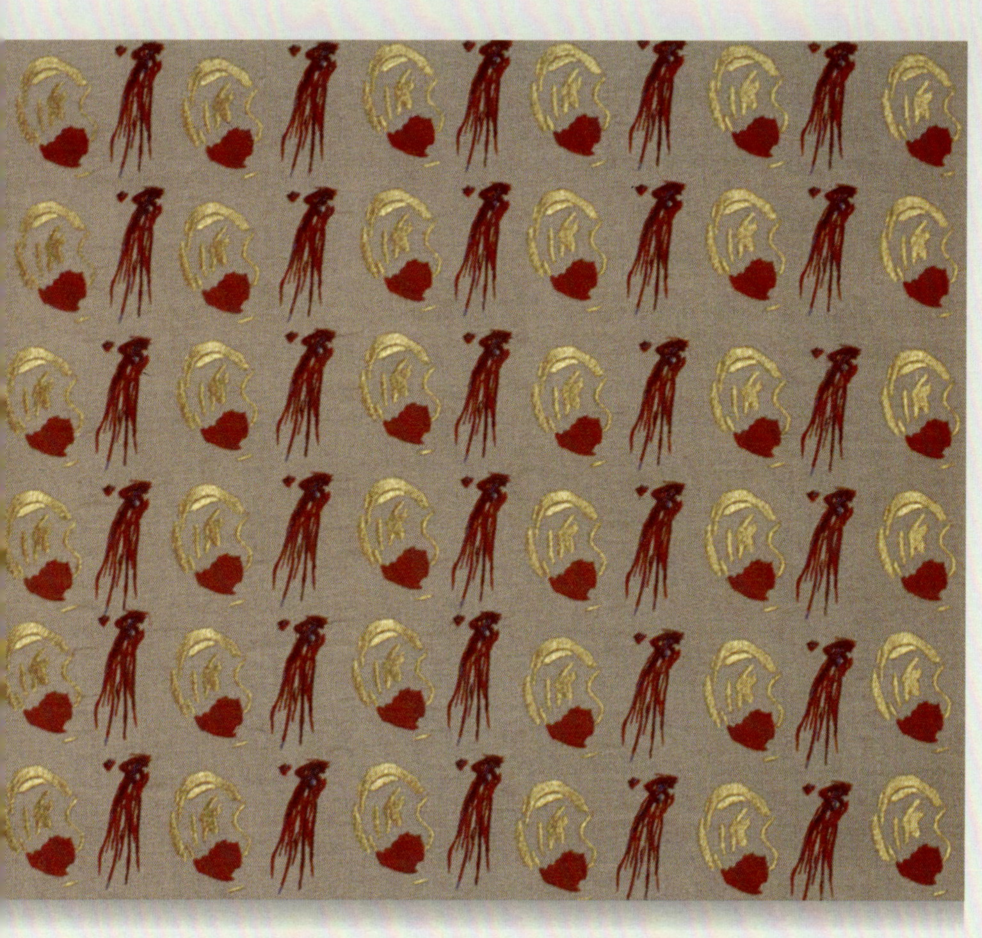

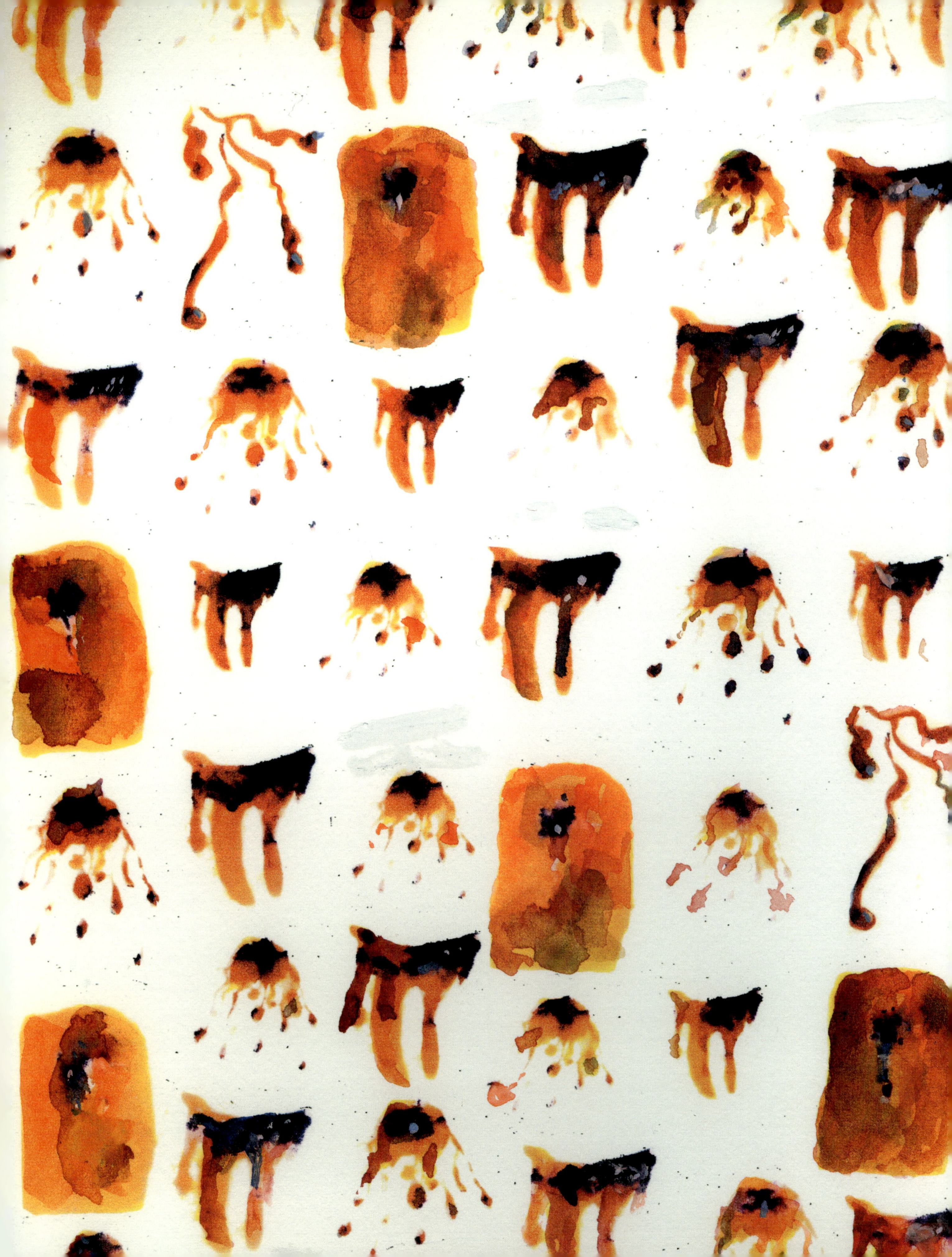

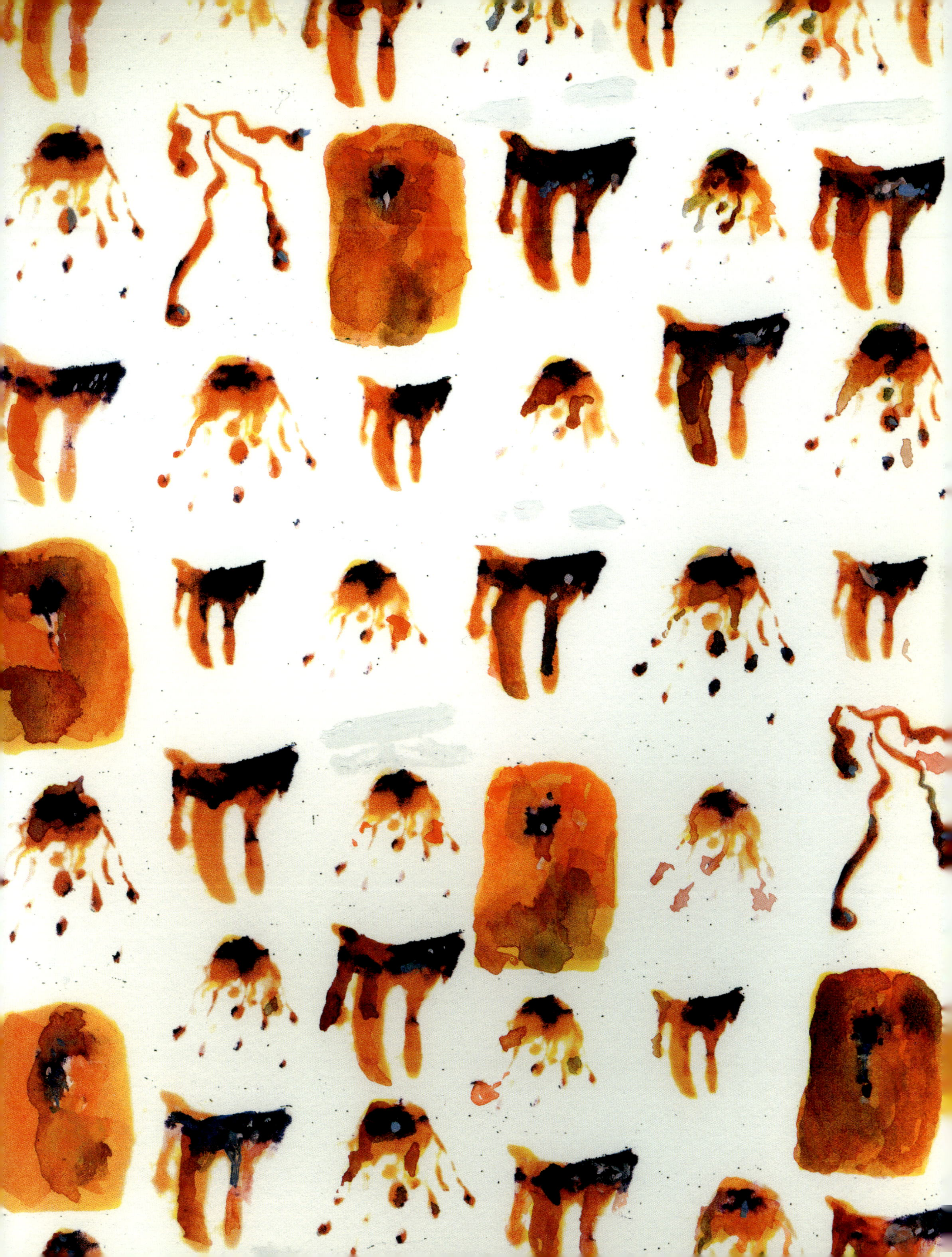

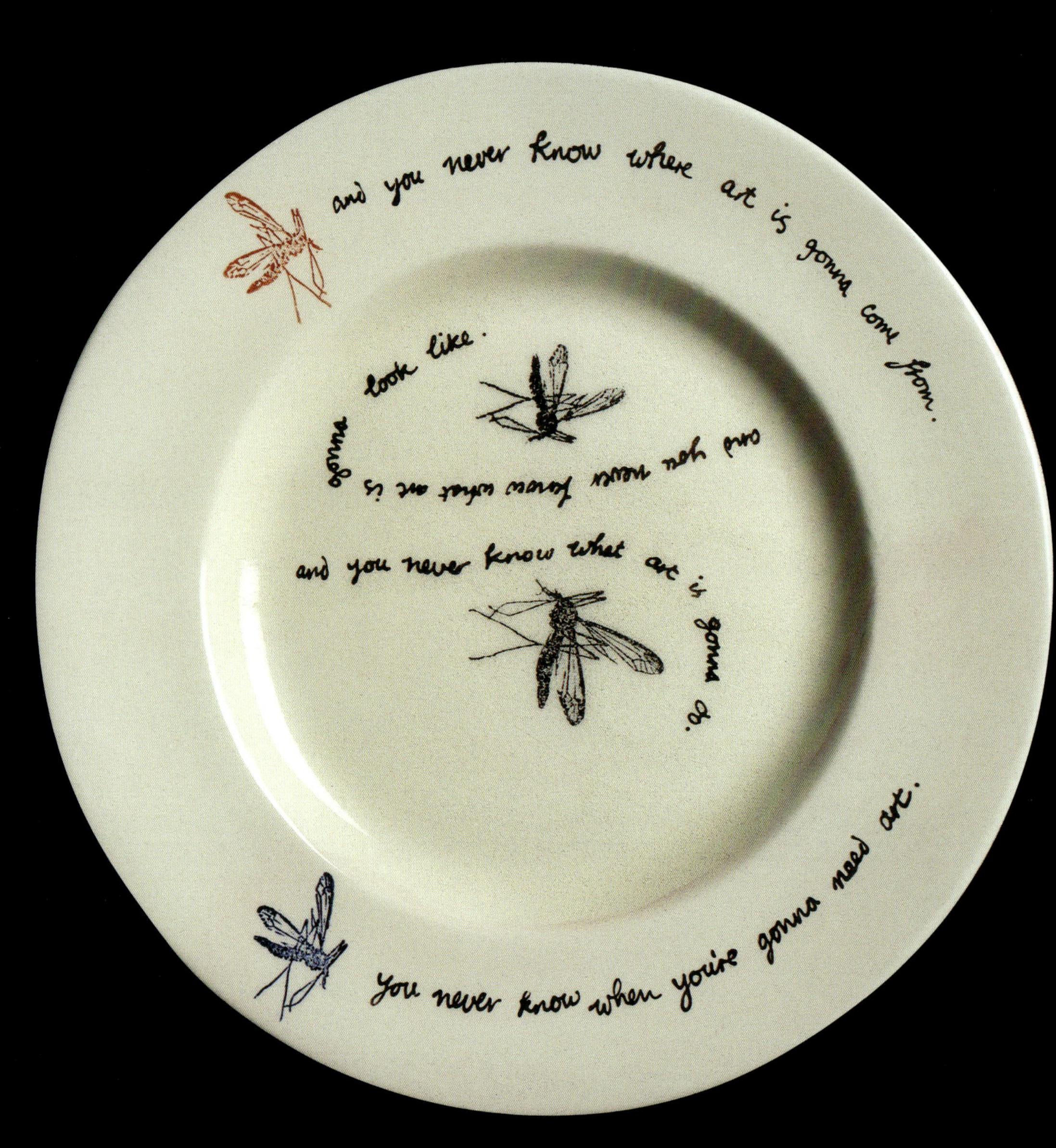
and you never know where art is gonna come from.
gonna look like.
and you never know what art is gonna look like.
and you never know what art is gonna do.
You never know when you're gonna need art.

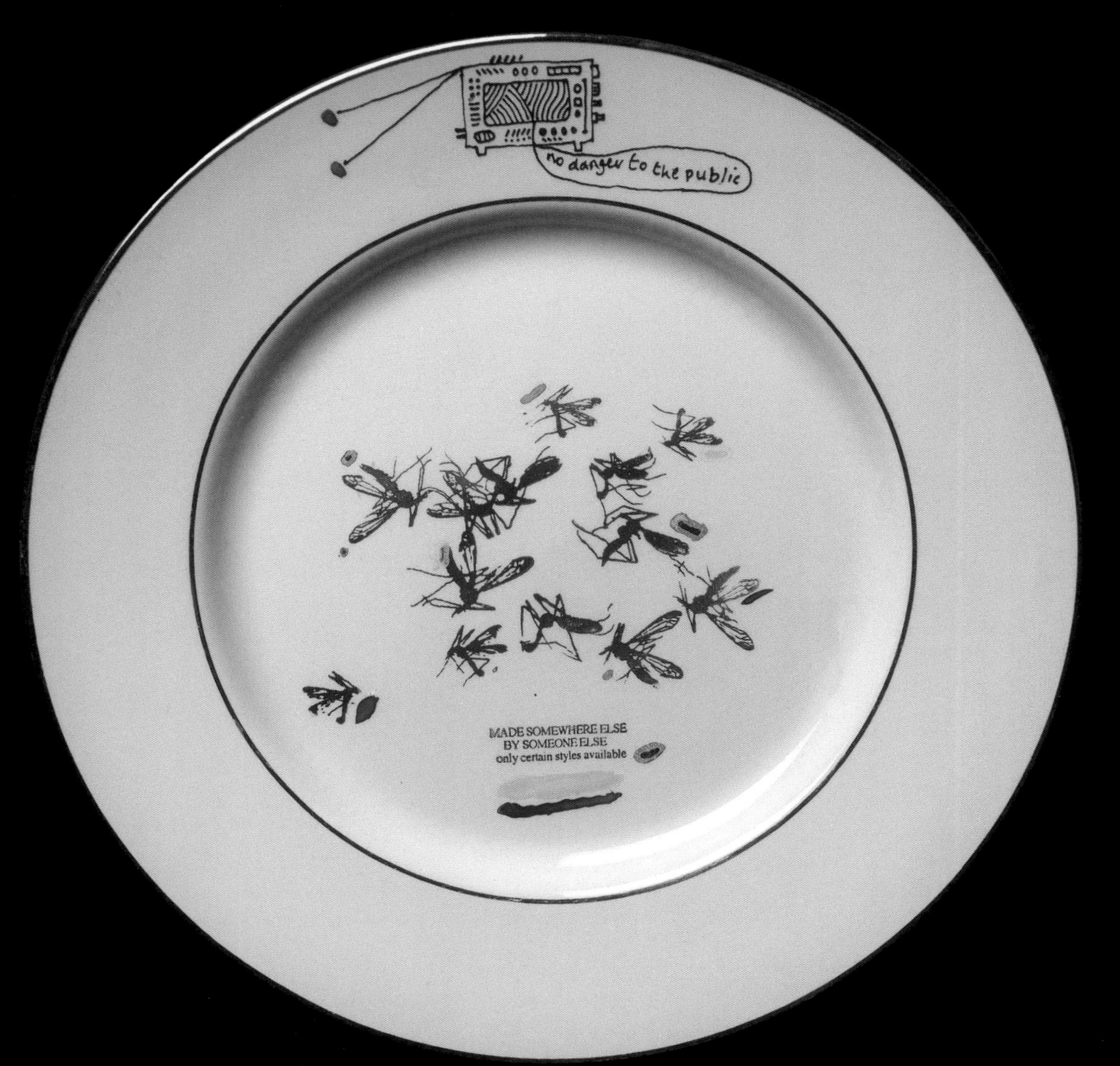

no danger to the public
MADE SOMEWHERE ELSE
BY SOMEONE ELSE
only certain styles available

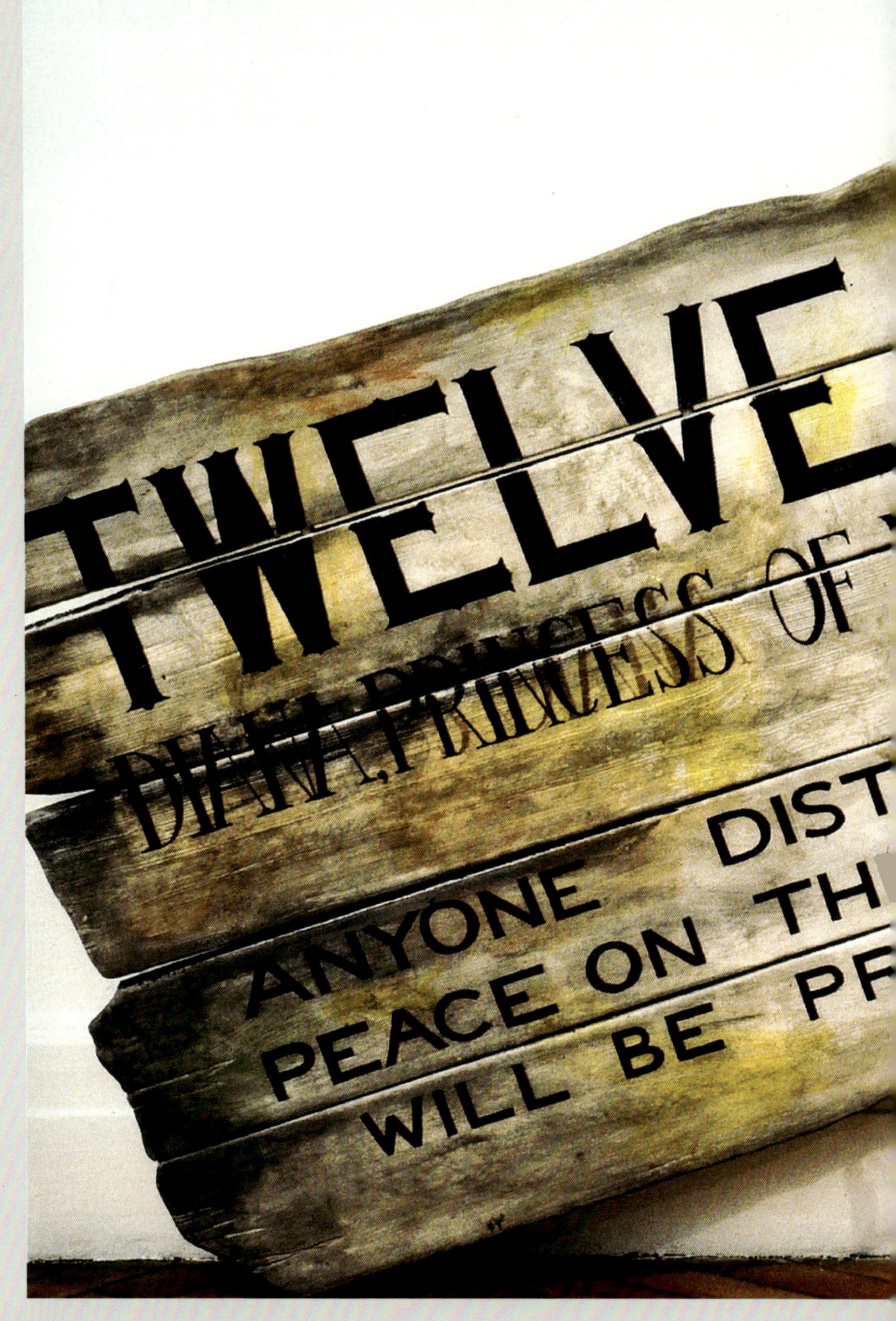
TWELVE
DIAN, PRINCESS OF
ANYONE   DIST
PEACE ON   TH
WILL   BE   PR

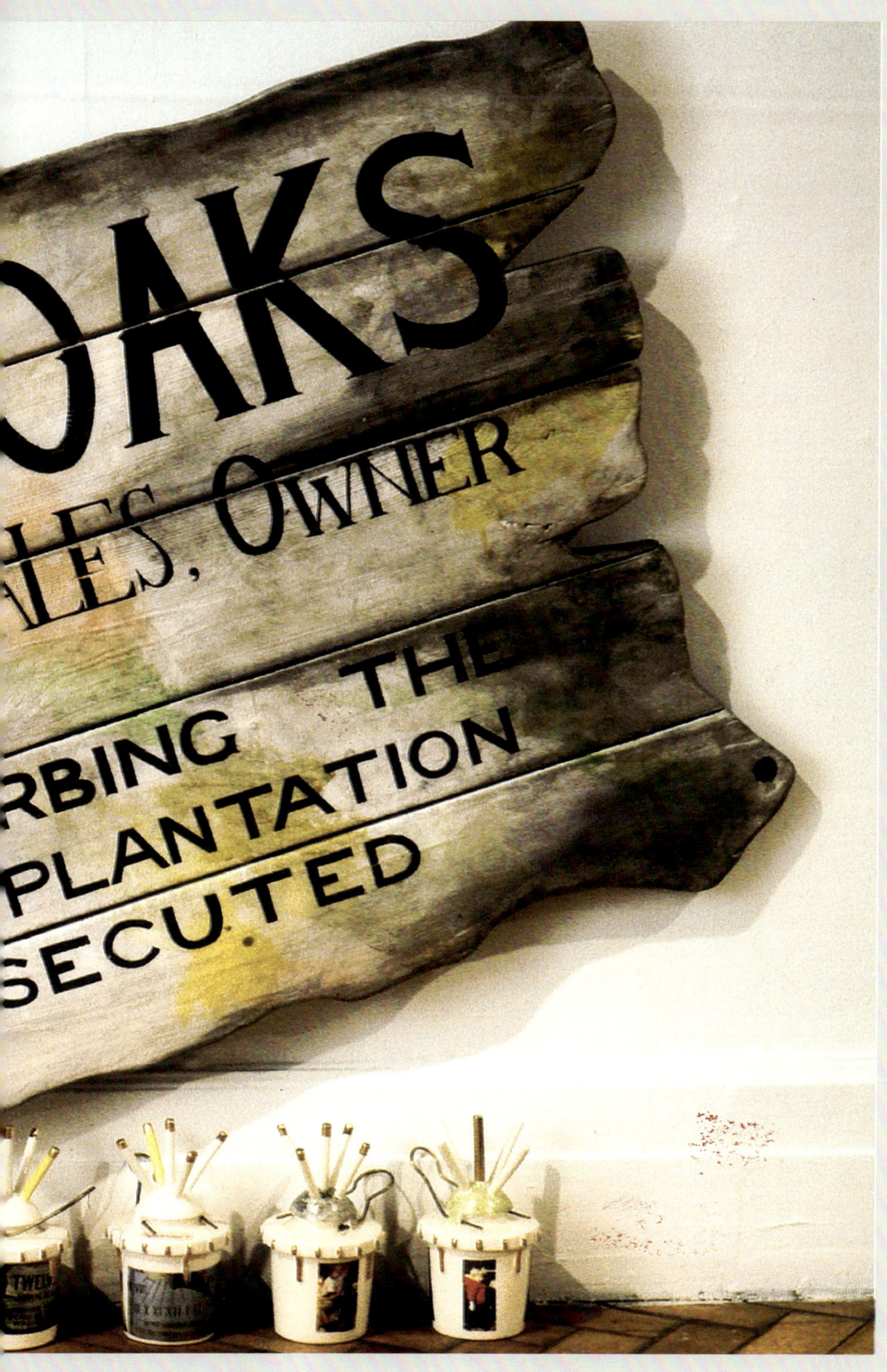
OAKS
ALES, OWNER
RBING   THE
PLANTATION
SECUTED

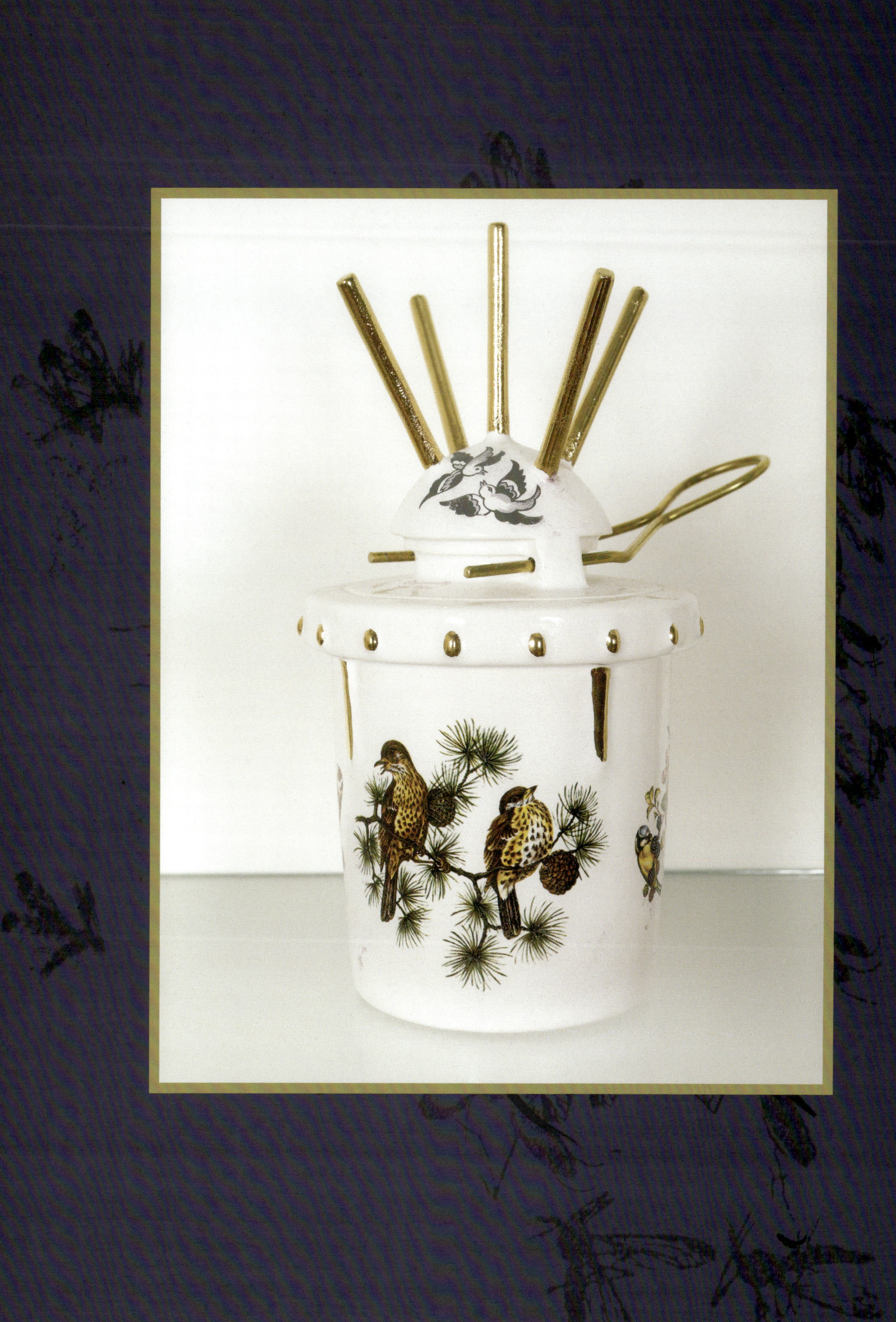

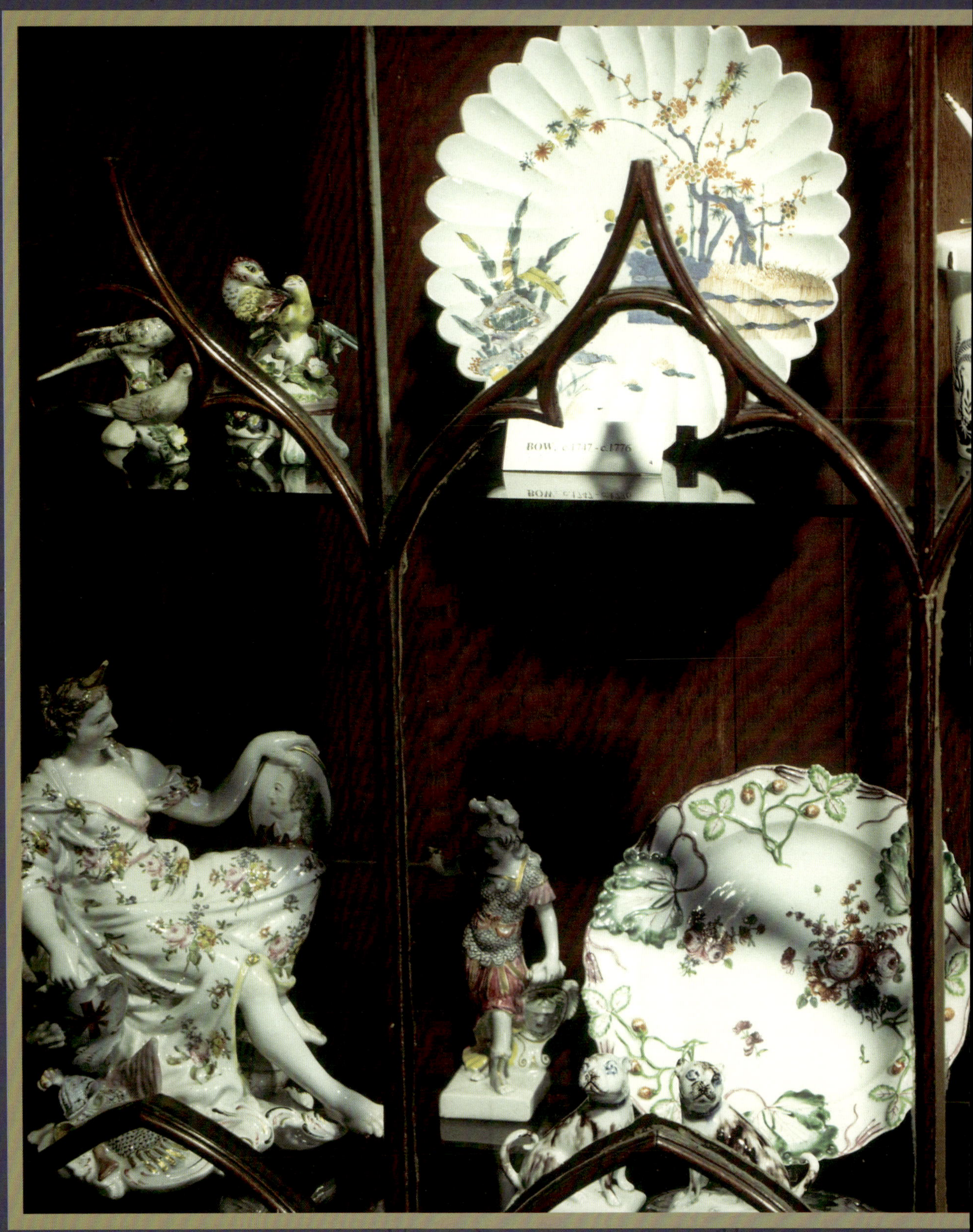

BOW, c.1747–c.1776

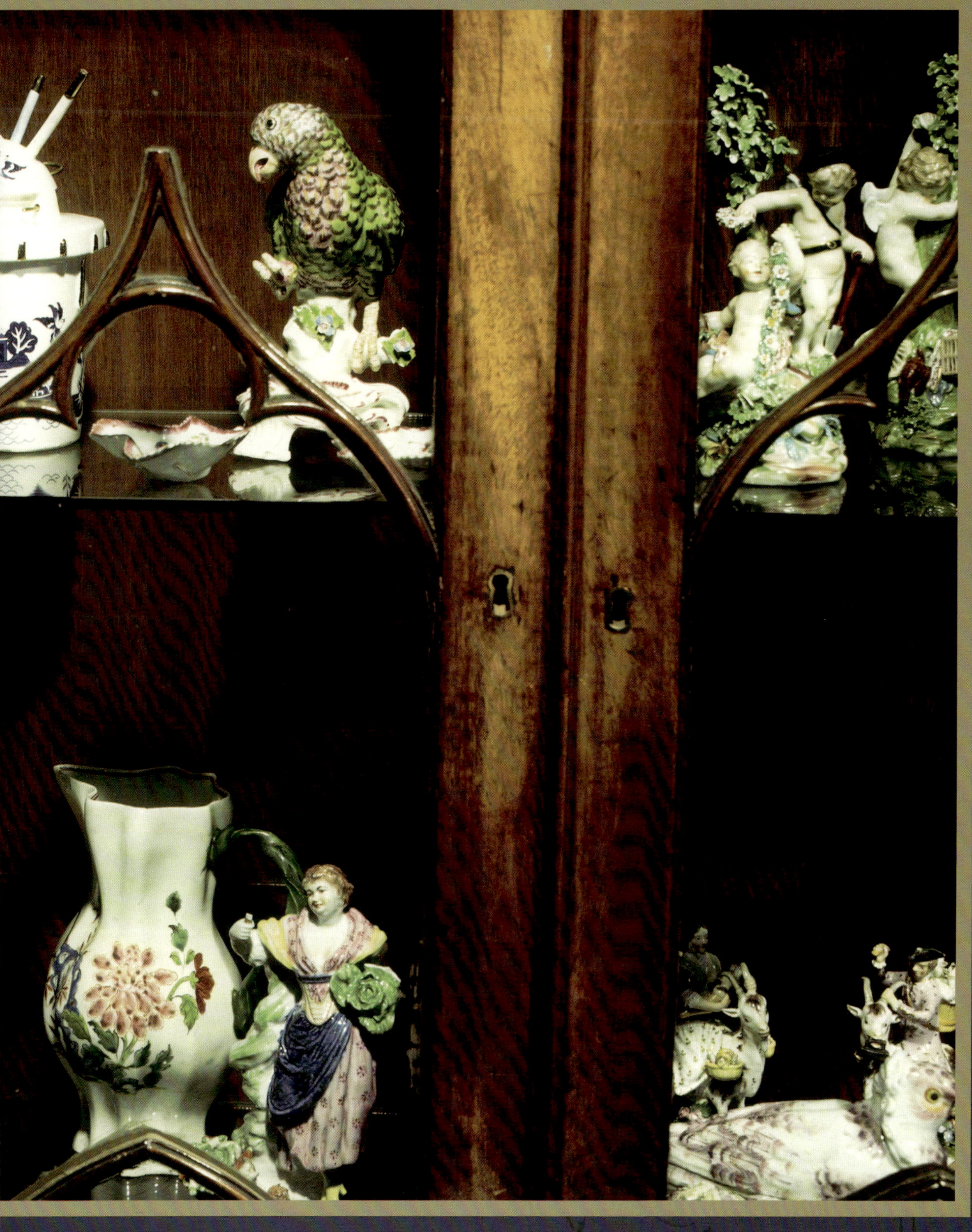

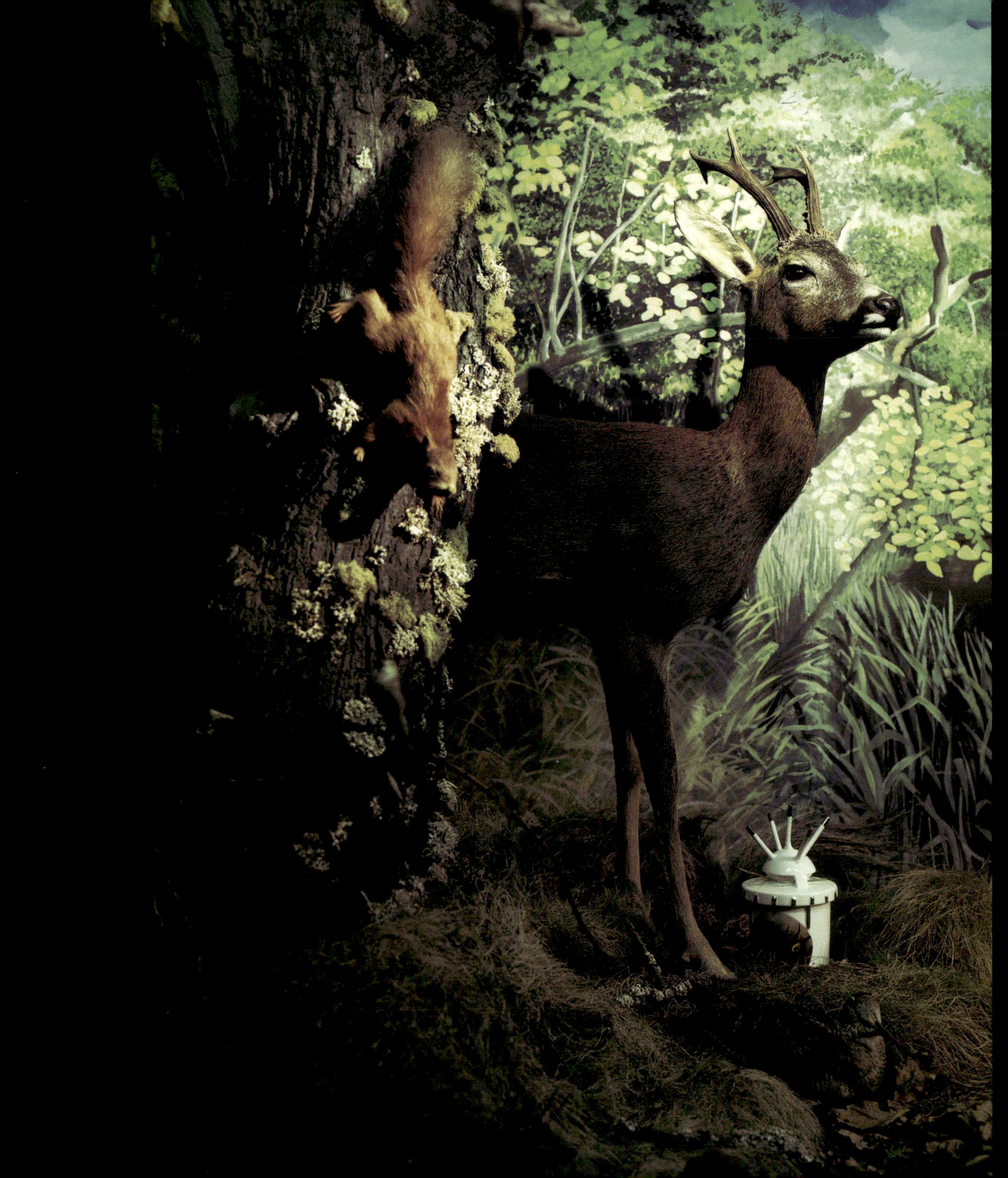

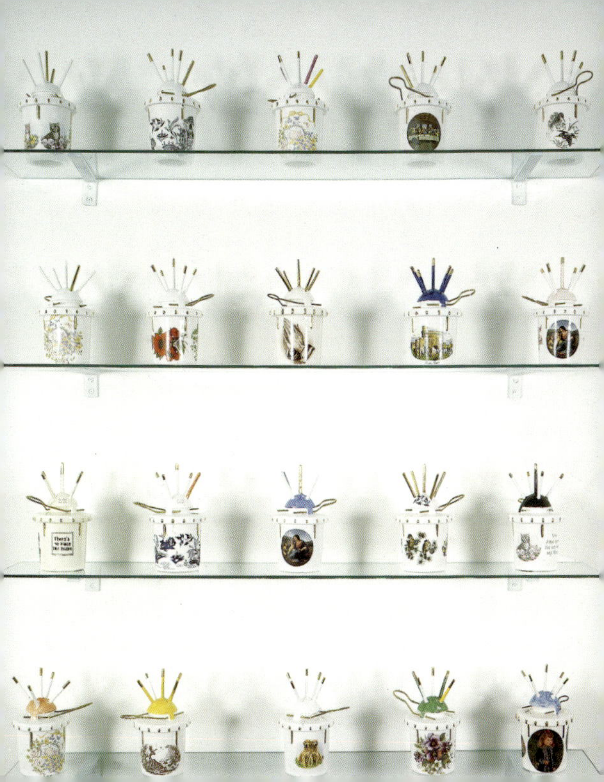

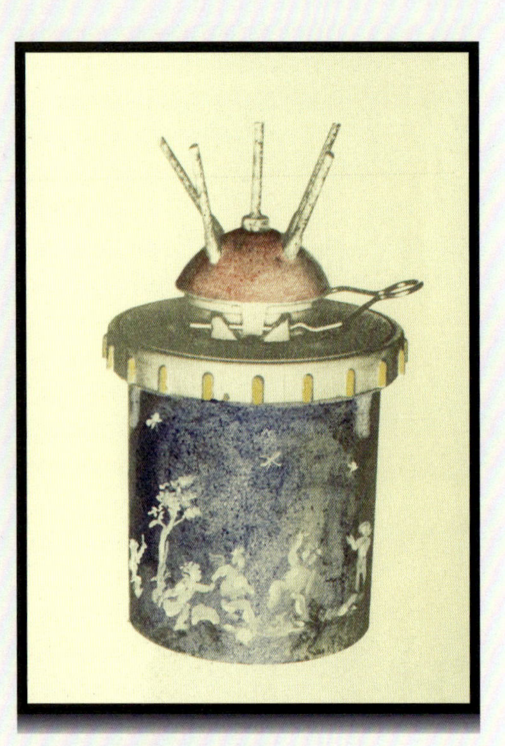 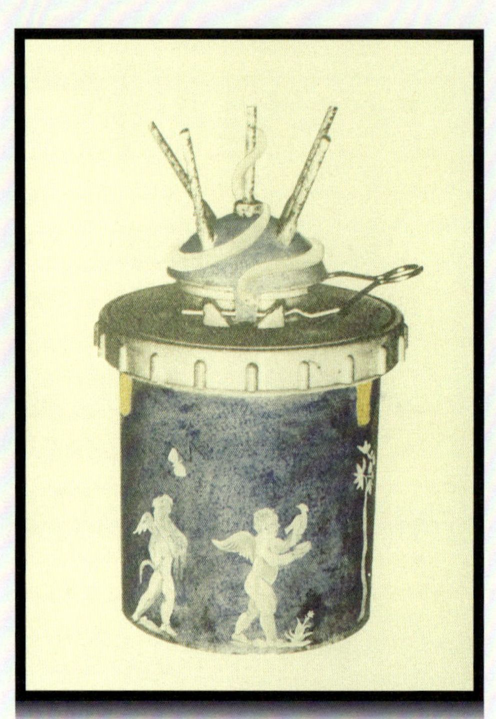

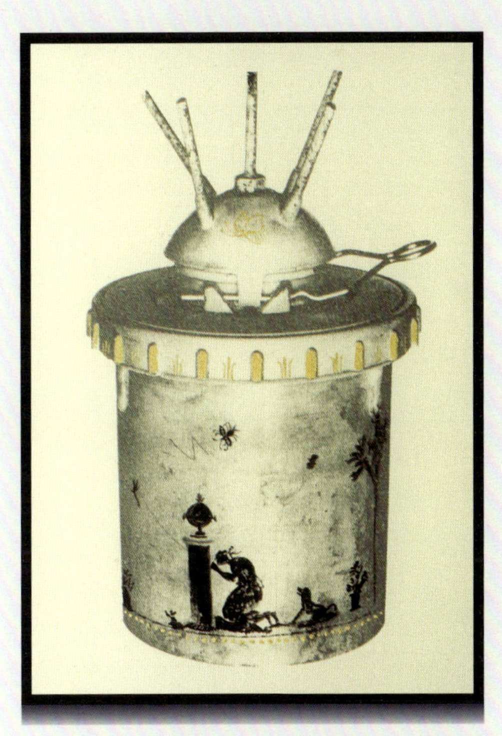
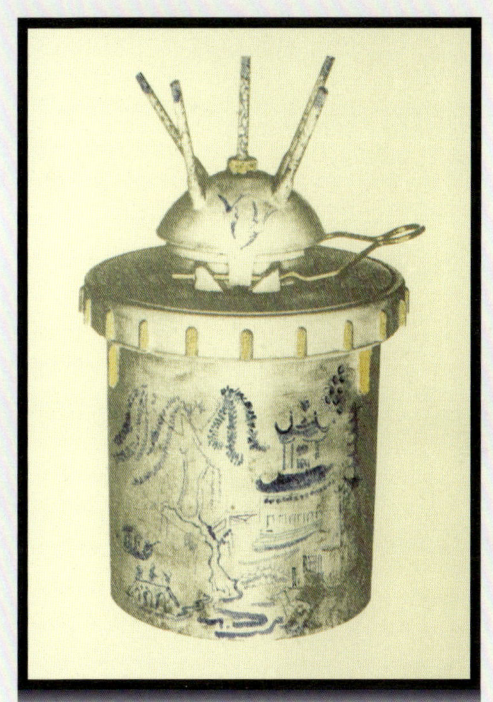

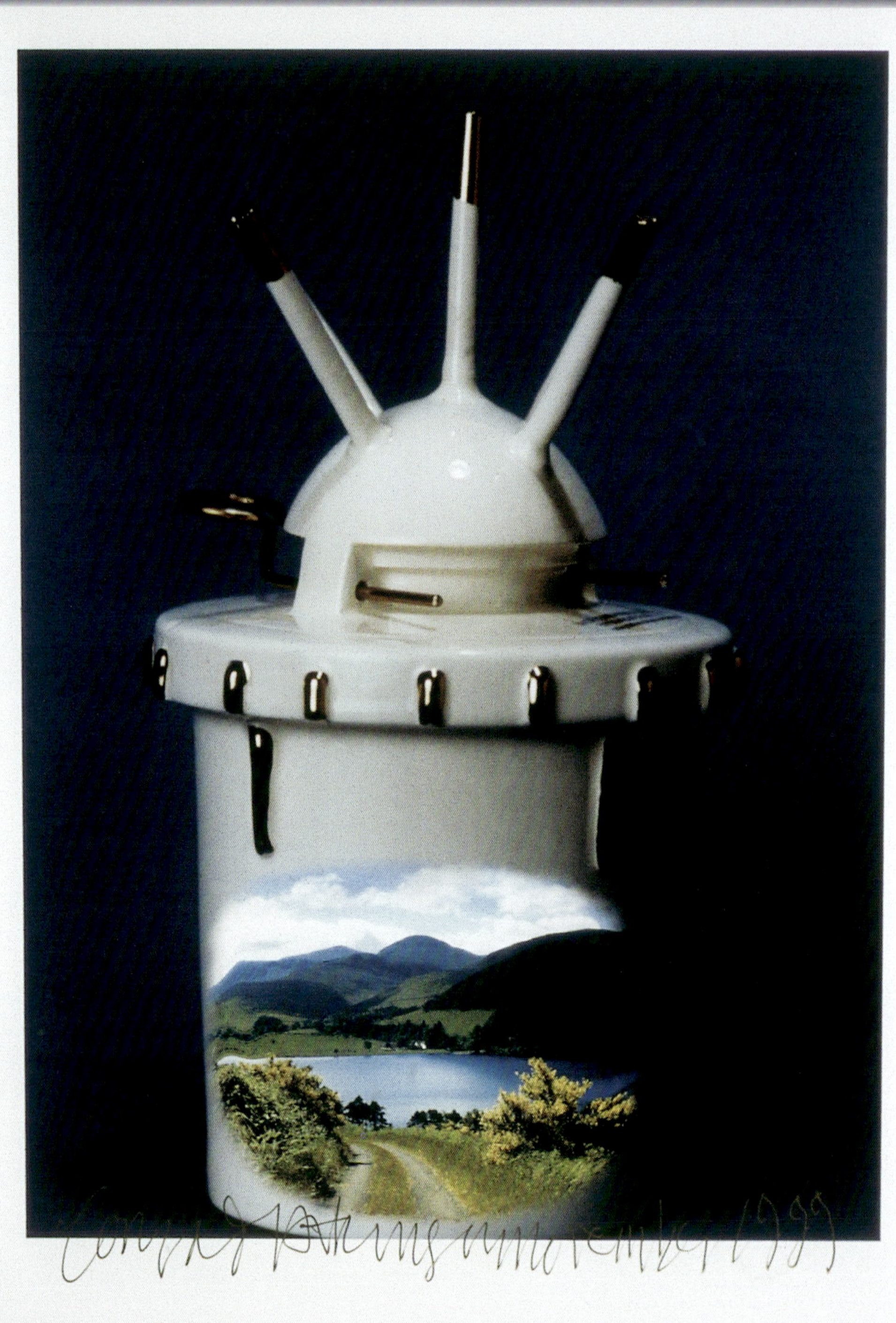

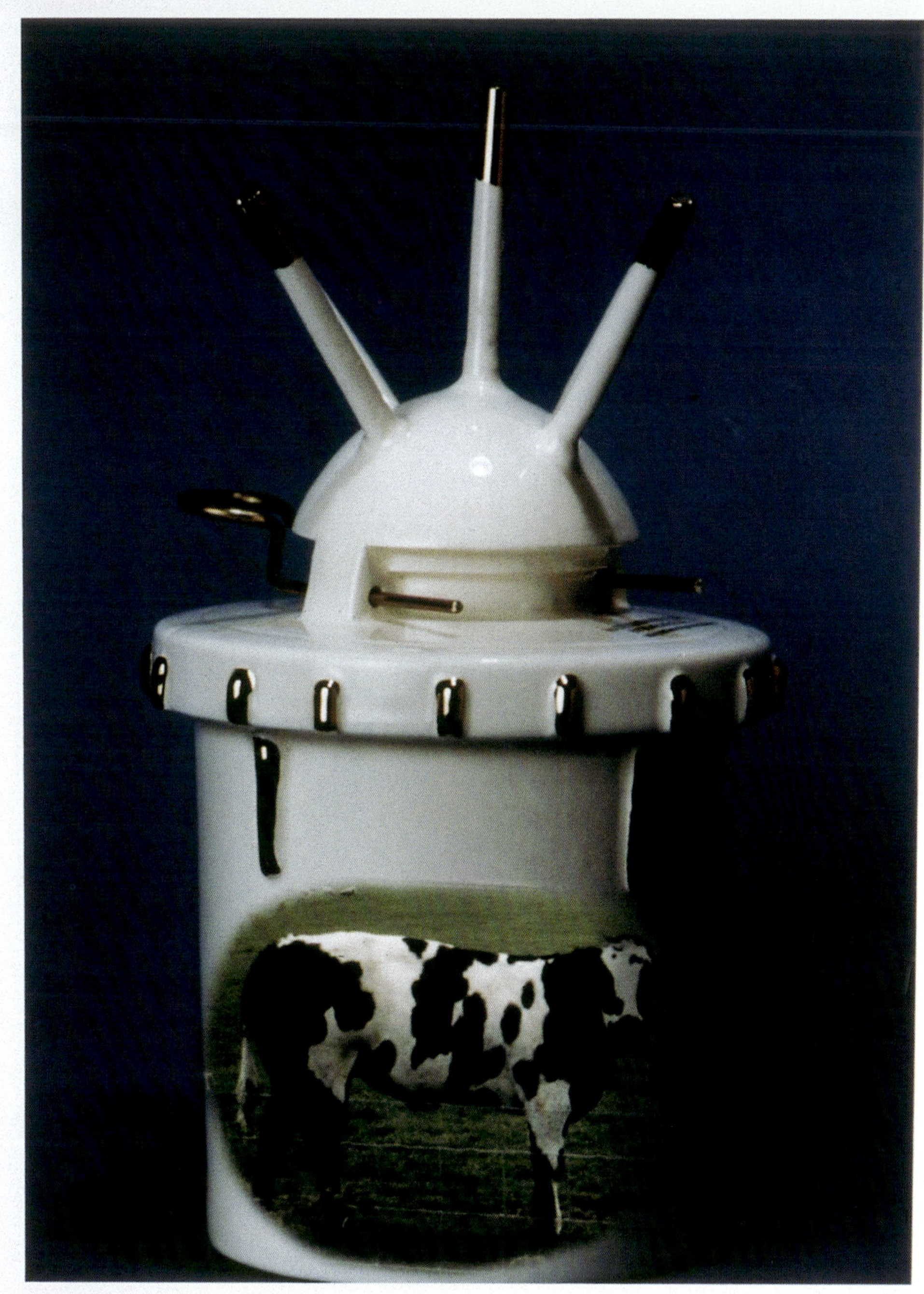

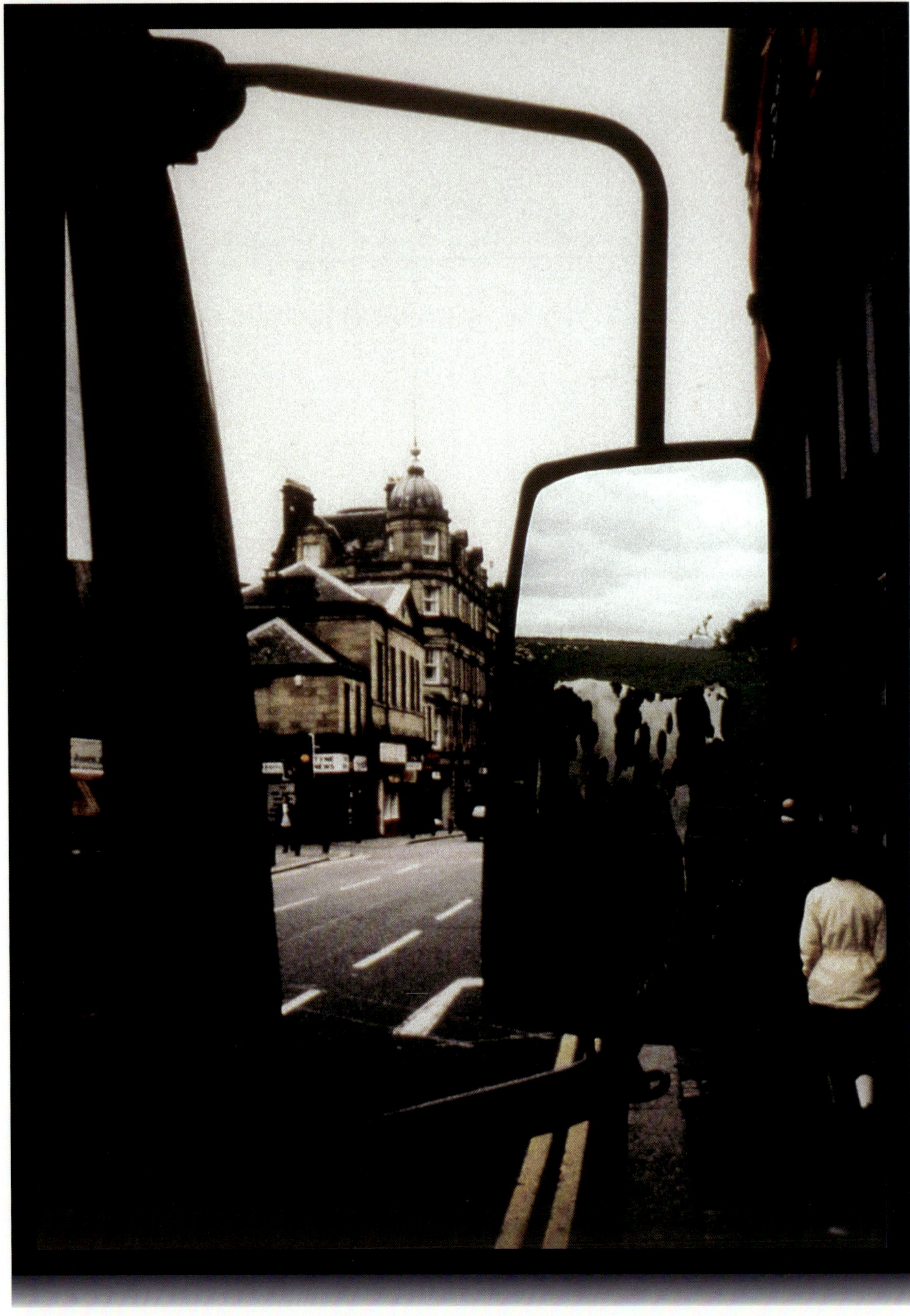

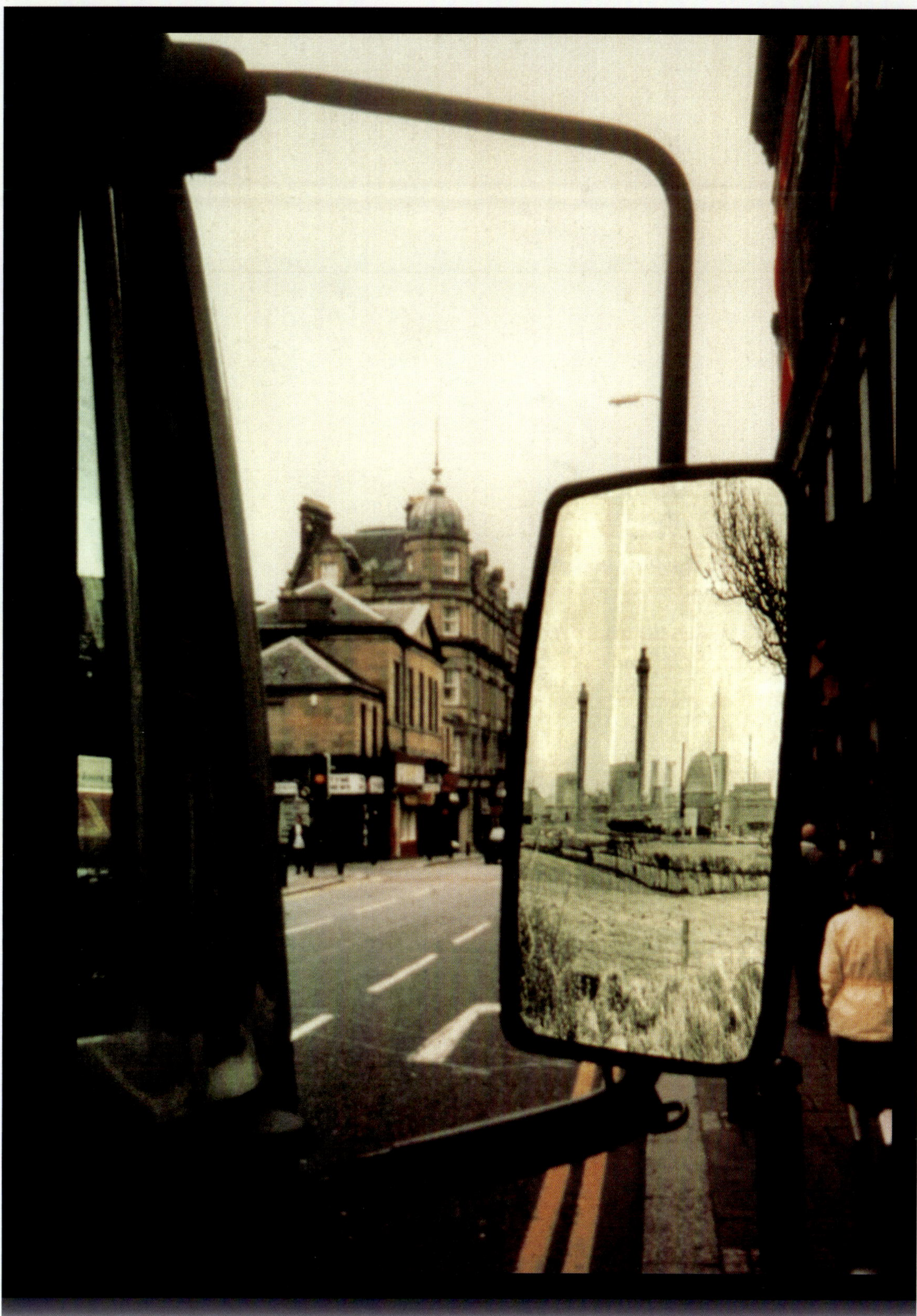

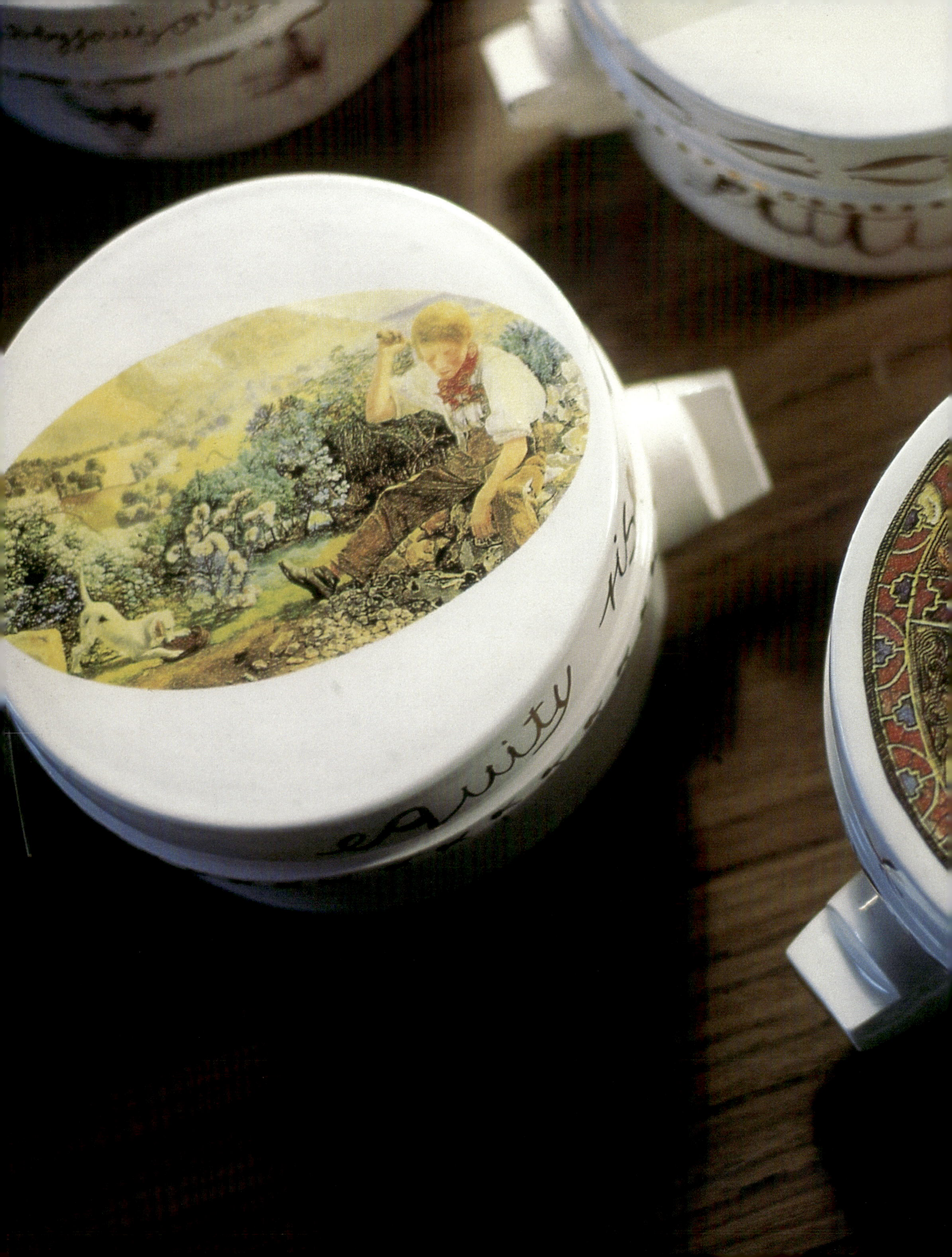

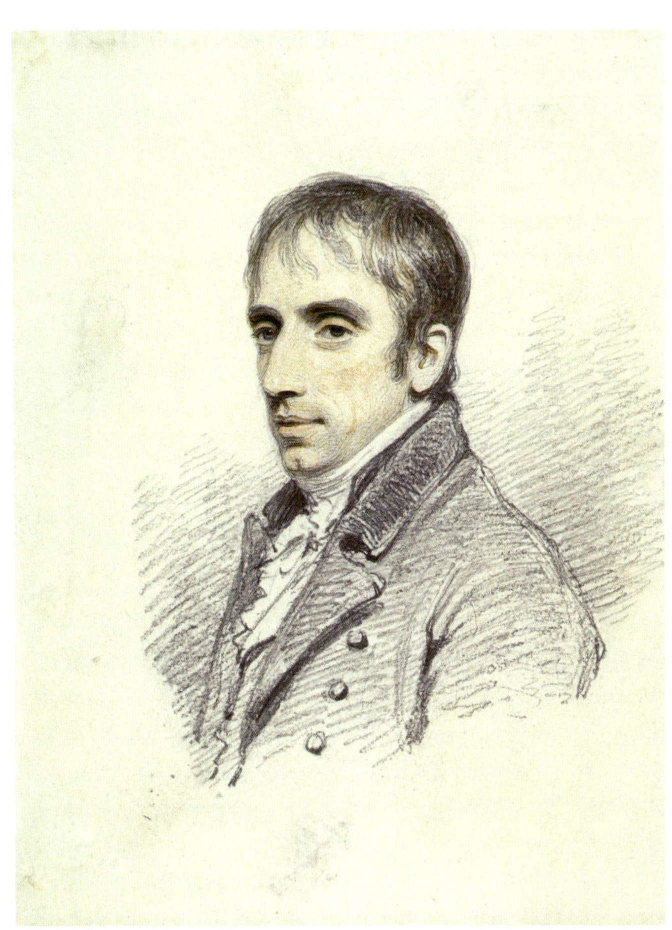

Henry Edridge, **William Wordsworth**, 1805

COMMON SIGHTS
BY CONRAD ATKINSON

The aspects underpinning my interest in Wordsworth and his work could be simply described as being focused upon the material world and the intellectual sphere and their concurrent relationship. The former is an apparently solid unyielding physical presence and the second less discernible with gray areas containing multiple notions including aesthetics and emotion, sensibility and subjectivity. Looking at these aspects of our existence and examining these twin concepts the phrase 'All that's solid melts into air' seems to contain enough truth that the slopes of the mountains and valleys of certainty and meaning are filled with so many attitudes and possibilities that we could be forgiven for freezing ourselves with a fear of acting or thinking about our environment and its meaning. Possibilities that have arisen in recent years might well be described as corporate and commercialized ways of seeing our surroundings and our landscapes which are so ubiquitous as to obliterate our presences and fill our visions with dubious other agendas. Constantly contesting these meanings could paralyze our desire and our will as well as our ability to act or even think 'cause every time I write a rhyme, these people think it's a crime'.

These concepts skate and slide and dance and reel; they flit and trip and slither and seep and trickle and crawl; they flow and stroll and run and wriggle and are tossed through our landscapes.

The temporary landscape flickers in and out of our vision and our mind because there was a time when every common sight did seem fixed and ok but then they change and every body loses itself.

Some strange landscapes both material and intellectual exist in the realm of landmines, with which I've worked for a decade. Working with landmines experts in Mines Advisory Group (MAG)) and with the US Campaign to Ban Landmines (Vietnam Veterans Trust) I was vividly made aware of this notion of the intangible interior reflecting the exterior landscape. A landmines removal expert came back from Cambodia recently and at one of my exhibitions said to me that when he returned to England he found it difficult to walk on an English lawn. Possibly the most famous example of this mental shift is the story of Gray drawing the curtains of his carriage as he drove through the Lake District in order not to view the brutal mountains. Wordsworth removed the curtains in a blinding flash. Subsequently after the death of his brother John at sea Wordsworth writes that he is no longer able to look at the sea...'the things I once could see I now can see no more'.

The notion that aboriginal people in Australia relate deeply to the landscape poetically and through stories and drawings and dreamings and coloring their bodies with red and yellow ochre they turn themselves into their landscapes as the distinctions and separations between their bodies and their minds and their landscapes slips away like a mirage...my own experience as a child in Cleator Moor of the 'redmen', the iron ore miners, the red iron ore dust seeping into everything and transforming their clothes into glittering fine silk like postmodern *haute couture* as they walked home with lungs filled with dust through a landscape permeated with red. The dust is now mined as a colorant for makeup. This landscape is colored by the vast hidden body of iron ore under the town; making the streams red, the town overlooked by two great slag banks studded with pumice reeked with familiar sulfur, garden rockeries made with spar, paths lined with crystals from the mines, crushed red gravel on the footpaths through the town, doorstops of polished hematite beside the reddened doorsteps, the red offcuts of pit props carried underarm at the end of the shift for the fire at home...St. Mary's Catholic Church with the grotto of life-sized saints embedded in iron ore spoil from the pits and built by the unemployed miners who made quartz boxes in a hall in Cleator Moor called The Blood Tub...all overlooked by two huge slag banks studded with pumice, and slag with sulfur seeping through the white and gray ash. These sulfurous fumes enabling the miners to grow beautiful disease free roses. An almost contrived fairytale paradox of beauty thriving in a poisonous atmosphere. The landscape from under the ground...the world turned upside down. I watched a couple of miners deep underground amongst glittering hematite fragments working with small pickaxes delicately and skillfully loosening a giant body of ore from the wall; they took over three hours sensing each transient vibration through the earth listening watching speaking.

This sense of landscape dissolving the body is reflected in other artists like Emily Brontë's *Wuthering Heights* where the characters names are taken from the landscape; Heathcliff, Hareton, Nellie Dean, Lockwood, Thrushcross Grange...people and the environment streaming through each other. The body and the mind the material and the emotional smearing themselves with each other's colors.

Pamela Woof talks about this in her essay on Daffodils:

> *How personal, even modern is Dorothy's reaction to the daffodils...Her perception of the flowers frail and mortal as we know they are, is original...no moral is drawn; it simply was so...this is deliberate writing*

Dorothy's precise observation of the daffodils moving as human bodies is resonant and unsentimental.

The way Wordsworth explores the emotional and intellectual and our landscapes relationships with the material world is both subtle and startlingly direct. There is astonishing clarity in his question to the old leech gatherer, a transient worker in the poem 'Resolution and Independence': 'How is it that you live, and what is it you do?'

The inquiry has no element of condescension and it is addressed to everyone and everything in the universe. It is perhaps the second most important question in literature after 'To be or not to be'.

A greeting in Cleator Moor I remember from the forties and fifties was "Are you working?"

Lyrical Ballads discovered the internal and external in a direct, radical and familiar language. Common stories about and about us. As the industrial revolution was turning whitehot from Whitehaven to Manchester and the migration to the cities increasingly put a gold frame turning the landscape into the picturesque. George Morland's rural poor disappear from Constable's landscapes.

We know the landscape is manipulated materially and physically, but more complex and less focused upon is how the landscape is managed internally, how is it manipulated aesthetically, emotionally, poetically, politically, ideologically; we know the production and marketing reasons which construct political apples and economic steaks but who constructs its meanings and for what purpose? How is the manipulation of the landscapes of our desires and emotions created and by what poetic, aesthetic and politics does it operate? How would the divinely and infinitely curious guy called Wordsworth have responded to the invisibility of the poetic residues of power? About the half life of things, the low thresholds, and americium, and strontium 90 and distorted insects and plutonium and seasonal labor patterns of the tourist industry and agribusiness and dioxin and 245t and genetically modified crops and global warming, West Nile disease and foot and mouth and the approaching blue tongue disease and BSE...and Africa moving slowly north in hunger. This is the man who democratized the landscape and the language with which it was constructed...paradoxically in his 'other' life as a sort of Tory he was famously hostile to democratic access to the land in his opposition to opening up the Lake District to the masses...but in essence his real life was elsewhere.

Robert Woof points out that 'a new question today is that cross pollination between the wild daffodil and the cultivar will lead to the destruction of the daffodils the Wordsworths celebrated. Left to the rigors of nature, it seems that the cultivars tend to revert to 'blind' plants, producing few if any flowers eventually.'

These common unseen sights are smothered or erased in gold and obliterated by corporate pictures. How can we mean? How can we see? How can we react? How can we speak? How can we mean? How can we feel? How can we desire? Whose desires, whose images, whose fantasy, whose life, whose meanings, for whose benefit, whose landscapes, whose pictures? Who is approaching to the nature of the ocular spectrum and every common sight? With no more wild daffodils.

'I've used the pen to express myself. You'll see that from day one my main focus was on self expression, no matter how lewd the subject matter.' This is Eminem talking recently about his work and acknowledging an acute awareness of the notion of lewdness and of the objections to his subject matter (as opposed to his language which is in itself innovative).

Compare this with the scorn directed at Wordsworth's subject matter, daffodils, in a letter by the poet Anna Seward to Walter Scott:

> *Surely if his worst foe had chosen to caricature this egoistic manufacturer of metaphysic importance upon trivial themes, he could not have done it more effectively.*

My early work (I make no mention of quality comparisons with myself and the two artists quoted) was attacked viciously for its subject matter...the lives of common people and their diseases...asbestosis, mercury poisoning, emphysema, pneumoconiosis the landscapes and their bodies.

The mind of man is married to this goodly universe – William Wordsworth

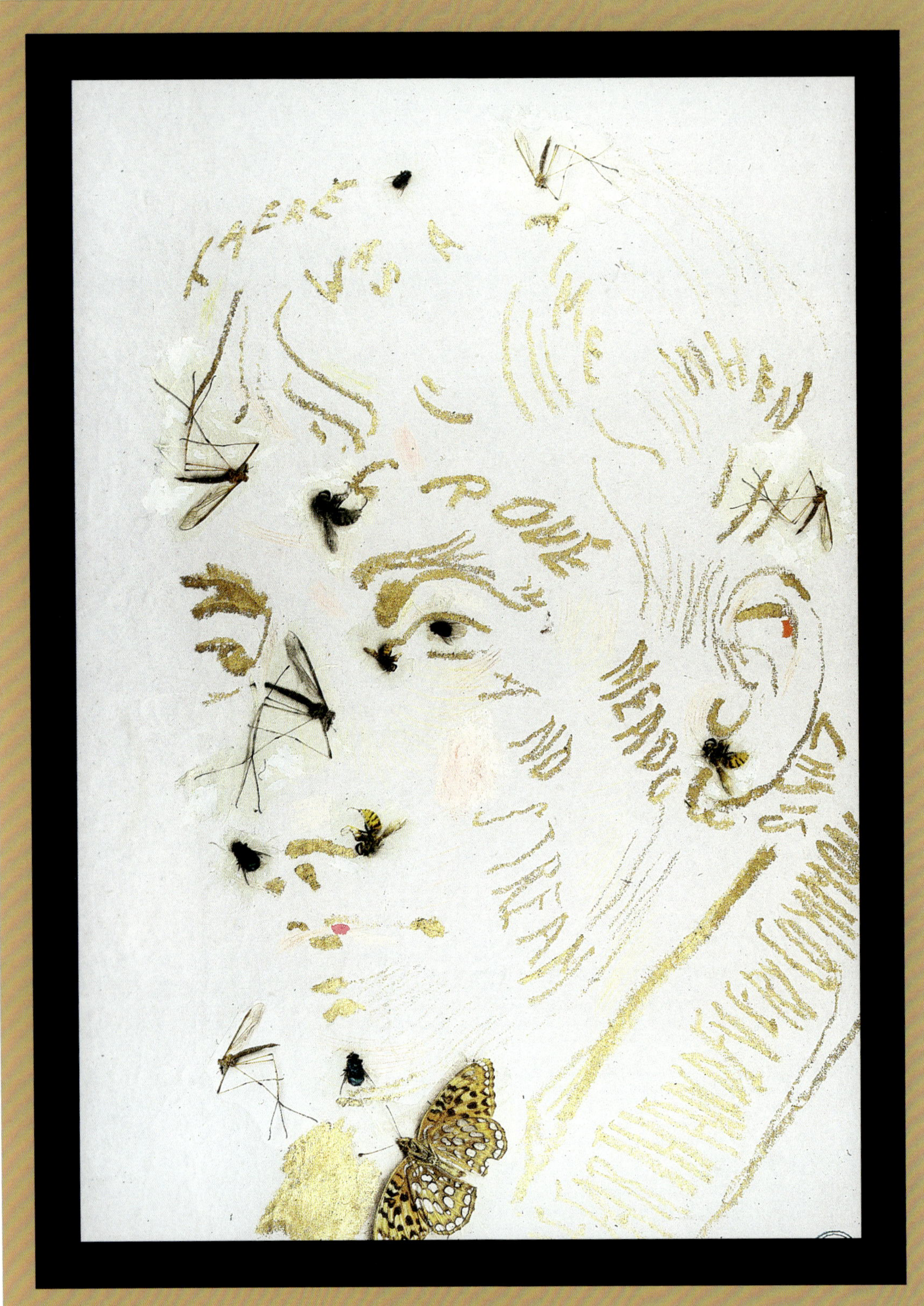

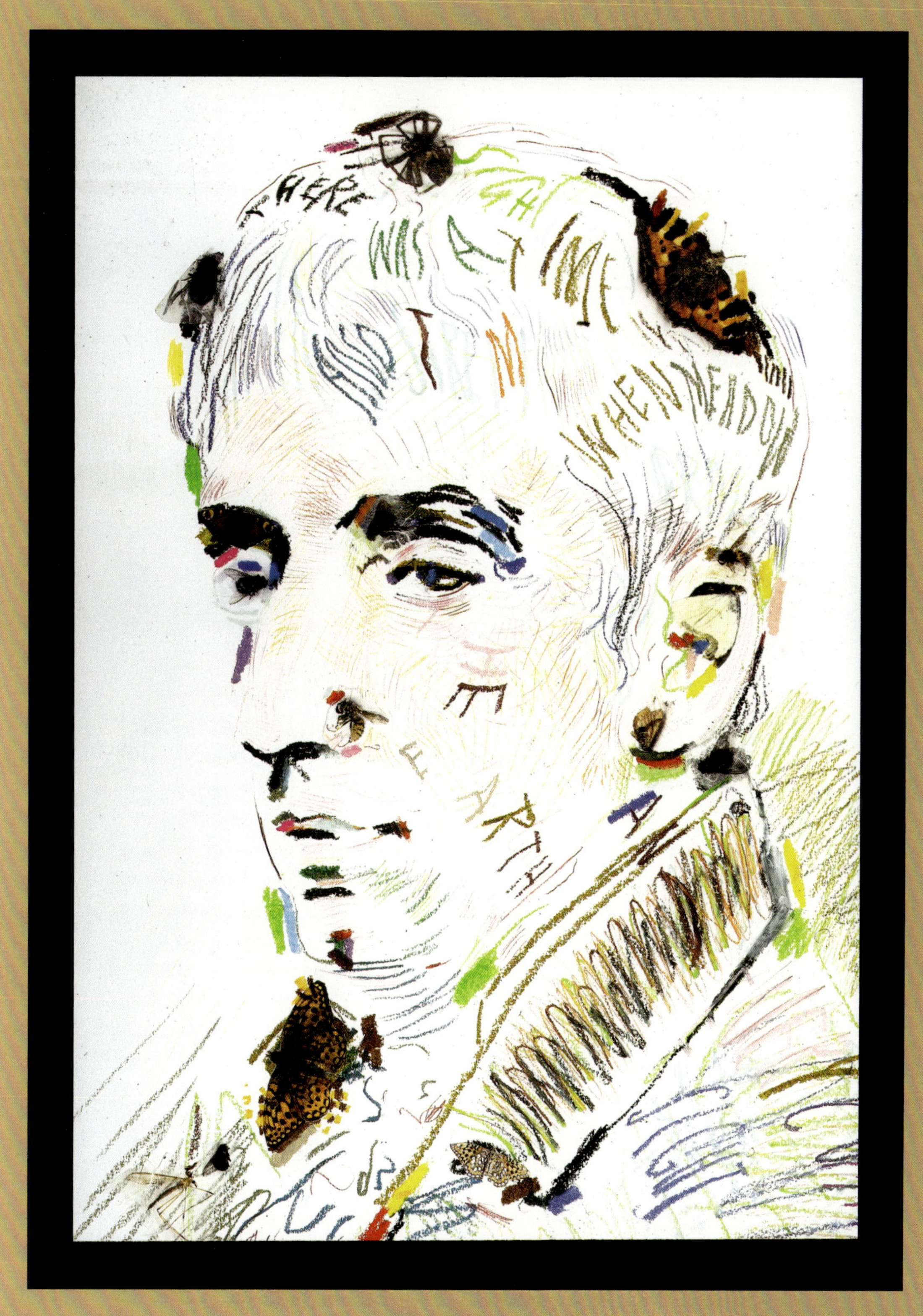

THERE WAS A TIME
WHEN MEADOW
THE EARTH

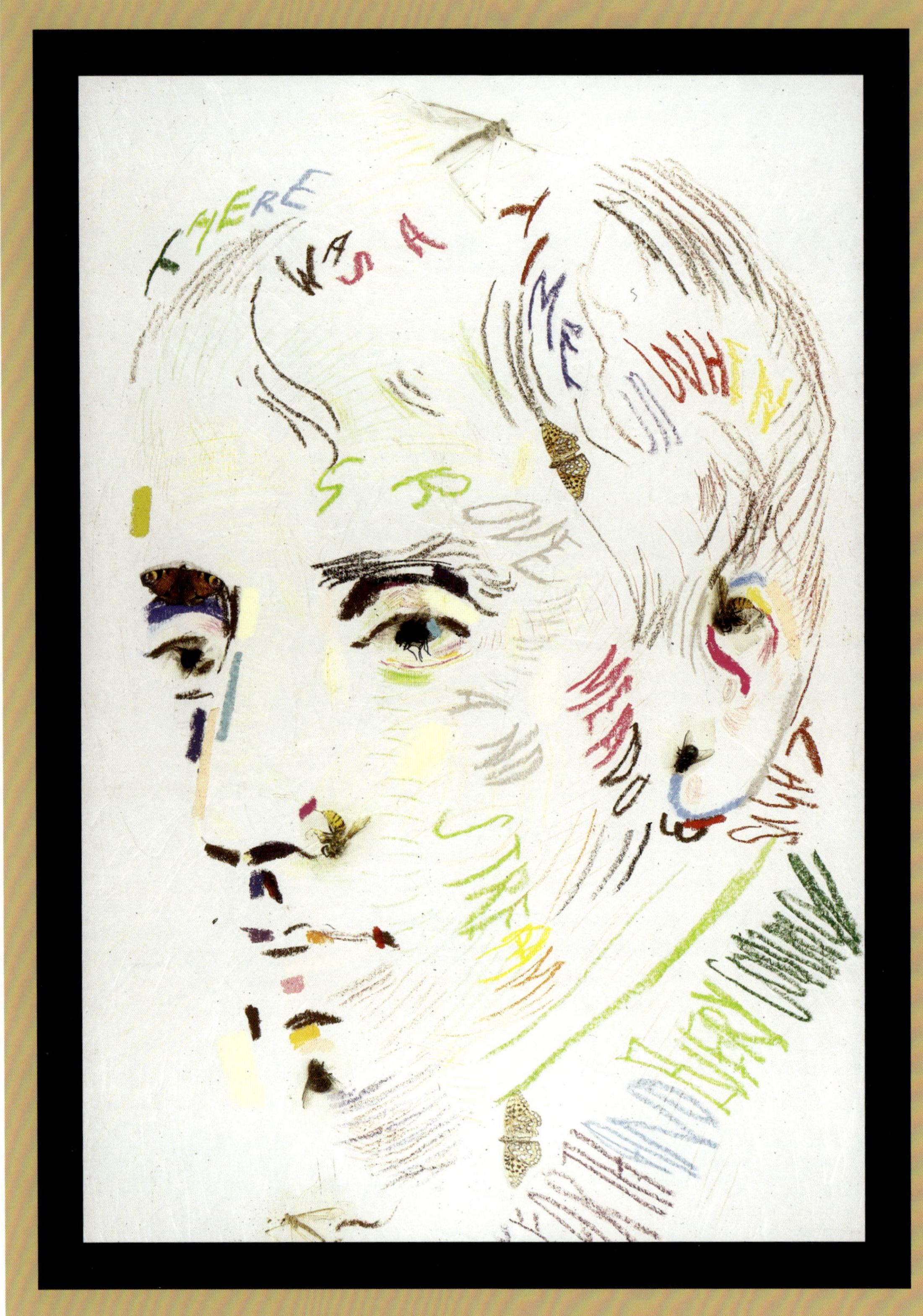

THERE
WAS A
TIME
WHEN
GROVE
MEADOW
AND STREAM

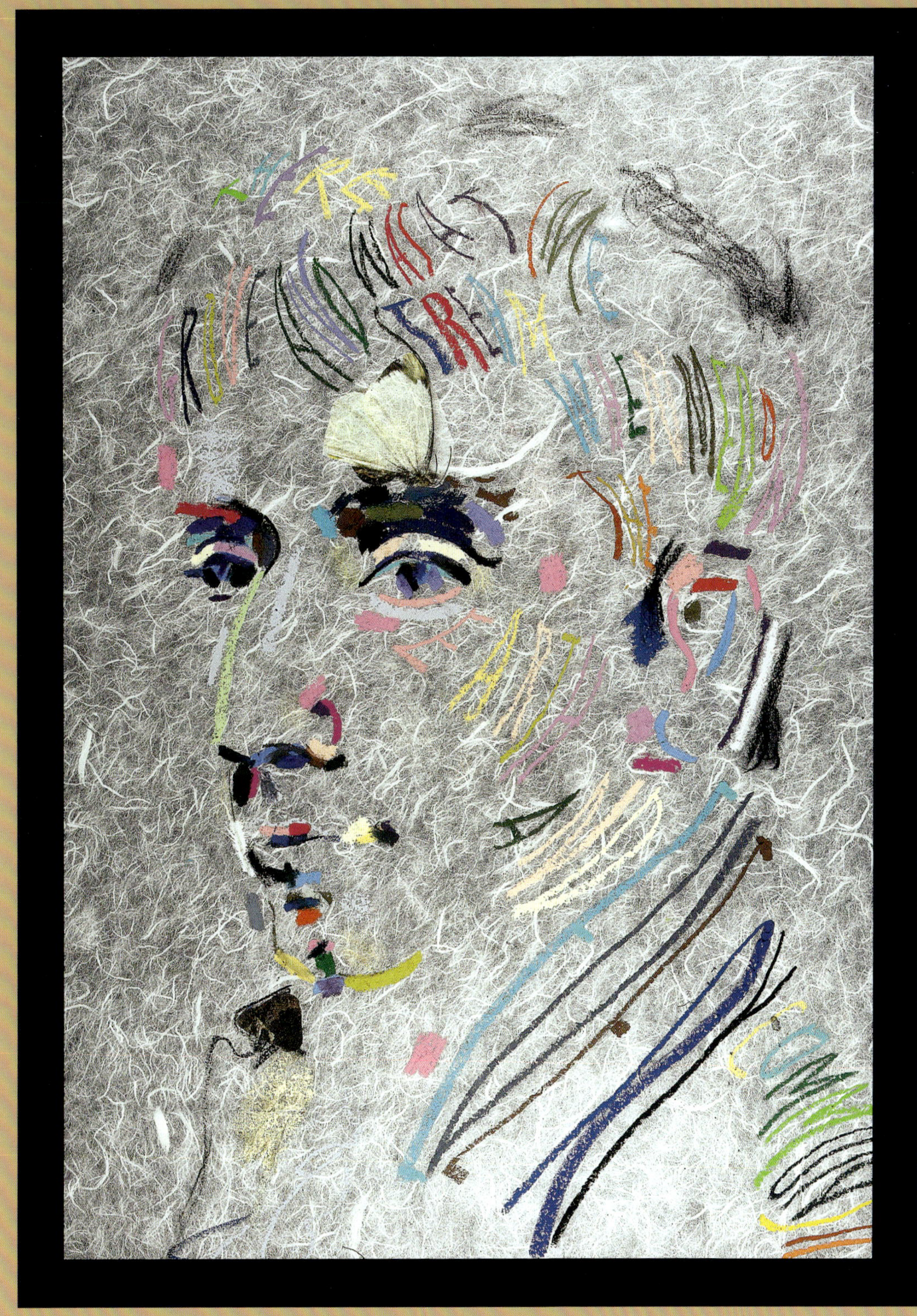

Hi there little boys and girls (FUCK YOU!)
There was a time when meadow grove and stream,
Today we're gonna learn how to poison squirrels
The earth, and every common sight,
But first I'd like you meet my friend Bob (Huh?)
To me did seem apparelled in celestial light
Say 'Hi Bob ("Hi Bob") Bob's thirty and still lives with his mom
The glory and the freshness of a dream
And he don't got a job, 'cause Bob sits at home and smokes pot
It is not now as it has been of yore;-
But his twelve year old brother looks up to him an awful lot
Turn wheresoer I may,
And bob likes
By night and day
To hangout at the local waffle spot
The things which I have seen I now can see no more
And wait in the parkin' lot for waitresses off the clock
The rainbow comes and goes
When it's late and the lot gets dark and fake like he walks his dog
And lovely the rose,
Drag 'em in the woods and go straight to the chopping block (AHH!)
The moon doth with delight
And even if they escaped and they got the cops
Look round her when the heavens are bare
The ladies would all be so afraid, they would drop the charge
Waters on a starry night
My penis is the size of a peanut, have you seen it?
And beautiful and fair
FUCK NO you ain't seen it, it's the size of a peanut (Huh?)
Speakin of peanuts, you know what else is bad for squirrels?
Ecstasy is the worst drug in the world
If someone ever offers it to you, don't do it
Kids two hits'll probably drain your spinal fluid
And spinal fluid is final, you wont get it back
So don't get attached, I'll jack every bone in your back

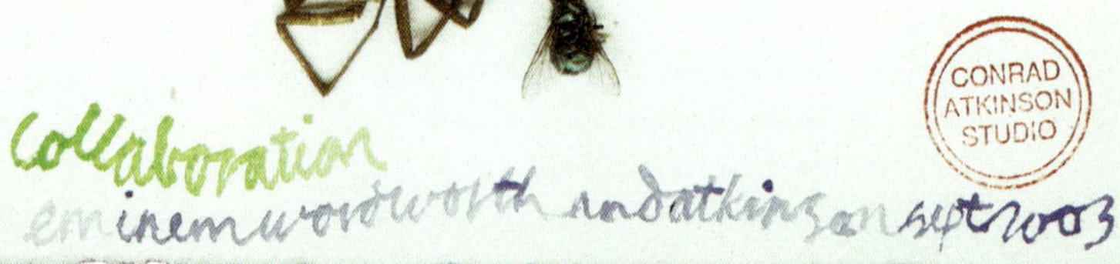

TO A BUTTERFLY

I've watched you now a full half-hour,
I'm not like them-but I can pretend
    Self-poised upon that yellow flower;
The sun is gone-but I have a light
    And, little butterfly! Indeed
The day is gone-but I'm having fun
    I know not if you sleep or feed.
I think I'm dumb-or maybe just happy
    How motionless! -not frozen seas
My heart is broke but I have some glue
    More motionless! And then
Help me inhale and mend it with you
    What joy awaits you, when the breeze
Well float around and hang out on clouds
    Hath found you out among the trees,
Then we'll come down and have a hangover
Skin the sun & fall asleep
    And calls you forth again!
Breathe away the soul so weak

    This plot of orchard ground is ours;
Lesson learned wish me luck
    My trees they are, my sister's flowers;
Soothe the sun wake me up
    Here rest your wings when they are weary;
    Here lodge as in a sanctuary!
    Come often to us, fear no wrong;
    Sit near us, on the bough!
We'll talk of sunshine and of song
    And summer days when we were young;
    Sweet childish days that were as long
    As twenty days are now.

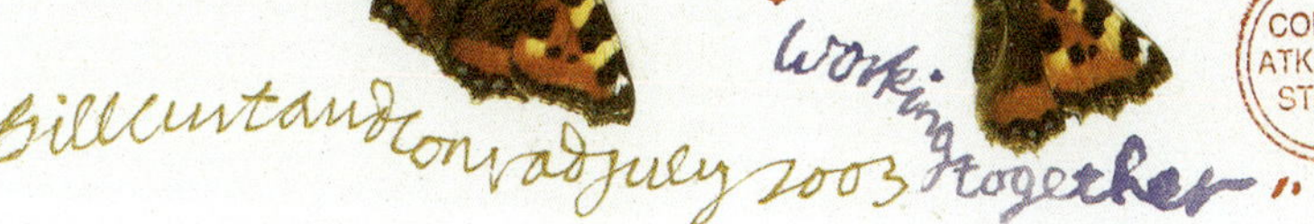

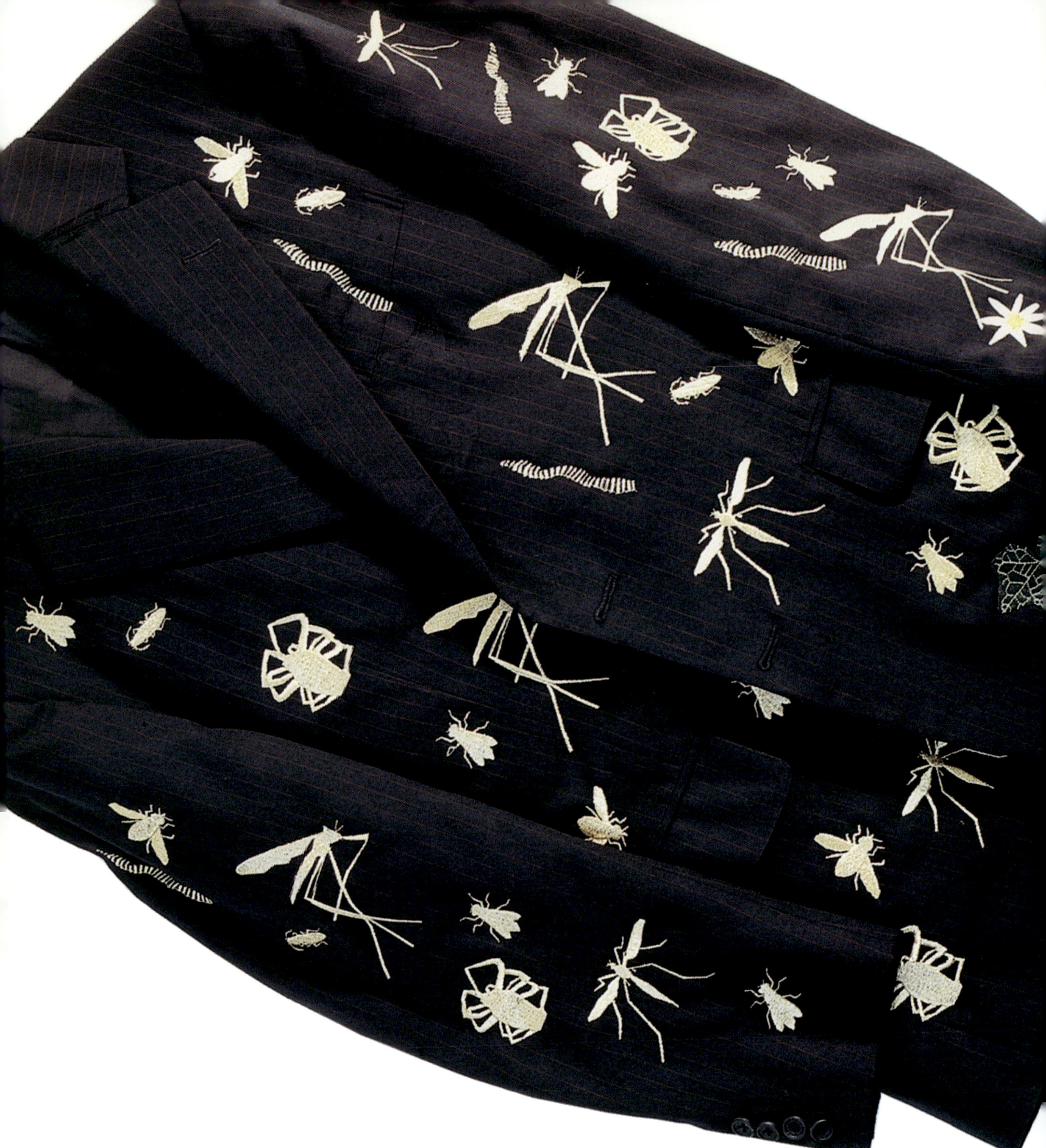

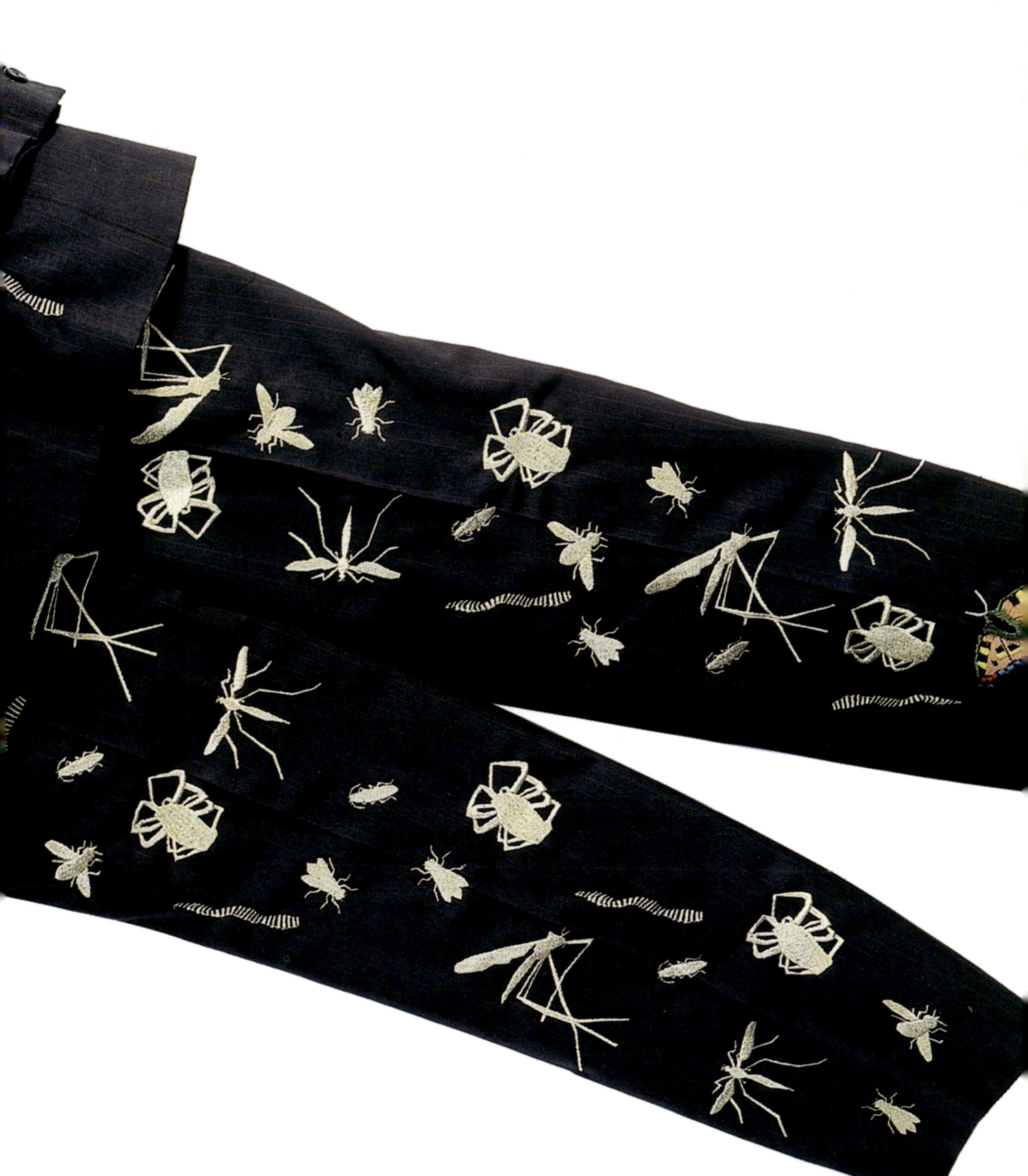

SUIT

The suit made in Savile Row which Wordsworth wore on Thursday 15th April 1802 whilst walking home from Eusmere to Grasmere with his sister Dorothy in a furious wind. It was on this walk that they observed many flowers and then fairly suddenly a large number of daffodils. A couple of years after this walk Wordsworth wore the suit to write the poem Daffodils and a little later he gave the suit to Coleridge to wear as a lucky literary suit in which to write popular poetry. Coleridge immediately wrote Kubla Khan which was an instant hit. The suit disappeared one night from a public house in Keswick in 1816 and was recently found in a thrift shop in San Francisco by Conrad Atkinson. Atkinson a minor Cumbrian artist living in San Francisco subsequently researched its provenance during lunch at Zuni Restaurant on Market Street (one of the best in San Francisco for Classic Californian cuisine) whilst eating a Caesar salad accompanied by a glass of chilled Hess Select Chardonnay. The suit contained pollen from the English native wild daffodil Narcissus pseudonarcissus L. It might be pointed out that this daffodil is under threat from the many hybrids produced in recent years by genetic modification. The pollen grain was identified by its morphology, which is ellipsoidal with a single long slit like aperture. Beneath the proteins and lipids on the surface of the pollen is a reticulum resembling lacelike vermicelli. The pollen grains are between 50 and 60 microns long. This pollen was then dated to about 1802 with an accuracy of plus or minus four years; it was then subjected to further tests which located the specific area by the lake mentioned in Dorothy's diary. An analysis of the ink stains on the suit were found to contain iron (possibly from Cleator Moor iron ore mine which was located just behind Atkinson's birthplace on Birks Road) which matched the extremely rare ink used by Coleridge in the original draft of the Kubla Khan. —*Conrad Atkinson, September 2003*

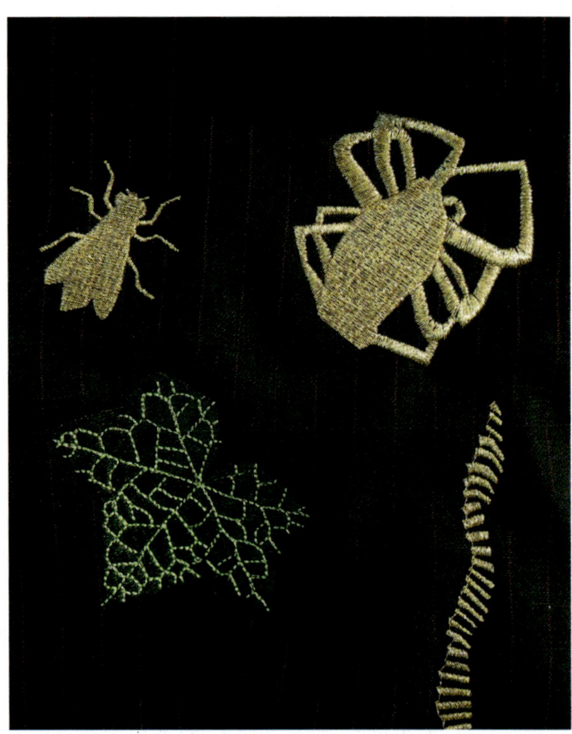

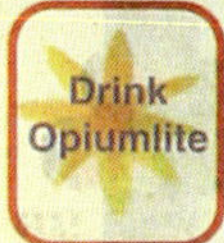
Drink Opiumlite

The Westmorland Gazette

Best poetic publication in the North · extra textual linguistic substance
Wordsworth Edition   Any Day Another Time

Formerly Resolution and Independence Gazette
No. Any number   Price: Any Price

Getting and Spending

POETRY South Lakes
Council to record minutes of finance committee in coloured rhyming couplets
Page 18

HIP HOPERA
Christina Aguilera & Dorothy Wordsworth in collaboration on new Hollywood production
Page 42   **2**   Leisure

GLOBAL WARMING
Paradise Lost poet John Milton in talks with Lancashire Police Authority
3

BRIEFLY

Editorial...
True love and desire poetry and beauty... pleasure and passion so often cynically manipulated for economic and political reasons

Artist appointed Chief Executive of Council

Wordsworth and the poetry of globalisation

Traffic shakeup causes fear, pain anguish, stress and the poetry of nostalgia

TS Eliot hits out at digital imaging wasteland & town centre tussle between Asda and Tesco

Dorothy Wordsworth approves G.M Daffodils... see gardening section

Bush rocked by senate rebellion over the poem The Prelude by local poet William Wordsworth

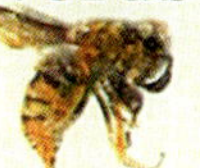

Conrad Atkinson and WB Yeats both agree that artists are the unacknowledged footballers of the world... See sports page 12 & 11

Emotional encounter between Catherine Zeta Jones, Posh Becks and the Brontë sisters in campaign against Atkins diet. Brontës to rewrite Wuthering Heights as centrally concerned with anorexia.

Secretary of State for Poetry vetos Treasury white paper cites lack of resonance and scan... instructs Chancellor to use iambicpentameters

London Poet Coleridge buys new porsche

Atkinson and Wordsworth in bust up about meaning of Lake District... Jack Straw to intervene.

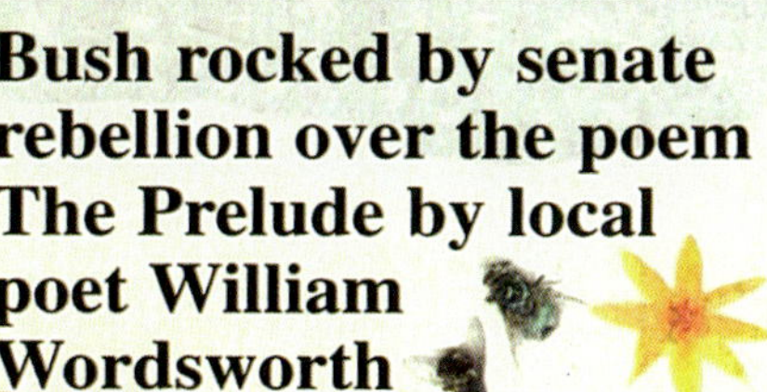
Average Lake District Scene

Traffic ticket shake up in Kendal...Wardens refuse to issue tickets propose to leave poems on car windscreens... argue this will improve traffic flow and curb road rage

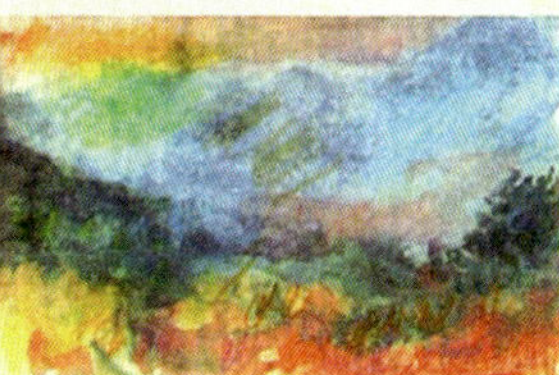

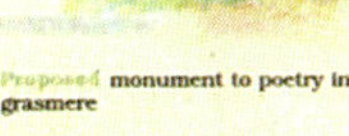
Proposed monument to poetry in grasmere

WILLIAM BLAKE challenges Blair on Iraq... possible peerage under threat

Row between Jordan and Raphael about meaning of beauty. Micheal Howard demands inquiry.

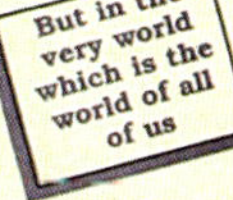
Monument to Wordsworth to be erected on Helvellyn

P.M office is considering a peerage for Conrad Atkinson for his services to British journalism and accurate reportage... see sports page

HISTORIC FIND IN SAN FRANCISCO
THE suit made in Savile Row which Wordsworth wore on Thursday 15th April 1802 whilst walking home from Eusemere to Grasmere with his sister Dorothy in a furious wind. It was on this walk that they observed many flowers and then fairly suddenly a large number of daffodils. A couple of years later he gave the suit to Coleridge to wear as a lucky literary suit in which to write popular poetry. Coleridge immediately wrote Kubla Khan which was an instant hit. The suit disappeared one night from a public house in Keswick in 1816 and was recently found in a thrift shop in San Francisco by Conrad Atkinson. Atkinson a minor Cumbrian artist living in San Francisco subsequently researched its provenance during lunch at Zuni Restaurant on Market Street (one of the best in San Francisco for Classic Californian cuisine) whilst eating a Caesar salad accompanied by a glass of chilled Hess Select Chardonnay.
The suit contained pollen from the English native wild daffodil Narcissus pseudo-narcissus. L. It might be pointed out that this daffodil is under threat from the many hybrids produced in recent years by genetic modification. The pollen grain was identified by its morphology, which is ellipsoidal with a single long slit like aperture. Beneath the proteins and lipids in the surface of the pollen is a reticulum resembling lacelike vermicelli. The pollen grains are between 50 and 60 microns long. This pollen was then dated to about 1802 with an accuracy of plus or minus four years; it was then subjected to further tests which located the specific area by the lake mentioned in Dorothy's diary. An analysis of the ink stains on the suit were found to contain iron (possibly from Cleator Moor iron ore mine which was located just behind Atkinsons birthplace on Birks Road) which matched the extremely rare ink used by Coleridge in the original draft of Kubla Khan.

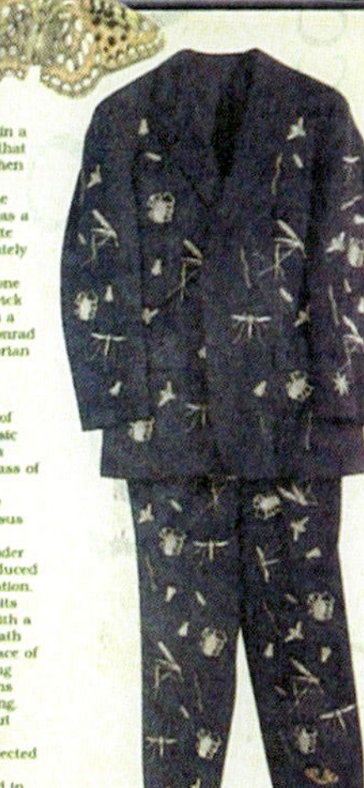

ALFRED LORD TENNYSON condemns lack of equipment for troops in Iraq...will compose angry poem. See sports page

Jobs in Lakeland
JOBS, mortgages, race, immigration not of great importance says new survey... poetry and art much more critical 87.72% of the people in the regions desire more meaning

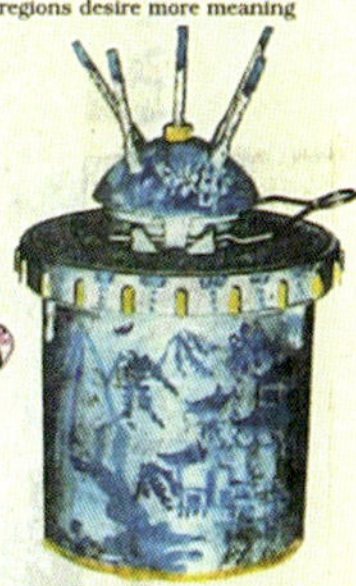
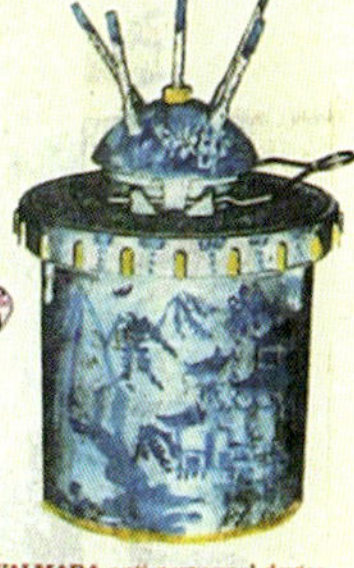

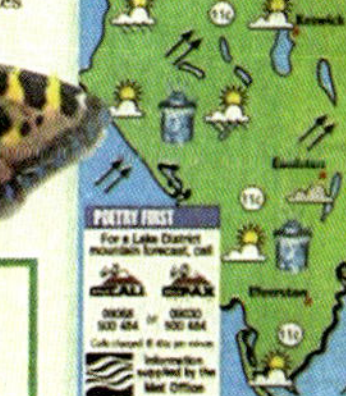
William Wordsworth Shopping Trolley

Robert Frost... soaring house prices threaten poetic inspiration in Lake District people too obsessed with poetry and art... deputy Prime Minister Prescott to act

Waterstones and Victoria & Albert Museum demand inquiry into poem Queen Mab by Shelley... PM says poem is not 95% true it is 100% wrong

Minister for Drawing criticizes defence outline

VALMARA anti personnel device
Defense chiefs to commission more aesthetically pleasing landmines... see leisure section
British sculptors negotiate fees Secretary of State for Sculpture to take control of the Defence Department... see sports page

Average distribution of art in South Lakeland

FAILURE is an oblique kind of success
Obliqueness is a certain kind of failure
Success is a permanent kind of obliqueness
Obliqueness is a failed kind of success
Oblique success is a kind of failure

GUEST editor next week is Eminem

Inside
- **POVERTY**
- **RAPTURE**
- **DESIRE**
- **FEAR**
- **PASSION**
- **A LITTLE PLEASURE**
- **THE FUTURE**
- **THE TRUTH**
- **THE PAST**
- **PAIN AND SPORT**
- **SPORT AND LOVE**
- **DISEASE AND SOMETHING ELSE (PROBABLY OBLIQUE ORGASMS)**

Conrad Atkinson april 2004

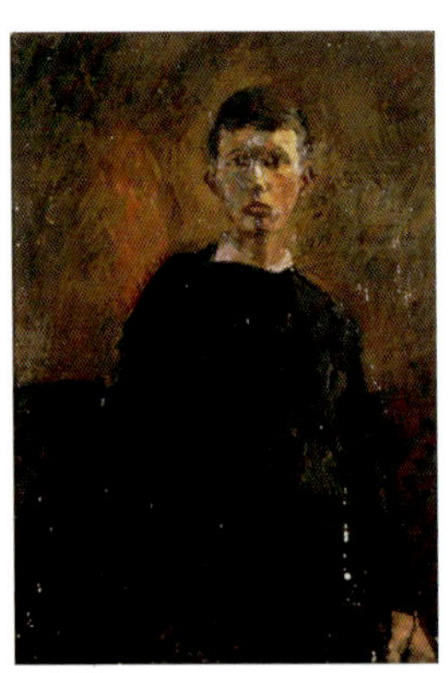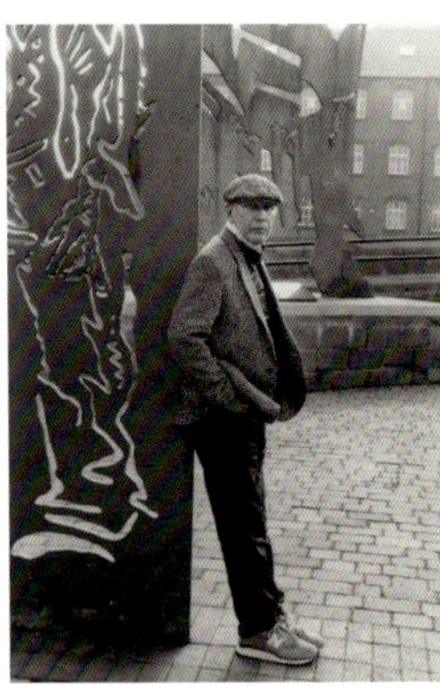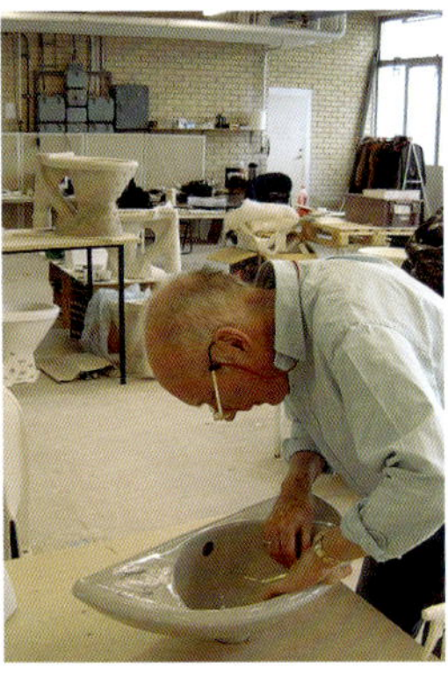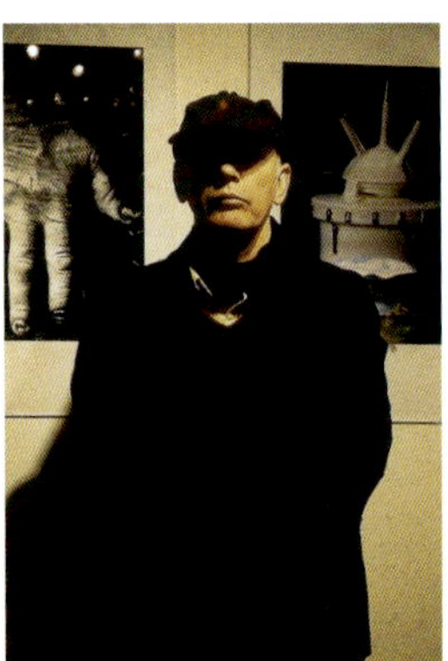

1940 Born, Cleator Moor, West Cumbria, England
Since **1992** Professor of Art and Chair of the Department of Art and Art History, University of California at Davis
Since **2002** Distinguished Visiting Professor/Artist in Residence, Courtauld Institute of Art, University of London

EDUCATION

1957–61 Carlisle College of Art, NDD
1961–62 Liverpool College of Art, ATD (distinction)
1962–65 Royal Academy Schools, London RAS (Honors), Painting & Drawing

SOLO EXHIBITIONS

1972 *Strike at Brannans*, ICA, London
1974 *Work, Wages and Prices*, ICA, London
Work, Wages and Prices, Northern Arts Gallery, Newcastle upon Tyne, England
1975 *Five Banners*, commissioned for the General and Municipal Workers Union, London
A Shade of Green, an Orange Edge, Arts Council of Northern Ireland Gallery, Belfast
1976 *Northern Ireland 1968, Mayday*, Art Net, London
Northern Ireland 1968, Mayday Midland Group Gallery, Nottingham, England
1977 *Approaching Reality*, Northern Arts Gallery, Newcastle upon Tyne, England
1979 *Material—Six Works*, Ronald Feldman Fine Arts, New York
1980 *Three Pieces for Dublin*, Project Arts Centre, Dublin
Graphics, Pentonville Gallery, London
Selected Works About the North, Carlisle Museum and Art Gallery, Carlisle, England
1981 *At the Heart of the Matter*, ICA, London
1982 *Conrad Atkinson*, Frank Watters Gallery, Sydney
Separate Peaces, Ronald Feldman Fine Arts, New York
1983 *Conrad Atkinson*, Power Gallery, Sydney
Conrad Atkinson, Roslyn Oxley Gallery, Sydney

1984 *Conrad Atkinson*, Touring Show: Sydney, Melbourne, Hobart, Brisbane, Adelaide, Perth, Newcastle, Australia
1985 *Conrad Atkinson*, Anna Leonowens Gallery, Halifax, Nova Scotia
Conrad Atkinson, Mercer Union, Toronto
Goldfish, Ronald Feldman Fine Arts, New York
1987 *Conrad Atkinson*, Talbot Rice Art Centre, Edinburgh
London Underground Posterworks, commissioned by Art Angel Trust, London, and Projects UK, Newcastle upon Tyne, England
Posterworks, Billboards commissioned by Projects UK London and Newcastle upon Tyne, England, and White Columns, New York
1988 *The Miners' Monument*, Commission, installed January 1988. Cleator Moor Town Council, Cleator Moor, England
1989 *Front Page*, Special project for *Art in America* 77, no. 6 (June, 1989)
Newspaper Works, Victoria and Albert Museum, London
Front Pages, Ronald Feldman Fine Arts, New York
Conrad Atkinson, Interim Art, London
1990 *Good Sports: Tales of New York*, Solo Gallery, New York
Moscow Exhibition Hall at Avtozavodskaya, Moscow. *"At last, we can no longer predict the future."*
Conrad Atkinson, Anne Berthoud Gallery, London
1992 *Zones of Gold*, Bradford City Art Gallery, Bradford, England
For Emily: New Works Made at the Henry Moore Sculpture Trust Studio, Henry Moore Sculpture Trust, Halifax, England (catalogue)
1993 *Newsfiles*, Moscow ICA, Moscow
New Works, Mandeville Gallery, San Diego
New Works, Richard Nelson Gallery, Davis, California
1994 *Conrad Atkinson*, Ruth Bloom Gallery, Los Angeles
1995 *Dorothy, Diego, Theodore and a horse of a different color*, University Art Gallery and Museum, Berkeley, California (catalogue)
Object, Paule Anglim Gallery, San Francisco
1996 Underground Gallery, Euston Station, London
Transient, Carlisle City Art Gallery and Museum, Carlisle, England
1997 *Mining Culture*, West Cumbria College, Workington, England
Dorothy Gale Meets Emily Brontë in Technicolor, Ronald Feldman Fine Arts, New York
1998 *Mining the School*, Atlanta International School, Atlanta
Mining Culture in Technicolor, Atlanta College of Art Gallery and High Museum, Atlanta
1999 Installation for First Liverpool Biennial. Liverpool City Museum, Liverpool, England
Mining Arts, Walker Art Gallery, Liverpool, England
Mining Culture and New Works, Bluecoats Gallery, Liverpool, England
2000 *Twenty Years—Ethical Viruses*, Abbot Hall Art Gallery, Kendall, England (catalogue)
Surplus: Cocktail Party, Intersection for the Arts. San Francisco
2002 *Tributes to Strike 1972-2002 by 100 Artists*, curated by Gavin Wade, Wolverhampton City Art Gallery, Wolverhampton, England
The Door to Cultures, Wolverhampton City Art Gallery, Wolverhampton, England
2003 *Constantly Contesting*, Rhode Island College, Providence, Rhode Island
Installation. Ronald Feldman Fine Arts, New York
Constantly Contesting, White Box, New York
Andersonstown, Belfast
Excavated Mutilations: New Work, Courtauld Institute of Art Gallery, London
2004 *Collaborations*, Ronald Feldman Fine Arts, New York
Constantly Contesting, Opalka Gallery, Albany, New York
Common Sights, Centre for British Romanticism, Grasmere, England
2006 Wolverhampton City Art Gallery, Wolverhampton, England

SELECTED GROUP EXHIBITIONS

1962 *London Group*, Mall Galleries, London
Royal Academy Summer Exhibition, London
1963–65 *Young Contemporaries*, RBA Gallery, London
1965 *Northern Young Artists*, City Art Gallery, Middlesborough, England
1967 *Two Painters*, Manchester City Art Gallery, Manchester, England
1968 *Royal Academy Bicentenary*, Royal Academy, London
1970 *Garbage Strike*, Sigi Krauss Gallery, London
1971 *Arts Spectrum*, Alexandra Palace, London
1973 *Critic's Choice*, Tooths Gallery, London
1974 *Solidarity with Chile*, Royal College of Art, London
1975 *Biennale de Paris*, Musee d'Art Moderne, Paris
1978 *Radical Attitudes Towards The Gallery*, Art Net, London
Art for Whom?, Serpentine Gallery, London
Art for Society, Whitechapel Art Gallery, London, and the Arts Council of Northern Ireland Gallery, Belfast
1979 *The Craft of Art*, Liverpool, England
Un Certain Art Anglais, Musee d'Art Moderne, Paris

1980   *Photography into Print*, Victoria and Albert Museum, London
Bringing it Home, Cockpit Gallery, London
Directions 4, Hirshhorn Museum and Art Gallery, Washington DC
Messages, Albright Knox Art Gallery, Buffalo, New York

1981   *Artists Against Nuclear War*, Acme Gallery, London
Landscapes, Tate Gallery, London

1982   *Artists Against Apartheid*, London
Contemporary Art Society Purchase Exhibition, Serpentine Gallery, London
War Games, Ronald Feldman Fine Arts, New York
The Atomic Salon, Ronald Feldman Fine Arts, New York, in collaboration with the *Village Voice*
The Art Record, Tate Gallery, London

1983   Art Institute of Chicago
Ronald Feldman Fine Arts, New York
Quarries, Camden Arts Centre, London
New Beginnings, Pentonville Gallery, London

1984   *Landscapes*, Victoria and Albert Museum, London
Content, Hirshhorn Museum, Washington DC
Social Spaces, Walter Phillips Gallery, Banff, Canada
Australian Prints, National Gallery, Canberra

1985   *Group Material* tour of U.S.
Prints, John Nicols Gallery, New York
Common Ground, Ecology Centre, London
Makkom, Amsterdam
Hand Signals, Ikon Gallery, Birmingham, England
New Acquisitions, Victoria and Albert Museum, London

1986   White Columns, New York
St. Martins School of Art Gallery, London
Laing Art Gallery, Newcastle upon Tyne, England
Brewery Arts Centre, Kendal, England
Artists and Social Commitment, Maryland Institute College of Art, Baltimore, Maryland
Arts and Leisure, The Kitchen, New York

1987   Photographers Gallery, London
University of Edinburgh, Edinburgh
Victoria and Albert Museum, London
Ecology Centre, London
PPOW, New York

1988   *BP British International Print Biennale*, Cartwright Hall, Bradford, England, and 7 other venues

1990   *Intaglio Printing in the 1980s*, Jane Voorhees Zimmerli Art Museum, Rutgers State University, New Brunswick, New Jersey
The Flag Project, Projects UK and Glasgow District Council
Club of Avantguardists, Moscow
Art Faculty Exhibition, Carnegie Mellon Art Gallery, Pittsburgh

1992   *Prints*, Frankel Nathanson Gallery, Maplewood, New Jersey
Gallery Artists, Ronald Feldman Fine Arts, New York

1994   *Elvis and Marilyn + 2x Immortal*, ICA Boston and traveling to: Contemporary Art Museum, Houston, Texas; Mint Museum of Art, Charlotte,
North Carolina; Cleveland Museum of Art, Cleveland, Ohio; Jacksonville Art Museum, Jacksonville, Florida; Portland Art Museum,
Portland, Oregon; Philbrook Academy, Tulsa, Oklahoma; Columbus Museum of Art, Columbus, Ohio; Tennessee State Museum,
Nashville, Tennessee; San Jose Museum of Art, San Jose, California; Honolulu Academy of Art, Honolulu, Hawaii
Flags for the Year 2000, Capp Street Project, San Francisco
Prints from Solo Impression, College of Wooster Art Museum, Wooster, Ohio
Moral Tales: Reading the 1980s, Tate Gallery, Liverpool, England

1995   *The Art of Justice Part II*, Lehman College Art Gallery, Bronx, New York
Artists' Valentines Richard Nelson Gallery, Davis, California
Parish Maps, Barbican Gallery, London
Elvis and Marilyn + 2x Immortal, (Touring USA)
Works on Paper, Victoria and Albert Museum, London

1996   *Withdrawing*, Ronald Feldman Fine Arts, New York
Fractured Fairy Tales, Duke University Fine Art Gallery, Durham, North Carolina
Blast Art Bernefit, X-Art Foundation, New York
Hot off the press, Carlisle City Art Gallery, Carlisle, England (touring)
Ten Years Printmaking, Peacock Gallery, Aberdeen, Scotland
Art at UC Davis, Shasta College Art Gallery, Redding, California
New Acquisitions II, University Art Gallery and Museum, Berkeley, California
Two times immortal, San Jose Art Museum, San Jose, California
Common Ground, British Council Gallery, Manchester, England

BBC film projected onto the side of the Baltic Exchange Building in Newcastle upon Tyne to celebrate *Year of the Visual Arts, U.K.*
Landscape, Barbican Art Gallery, London
Drawings For the Miners Monument, Abbott Hall Art Gallery, Kendal, England

1997 *Face a l'histoire*, Centre Georges Pompidou, Paris
Hot Off the Press, Crafts Council Gallery, London

1998 *Works in Ceramic*, Kecskemet, Hungary
Ceramic Works, HOTP2, Budapest
Works on Paper, R L Nelson Gallery, University of California, Davis, California
Elvis and Marilyn + 2x Immortal, Touring south-east Asia
Fantasy Football Art League, Walsall Museum and Art Gallery, Wallsall, England

1999 *The Plate Show*, Collins Gallery, Glasgow, Scotland (catalogue)
Degree Show, University Gallery, Leeds, England
1984, Camden Arts Centre, London

2000 *The Watercloset Workshop*, Konstfak. University of Stockholm
The Watercloset Workshop, Gustavsburg Museum, Sweden
Willow Pattern Show, Bluetit Gallery, Newcastle upon Tyne, England
Live in Your Head—Art 1965/1975, Whitechapel Art Gallery, London

2001 *Live in your head*, National Gallery, Lisbon
The Lab, San Francisco
In Print, Ferens Gallery, Hull, England (catalogue)
The Watercloset Workshop, Rohsska Museum, Gothenberg, Sweden

2002 *The Watercloset Workshop*, Hatton Gallery, University of Newcastle upon Tyne, Newcastle upon Tyne, England
The Watercloset Workshop, Technicens Hus, Sweden

2003 Grossmount College, San Diego

2004 *Democracy*, White Box, New York
Auction for Landmines Campaign: *Adopt a Mine*, Beverly Hills Hilton, Los Angeles
Landmines Auction, Pace Wildenstein, New York
The State of Art, Intersection for the Arts, San Francisco

2005 *Prints Portfolio Exhibit*, Intersection for the Arts, San Francisco
Arbeit, Taxis im Palais, Innsbruck, Austria
A Picture of Britain, Tate Gallery, London
Blueprint, Intersection for the Arts, San Francisco (traveling to Seville, Spain in 2006)
Big Glass, Edge: Suit for Marcel Duchamp and Iraq, National Glass Centre, Sunderland, England

SELECTED WORK IN PUBLIC AND PRIVATE COLLECTIONS

Abbots Hall Gallery, Kendal, England
Aberdeen Art Gallery, Aberdeen, Scotland
Arts Council of Great Britain
Birmingham City Art Gallery, Birmingham, England
Bradford City Art Gallery, Bradford, England
British Centre for Romanticism, Grasmere, England
British Council Collection
British Museum, London
Brooklyn Museum, Brooklyn, New York
Carlisle City Art Gallery and Museum, Carlisle, England
Carlton University, Ottawa
Contemporary Art Society, London
General and Municipal Workers Union, London
Leeds Armory Museum, Leeds, England
Middlesborough City Art Gallery, Middlesborough, England
Museum of Modern Art, New York
National Ceramic Centre, Aberystwyth, Wales
National Gallery of Australia, Canberra
Power Gallery, University of Sydney, Sydney, Australia
Pushkin Museum, Moscow
R L Nelson Gallery, Davis, California
Sheffield City Art Gallery, Sheffield, England
Talbot Rice Gallery, Edinburgh
Tate Gallery, London
University Museum and Gallery, Berkeley, California
Victoria and Albert Museum, London
Wakefield City Art Gallery, Wakefield, England
Whitworth Gallery, Manchester, England
Wolverhampton City Art Gallery, Wolverhampton, England

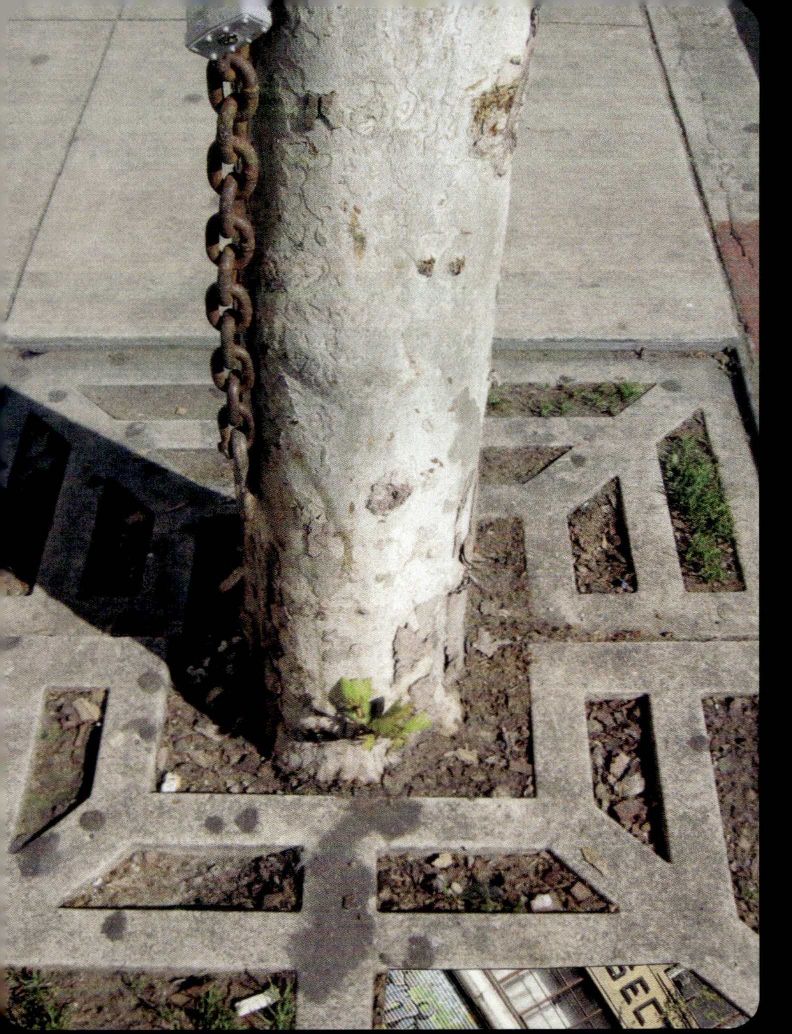

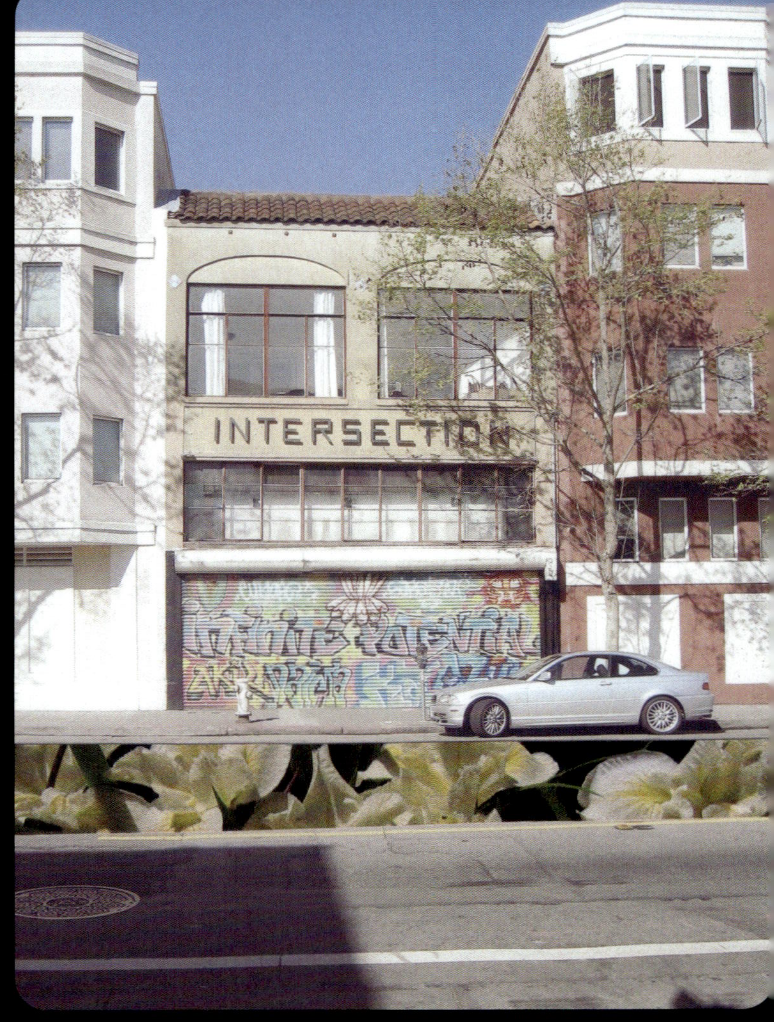
INTERSECTION

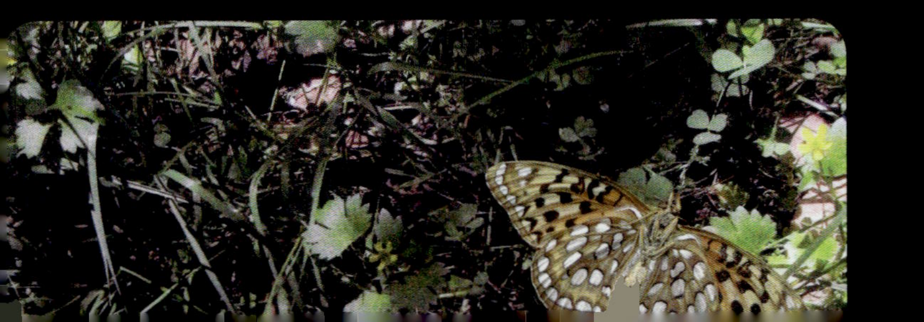

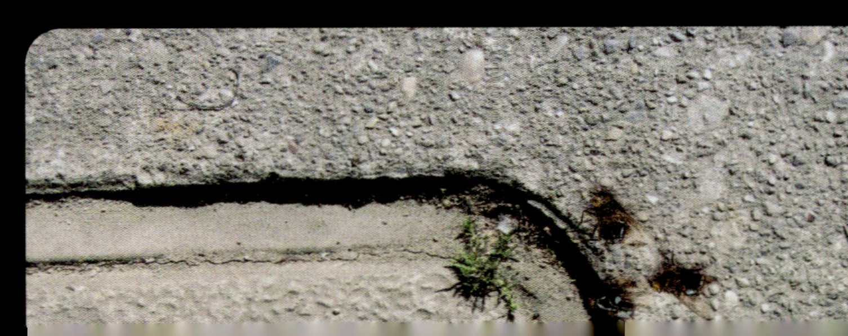

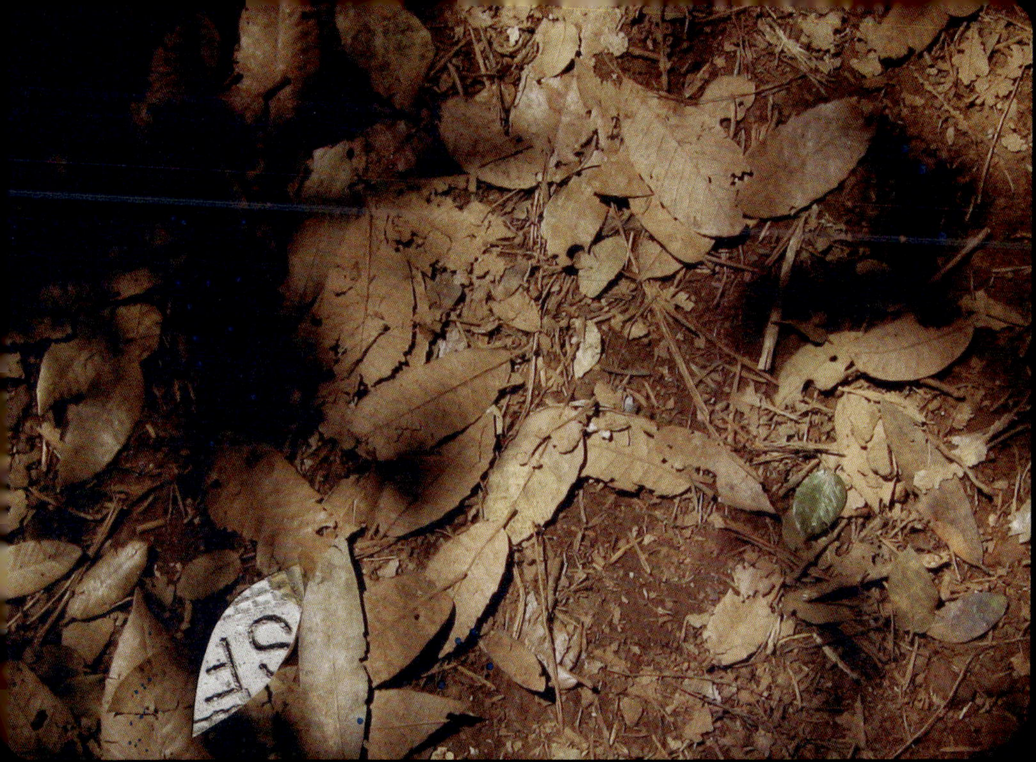

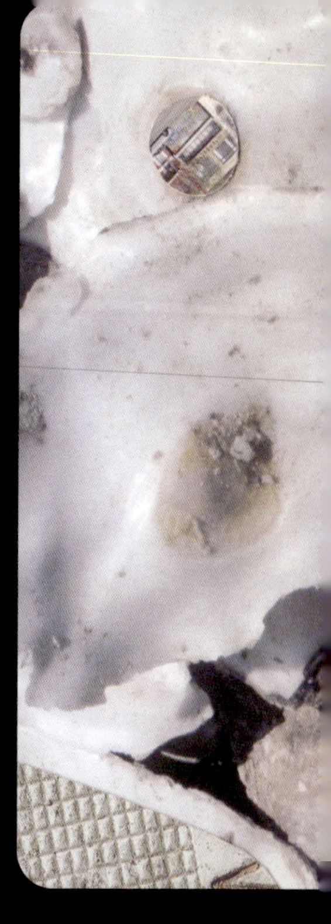
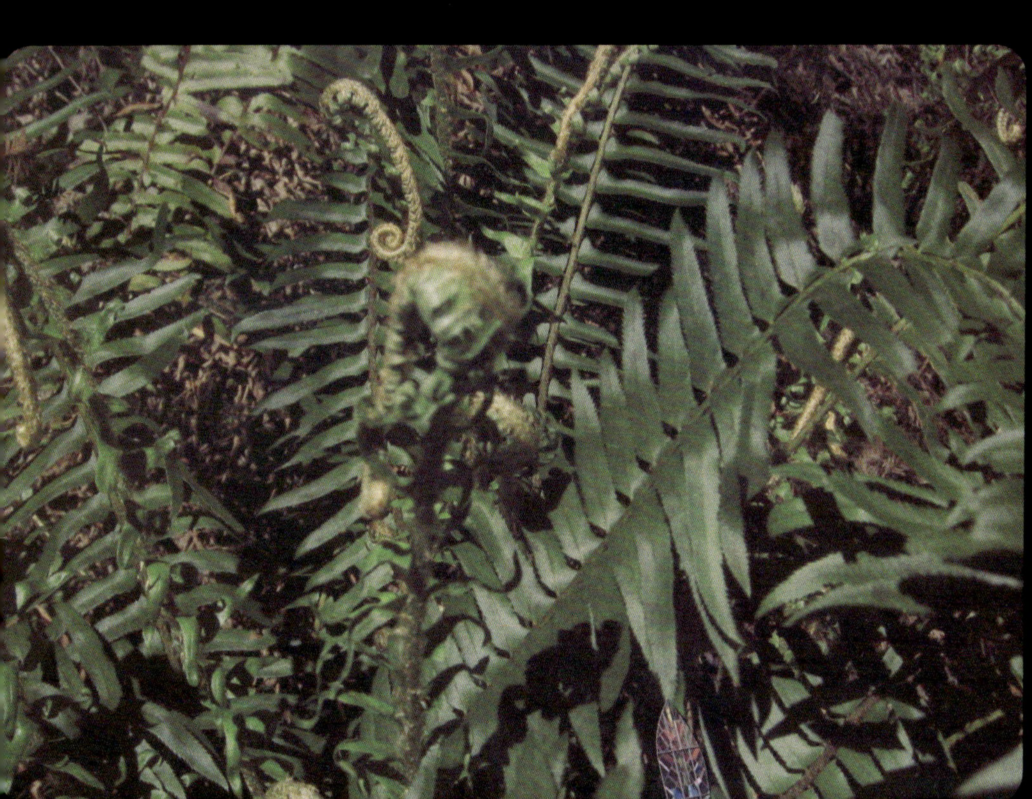
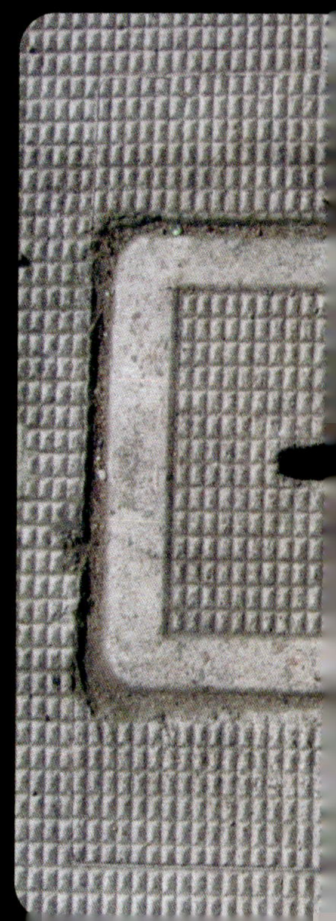

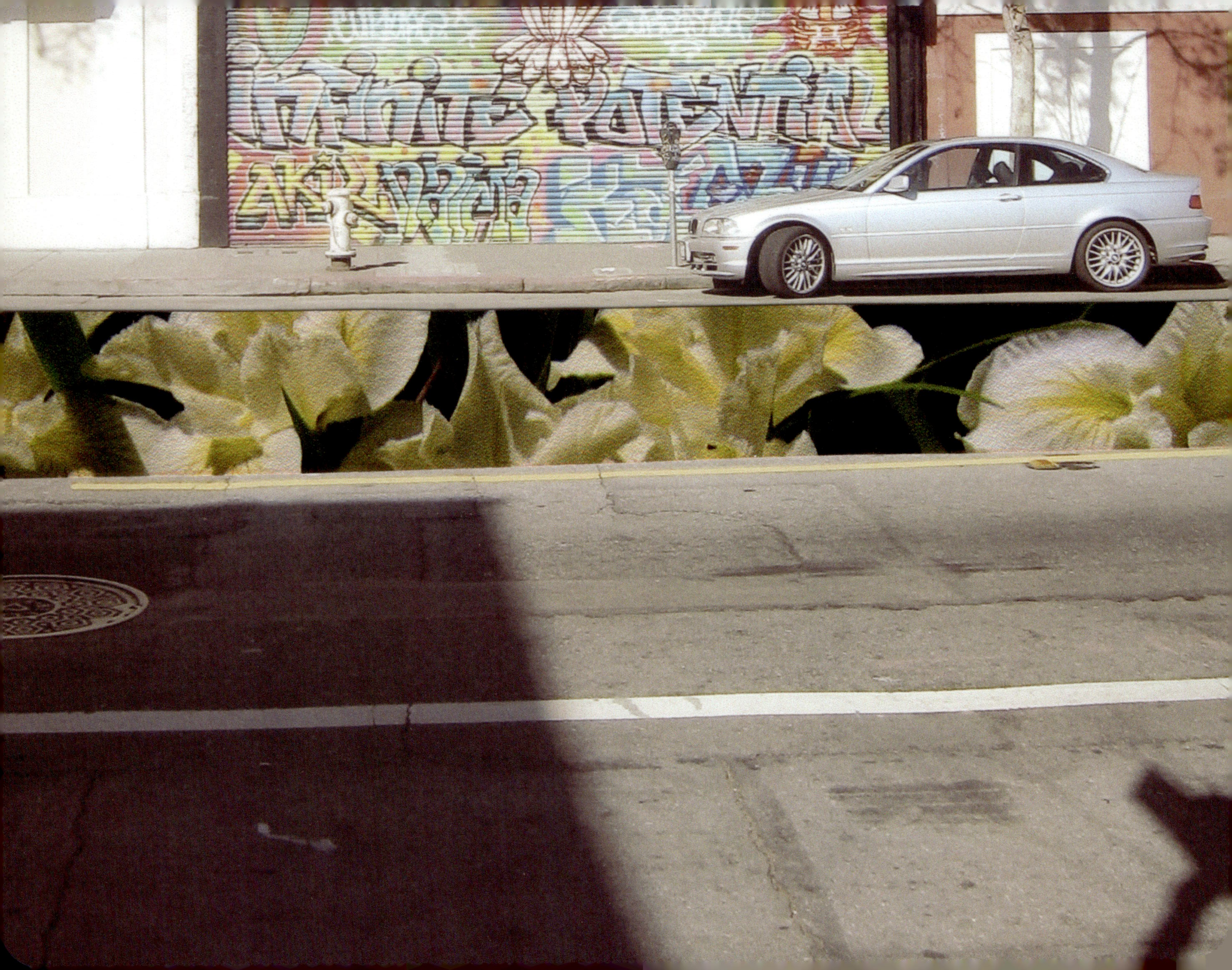
INFINITE POTENTIAL
AKA

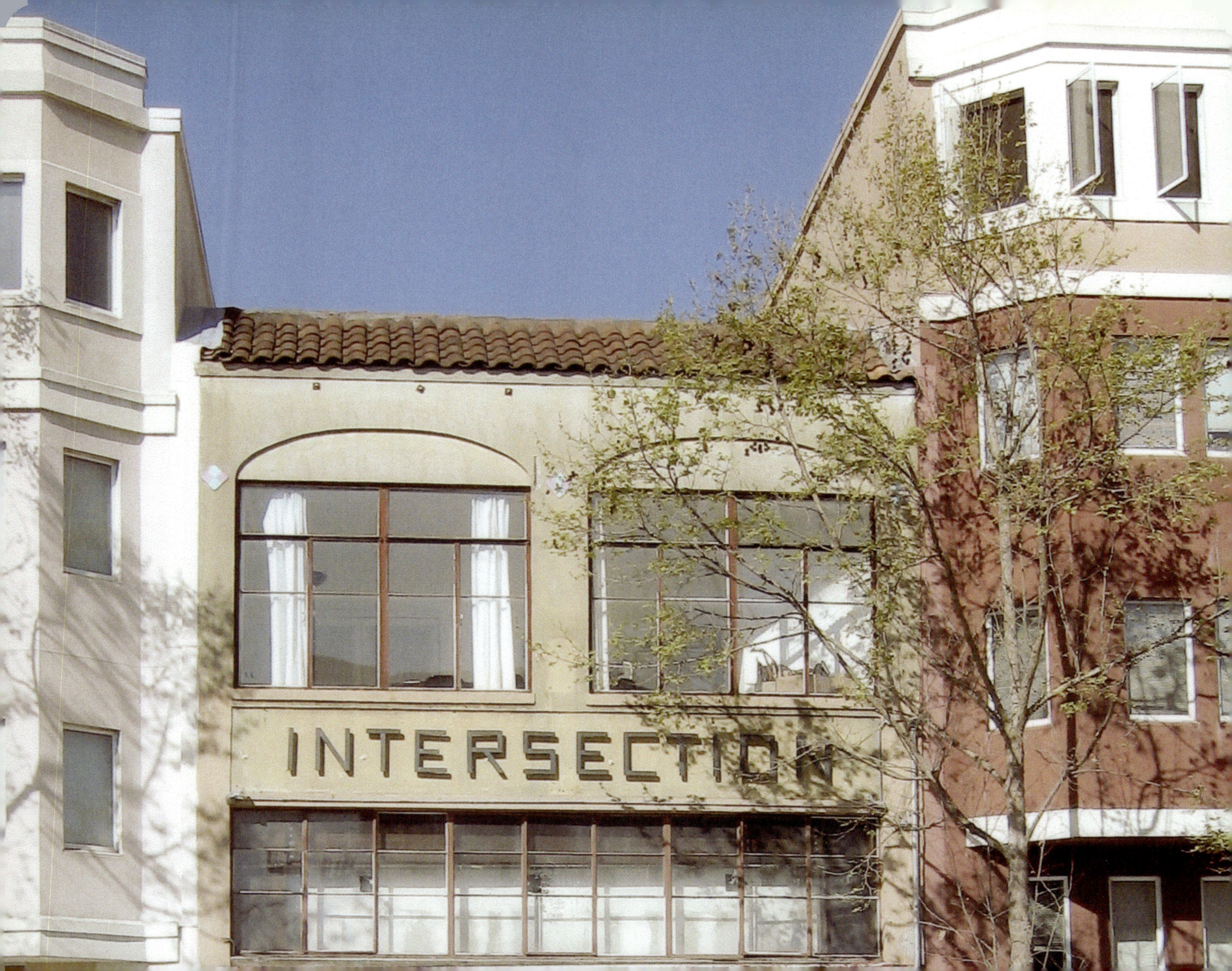
INTERSECTION

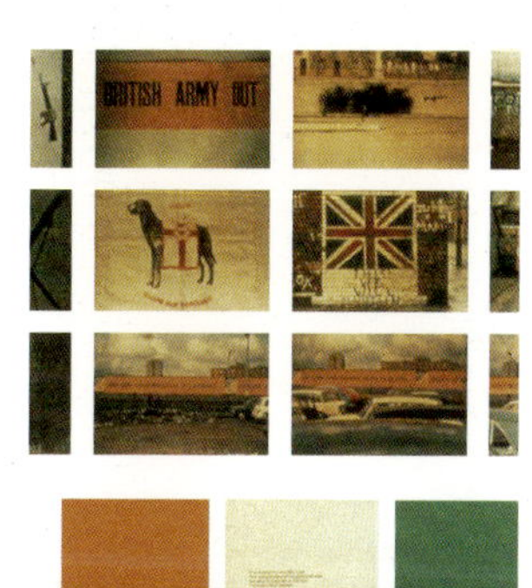

Northern Ireland 1968—May Day, 1975
(section of total work)
75 color photographs mounted on board, each 5 x 7 inches (12.7 x 17.8 cm)
64 typewritten sheets mounted on board, each 8¼ x 5¾ inches (21 x 13.6 cm)
Photo: eeva-inkeri
Courtesy Wolverhampton City Art Gallery

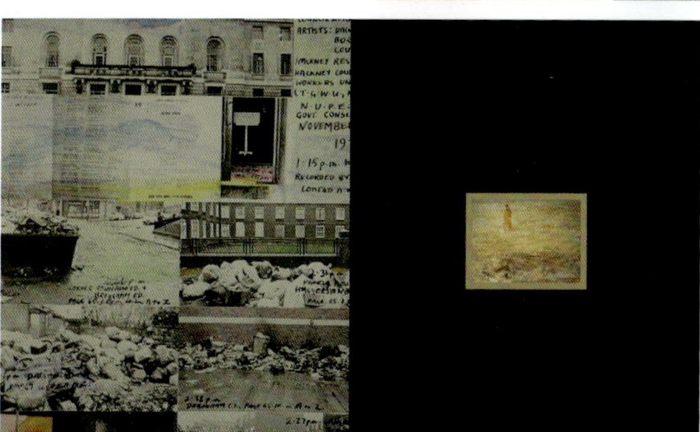

Garbage, 1970
(detail)
Photocollage with hand-coloring
30 x 96 inches (76.2 x 243.8 cm)
Photo: Rainer Iglar
Courtesy Galerie im Taxispalais, Innsbruck

Woman on Beach, 1959
Oil on canvas
28 x 36 inches (71.1 x 91.4 cm)
Photo: Richard Hearn
Courtesy Sophie Atkinson and Richard Hearn

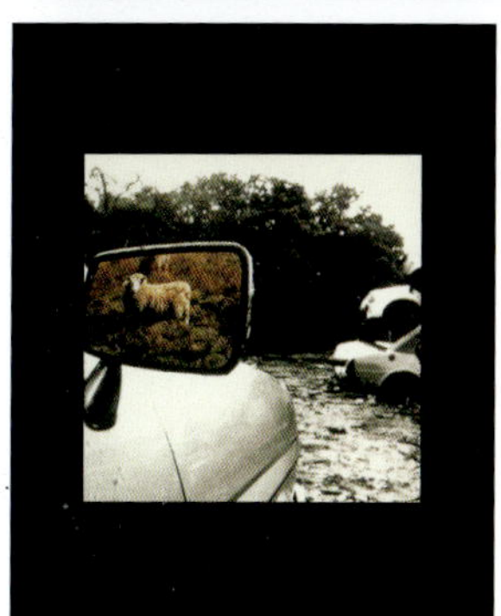

Cumbrian Landscape (from Landescape), 1978
Iris print on handmade paper
17 x 21 inches (43.2 x 53.3 cm)
Photo: Conrad Atkinson
Courtesy Ronald Feldman Fine Arts / Northern Arts Board

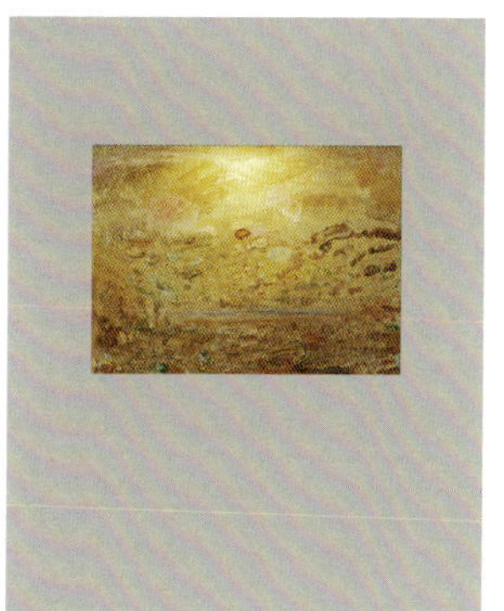

Golden Landscape, 2003
Oil and gold dust, and lipstick on canvas
12 x 16 x 1½ inches (30.5 x 40.6 x 3.8 cm)
Photo: Alan Zindman
Courtesy The Wordsworth Trust

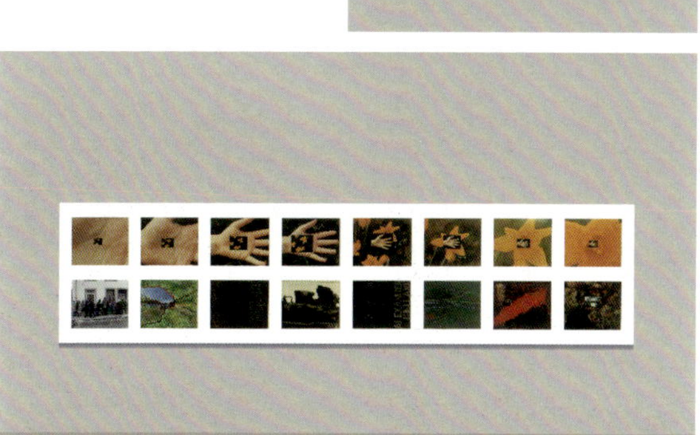

For West Cumbria, For Wordsworth, 1980
Photographs, acrylic, iron ore and coal on hardboard and card
Polyptych: 16 panels. each 20 x 24 inches (50.8 x 61 cm)
Photo: Conrad Atkinson
Courtesy Tate Gallery

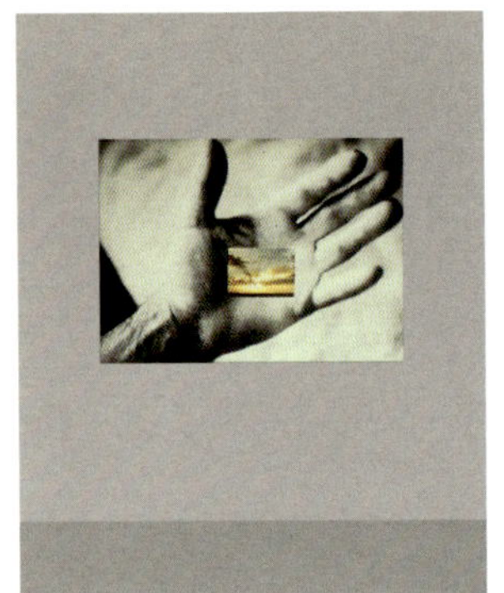

Sunset: for Shelley/Wordsworth, 1978
(section of total work)
10 photocollages framed in plexiglas boxes
20 x 24 inches (50,8 x 61 cm) each
Photo: Conrad Atkinson
Courtesy Berkeley Art Museum / Pacific Archive

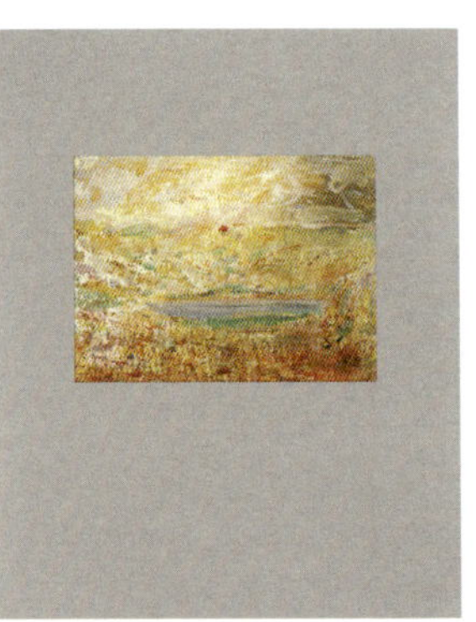

Landscape with Pain, 2003
Oil on canvas
12 x 15¾ x 1 inches (30.5 x 40 x 2.5 cm)
Photo: Alan Zindman
Courtesy The Wordsworth Trust

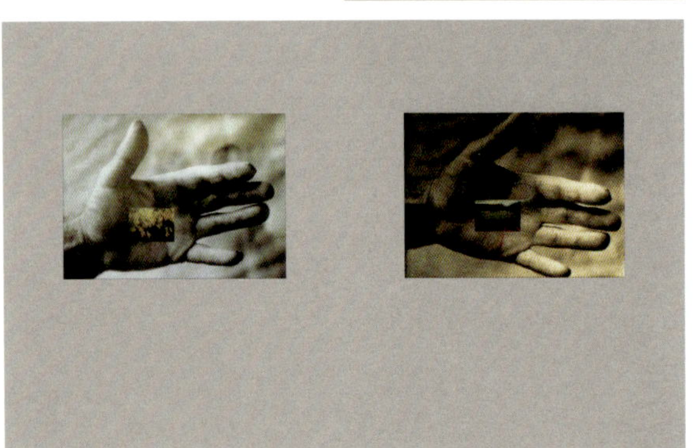

Sunset: for Shelley/Wordsworth, 1978
(section of total work)
10 photocollages framed in plexiglas boxes
20 x 24 inches (50.8 x 61 cm) each
Photo: Conrad Atkinson
Courtesy Berkeley Art Museum / Pacific Archive

Sunset: for Shelley/Wordsworth, 1978
(section of total work)
10 photocollages framed in plexiglas boxes
20 x 24 inches (50.8 x 61 cm) each
Photo: Conrad Atkinson
Courtesy Berkeley Art Museum / Pacific Archive

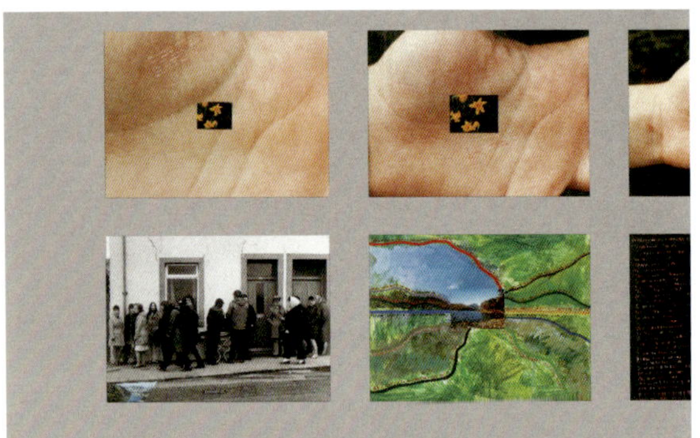

For West Cumbria, For Wordsworth, 1980
(section of total work)
Photographs, acrylic, iron ore and coal on hardboard and card
Polyptych: 16 panels. each 20 x 24 inches (50.8 x 61 cm)
Photo: Conrad Atkinson
Courtesy Tate Gallery

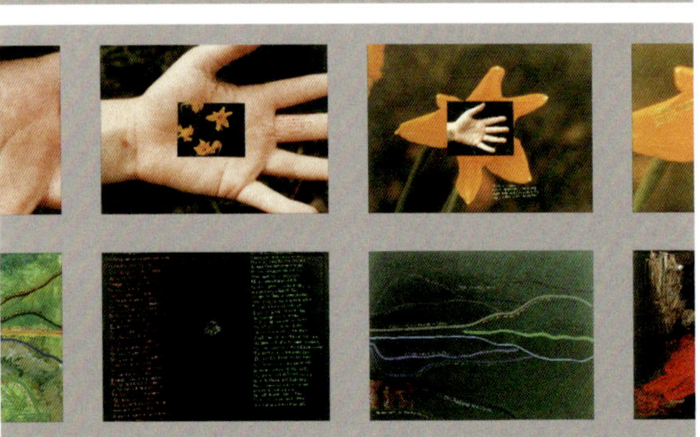

For West Cumbria, For Wordsworth, 1980
(section of total work)
Photographs, acrylic, iron ore and coal on hardboard and card
Polyptych: 16 panels. each 20 x 24 inches (50.8 x 61 cm)
Photo: Conrad Atkinson
Courtesy Tate Gallery

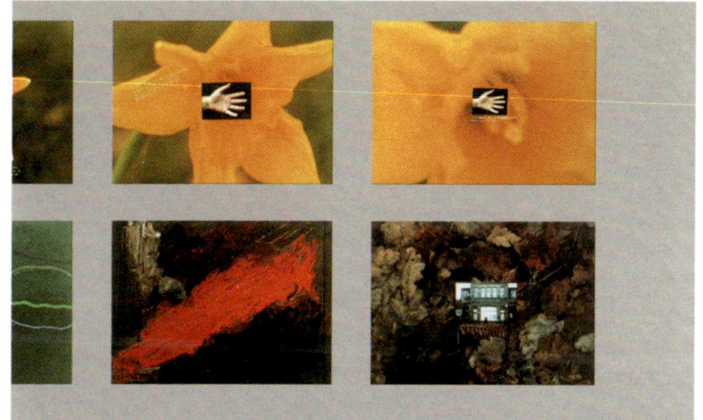

For West Cumbria, For Wordsworth, 1980
(section of total work)
Photographs, acrylic, iron ore and coal on hardboard and card
Polyptych: 16 panels. each 20 x 24 inches (50.8 x 61 cm)
Photo: Conrad Atkinson
Courtesy Tate Gallery

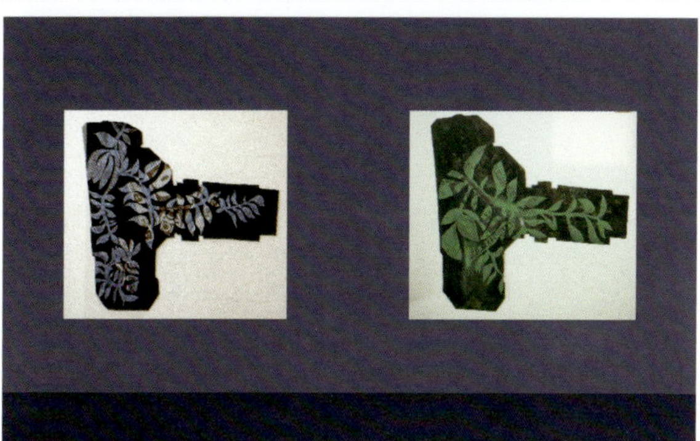

William Morris's Camera of the E.E.C., 1983
Acrylic and plastic on canvas (shaped)
48 x 48 inches (121.9 x 121.9 cm)
Photo: eeva-inkeri
Courtesy the Artist / Ronald Feldman Fine Arts

William Morris's Camera and Fertilizer Bag, 1983
Acrylic and plastic on canvas (shaped)
48 x 48 inches (121.9 x 121.9 cm)
Photo: eeva-inkeri
Courtesy the Artist / Ronald Feldman Fine Arts

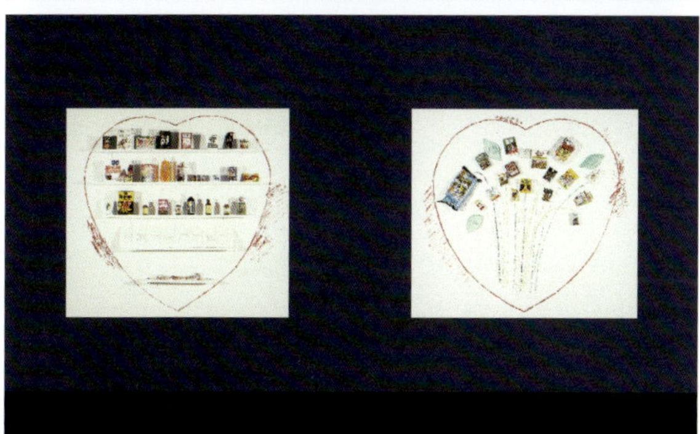

At the Heart of the Matter, 1981
(section of total work)
Assemblage
48 x 48 inches (121.9 x 121.9 cm)
Photo: Chris Davies
Courtesy Ronald Feldman Fine Arts

At the Heart of the Matter, 1981
(section of total work)
Assemblage
48 x 48 inches (121.9 x 121.9 cm)
Photo: Chris Davies
Courtesy Ronald Feldman Fine Arts

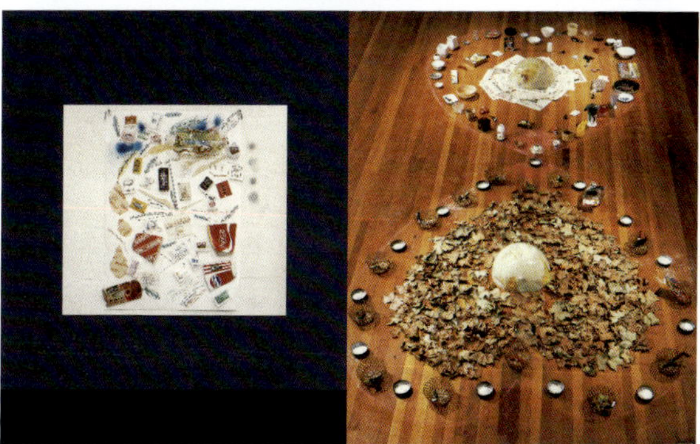

Energy, 1972
Assemblage: airline food, utensils
20 x 14 inches (50.8 x 35.6 cm)
Photo: Chris Davies
Courtesy Ronald Feldman Fine Arts

Developed and Underdeveloped Food (from *At the Heart of the Matter*), 1981
flour, bowls, foods, globe, leaves
14 x 6 feet (426.7 x 182.9 cm)
Photo: Chris Davies
Courtesy Institute of Contemporary Arts

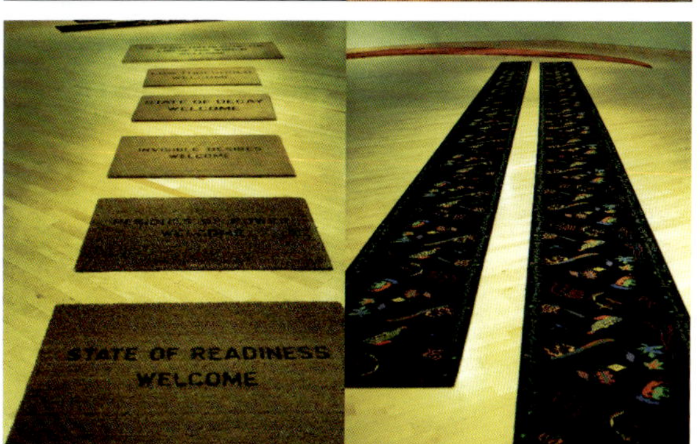

Critical Mats for Sellafield, 1986
Series of eight mats
36 x 48 inches (91.4 x 121.9 cm) each
Photo: Unknown
Courtesy Talbot Rice Art Gallery, Edinburgh University / Washington University, St. Louis

Equals, 1992
Wilton carpet
472½ x 27 inches (1200 x 69 cm)
Photo: Conrad Atkinson
Courtesy Syd Banks

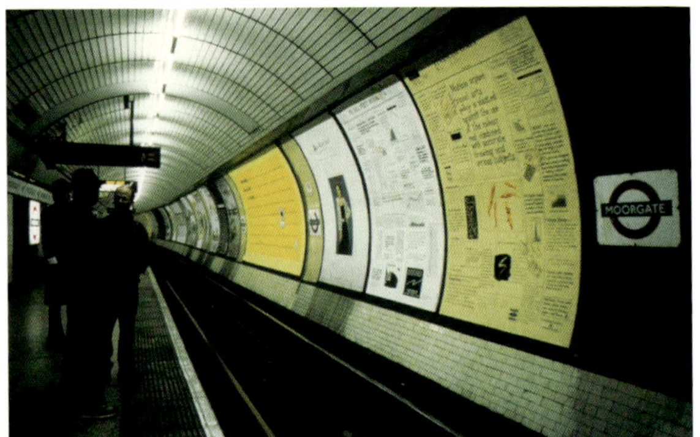

Wall Street Journal and Financial Times Posterworks, 1989
Litho print and acrylic on paper
60 x 120 inches (152.4 x 304.8 cm)
Photo: Art Angel Trust
Courtesy Art Angel Trust / Victoria and Albert Museum

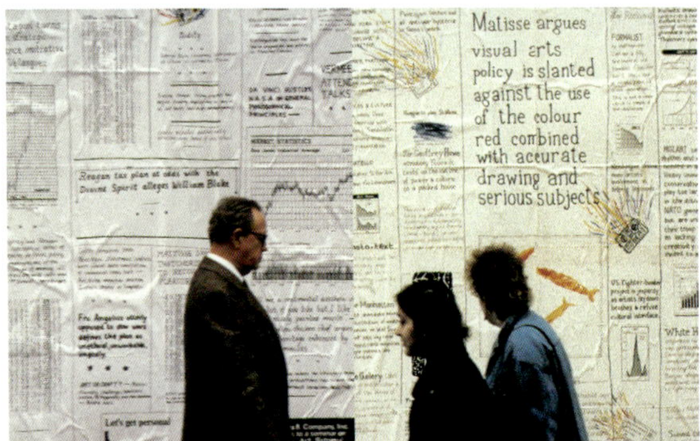

Wall Street Journal and Financial Times Posterworks, 1989
Litho print and acrylic on paper
60 x 120 inches (152.4 x 304.8 cm)
Photo: Art Angel Trust
Courtesy Art Angel Trust / Victoria and Albert Museum

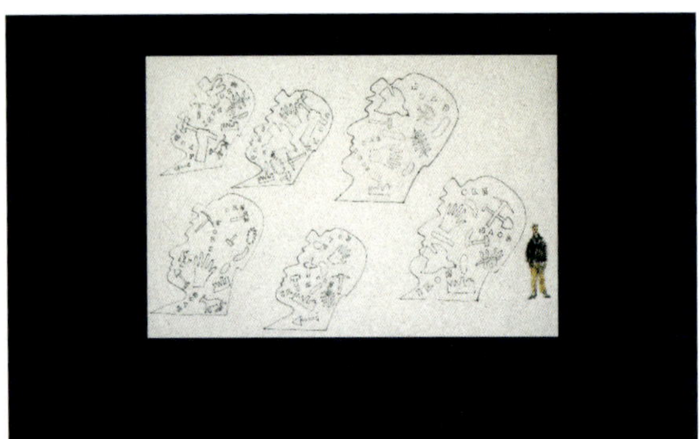

Drawing for The Miners' Monument, Cleator Moor, 1989
Pen and ink on Japanese handmade paper
20 x 30 inches (50.8 x 76.2 cm)
Photo: Guy Pawle
Courtesy Cleator Moor Town Council

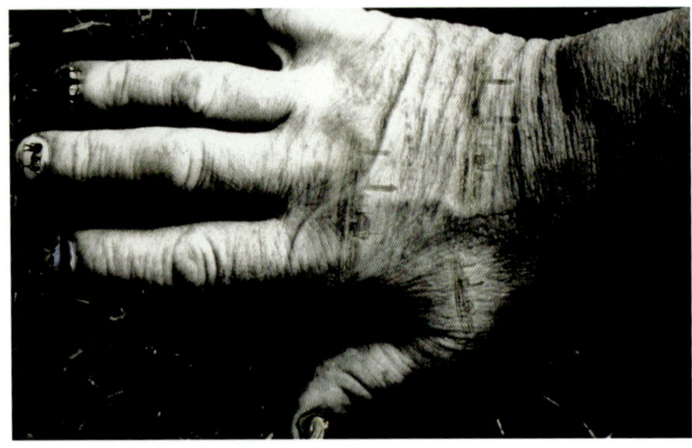

Hand (from *Landescape*), 1997
Unique digital print
image 15¼ × 21¾ inches (38.7 x 55.6 cm) paper 20 x 30 (50.8 x 76.2 cm)
Photo: Conrad Atkinson
Courtesy Northern Arts Board

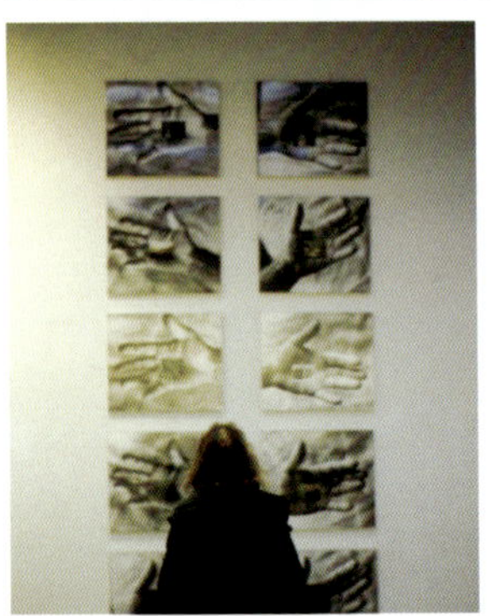

Sunset: for Shelley/Wordsworth, 1978
(section of total work)
10 photocollages framed in plexiglas boxes
20 x 24 inches (50.8 x 61 cm) each
Photo: Conrad Atkinson
Courtesy Berkeley Art Museum / Pacific Archive

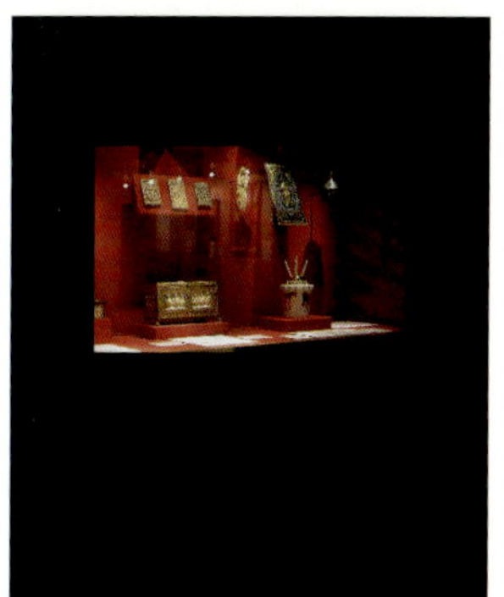

Ceramic Landmine with Fra Angelico Scar
(from installation in Courtauld Institute Gallery), 2002
On glaze transfer and gold luster on ceramic
approx. 7½ x 5 inches (19 x 12.7 cm)
Photo: Peter Carey
Courtesy Courtauld Institute of Art

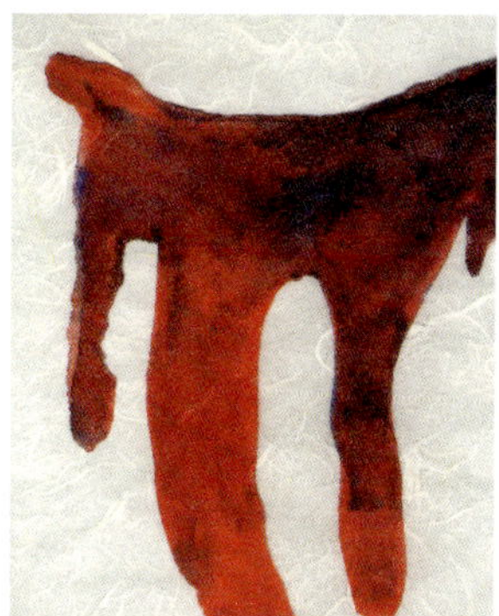

Fra Angelico Wound, 2002
Watercolor on handmade paper
6 x 6 inches (15.2 x 15.2 cm)
Photo: Peter Carey
Courtesy Courtauld Institute of Art

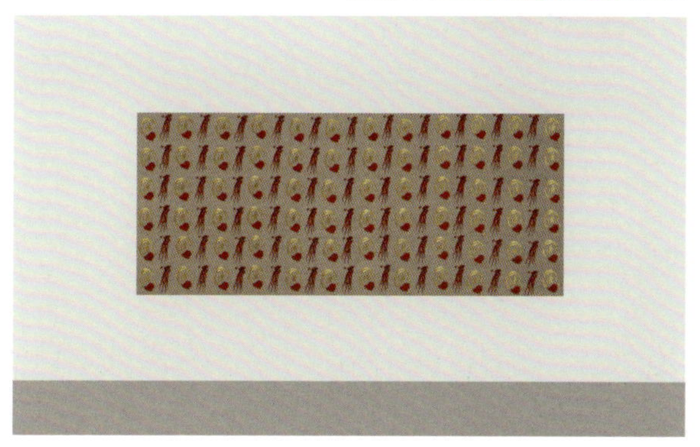

Vincent's Uncovered Ear and Euphonious Wound, 2004
(from a vase in the collection of the Metropolitan Museum of Art)
Metallic gold embroidery digitally produced on linen
25 x 66 inches (63.5 x 167.6 cm)
Photo: Alan Zinderman
Courtesy Ronald Feldman Fine Arts

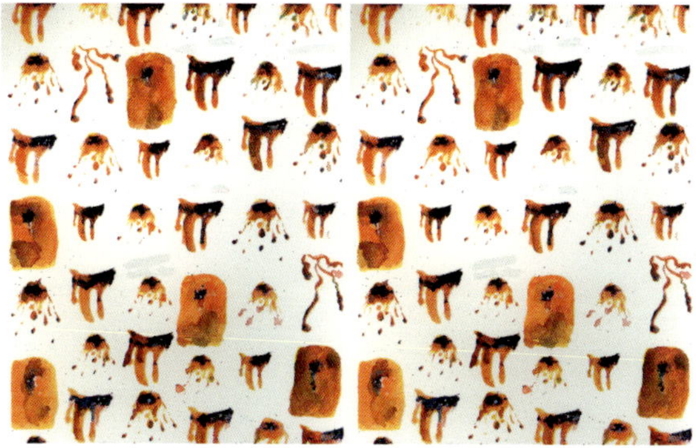

Scars and Wounds, 2002
(from the collections of the Metropolitan Museum of Art and the Courtauld Institute of Art)
Digitally printed wallpaper
25 x 144 inches (63.5 x 365.8 cm)
Photo: Conrad Atkinson
Courtesy White Box, New York

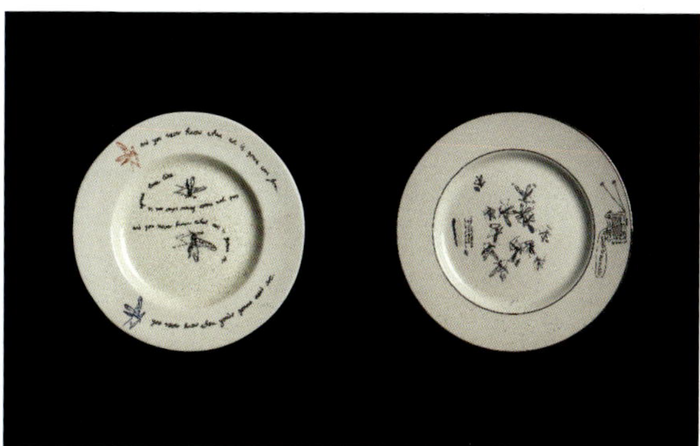

"You never know where art is gonna come from", 1996
Ceramic plate with on glaze and luster
10 inches (25.4 cm) diameter
Photo: Guy Pawle
Courtesy Ronald Feldman Fine Arts

No danger to the public, 1996
Ceramic plate with on glaze and luster
10 inches (25.4 cm) diameter
Photo: Guy Pawle
Courtesy Ronald Feldman Fine Arts

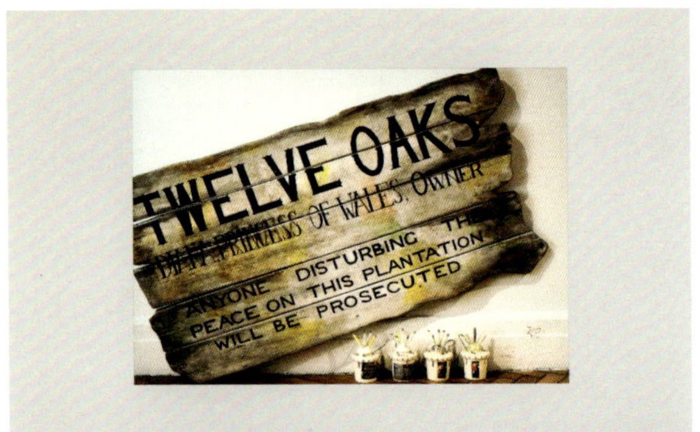

Souvenir for Diana, 1998
Wood, acrylic, ceramic landmines
60 x 96 inches (152.4 x 243.8 cm)
Photo: unknown
Courtesy Atlanta College of Art Gallery

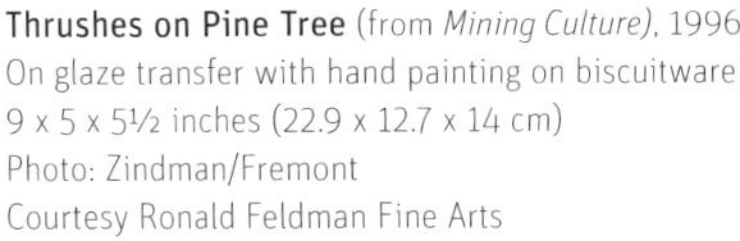
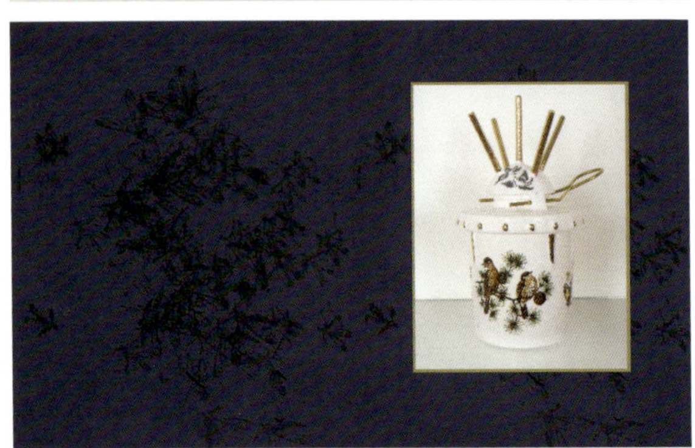

Thrushes on Pine Tree (from *Mining Culture*), 1996
On glaze transfer with hand painting on biscuitware
9 x 5 x 5½ inches (22.9 x 12.7 x 14 cm)
Photo: Zindman/Fremont
Courtesy Ronald Feldman Fine Arts

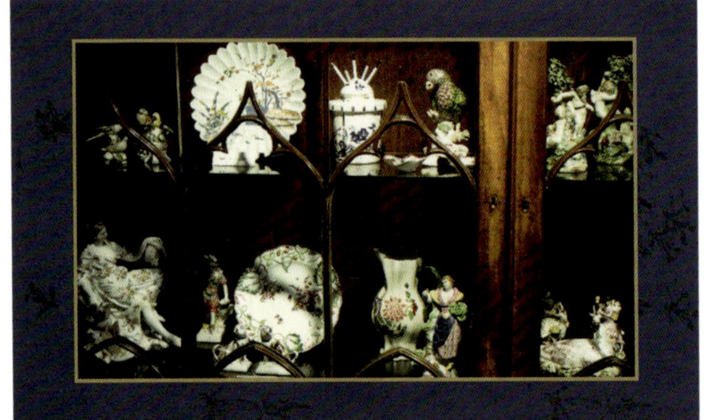

Mining Culture, 1995
(section of work: installation in Tullie House Museum Ceramic Collection)
Willow pattern Valmara ceramic landmine with on glaze
60 x 108 inches (152.4 x 274.3 cm)
Photo: Guy Pawle
Courtesy Tullie House Museum

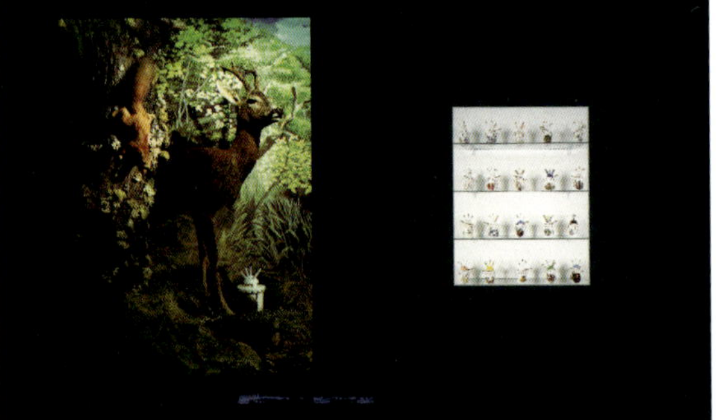

Mining Culture, 1996
(section of work: installation in *Stag at Bay* diorama)
Ceramic landmine
108 x 60 inches (274.3 x 152.4 cm)
Photo: Guy Pawle
Courtesy Tullie House Museum

Mining Culture, 1996
(section of work)
20 ceramic landmines
On glaze transfer with hand painting on biscuitware
9 x 5 x 5½ inches (22.9 x 12.7 x 14 cm) each
Photo: Zindman/Fremont
Courtesy Ronald Feldman Fine Arts

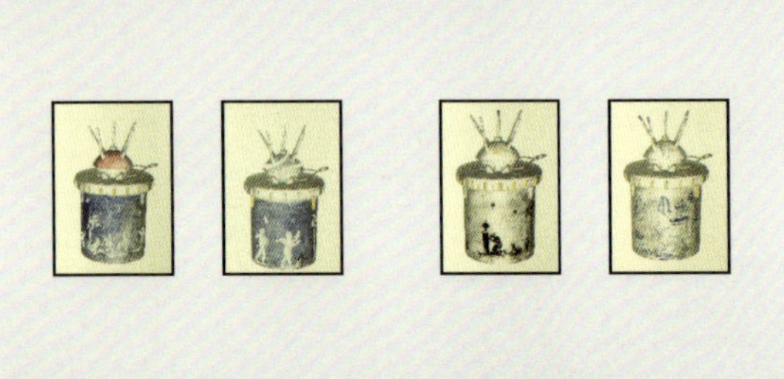

Landmine prints, 1997
Iris prints with watercolor on handmade paper
24 x 30 inches (61 x 76.2 cm) each
Photos: Conrad Atkinson
Courtesy the artist / Victoria and Albert Museum

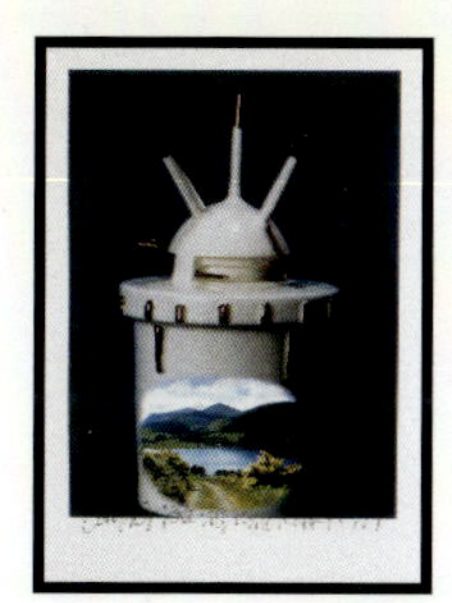 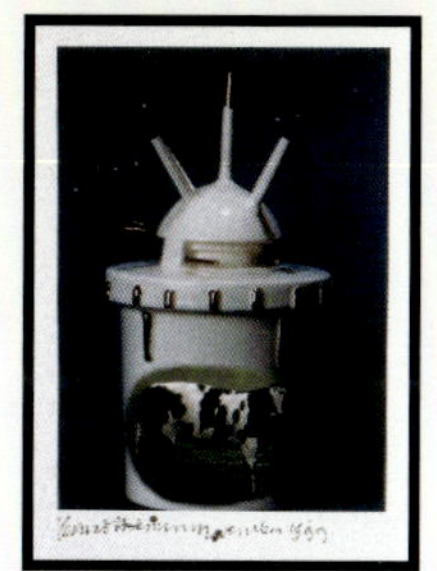

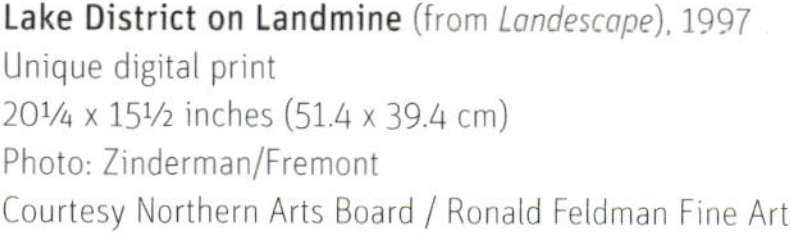

Lake District on Landmine (from *Landescape*), 1997
Unique digital print
20¼ x 15½ inches (51.4 x 39.4 cm)
Photo: Zinderman/Fremont
Courtesy Northern Arts Board / Ronald Feldman Fine Arts

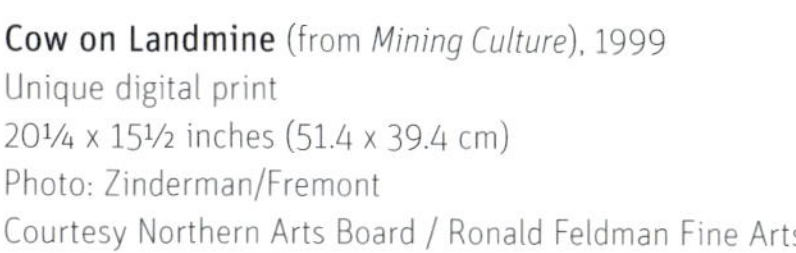

Cow on Landmine (from *Mining Culture*), 1999
Unique digital print
20¼ x 15½ inches (51.4 x 39.4 cm)
Photo: Zinderman/Fremont
Courtesy Northern Arts Board / Ronald Feldman Fine Arts

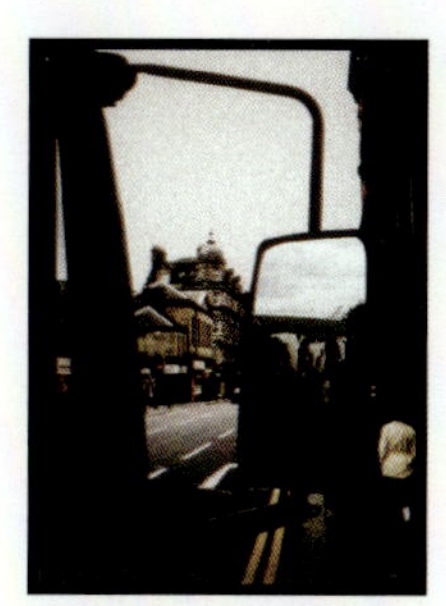 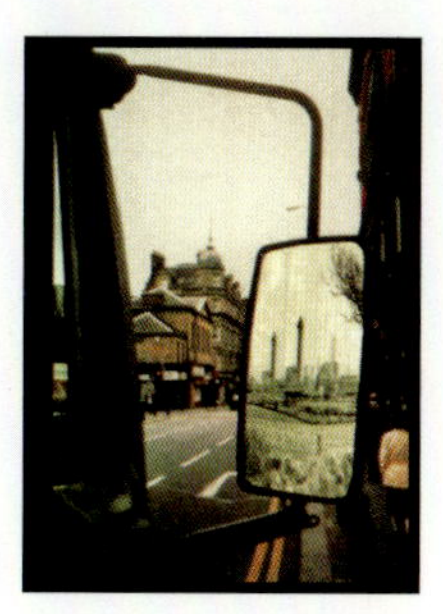

Cows in Bus Mirror (from *Landescape*), 1997
Unique digital print
image 20¼ x 15½ inches (51.4 x 39.4 cm)
Photo: Zindman/Fremont
Courtesy Northern Arts Board

Sellafield in Bus Mirror (from *Landescape*), 1995
Unique digital print
image 20¼ x 15½ inches (51.4 x 39.4 cm)
Photo: Zindman/Fremont
Courtesy Northern Arts Board / Ronald Feldman Fine Arts

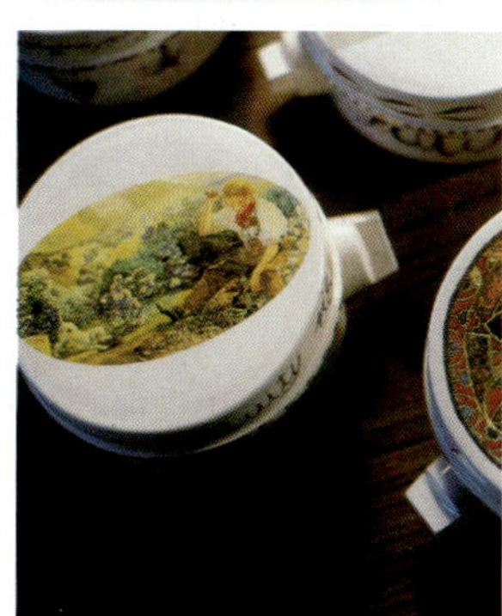

Landmines (installation in Walker Art Gallery/First Liverpool Biennial), 1999
Ceramic personnel mine (Chinese copy of Russian mine) with on glaze print of images
from Walker Art Gallery collection
9 x 9 inches (22.9 x 22.9 cm) each
Photo: Conrad Atkinson
Courtesy Margaret Harrison

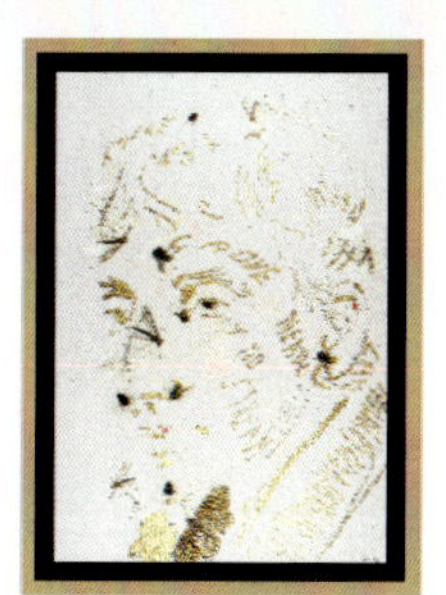 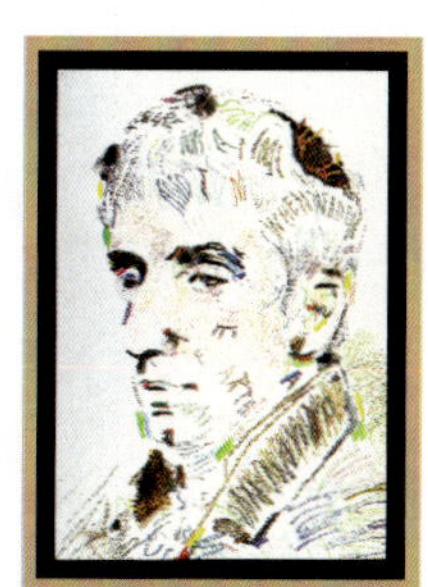

William Wordsworth I, 2003
Oil pastel and inkjet print
30 x 22 inches (76.2 x 55.9 cm)
Photo: Alex Black
Courtesy The Wordsworth Trust

William Wordsworth II, 2003
Oil pastel and inkjet print
30 x 22 inches (76.2 x 55.9 cm)
Photo: Alex Black
Courtesy The Wordsworth Trust

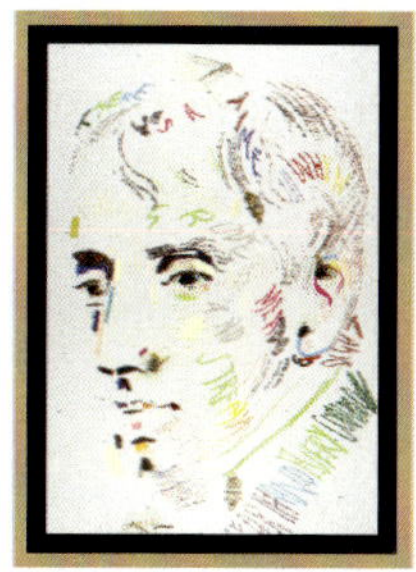 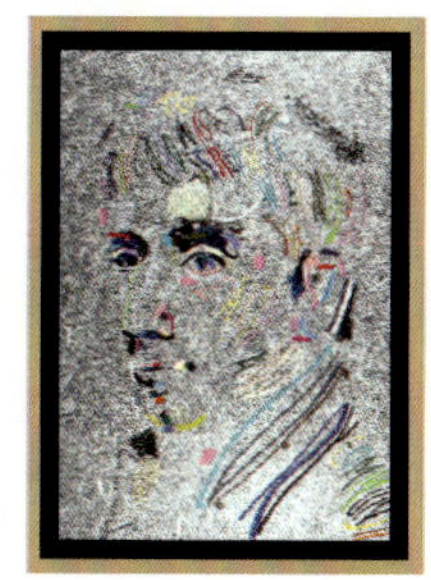

William Wordsworth III, 2003
Oil pastel and inkjet print
30 x 22 inches (76.2 x 55.9 cm)
Photo: Alex Black
Courtesy The Wordsworth Trust

William Wordsworth IV, 2003
Oil pastel and inkjet print
30 x 22 inches (76.2 x 55.9 cm)
Photo: Alex Black
Courtesy The Wordsworth Trust

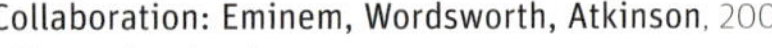

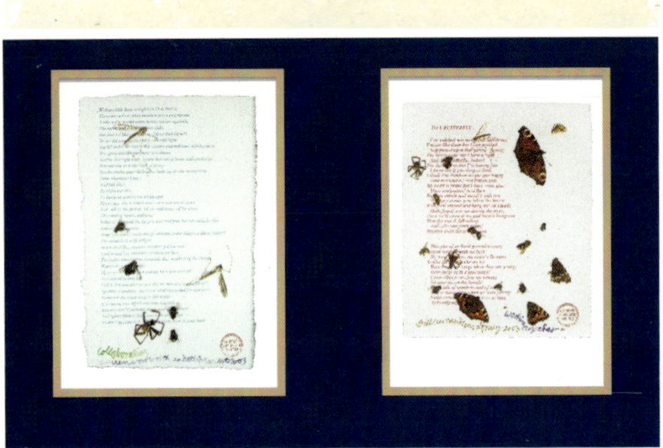

Collaboration: Eminem, Wordsworth, Atkinson, 2003
Inkjet on handmade paper
11 x 8 inches (27.9 x 20.3 cm)
Photo: Alex Black
Courtesy The Wordworth Trust

Working together: Bill, Kurt and Conrad, 2003
Inkjet on handmade paper
11 x 8 inches (27.9 x 20.3 cm)
Photo: Alex Black
Courtesy The Wordworth Trust

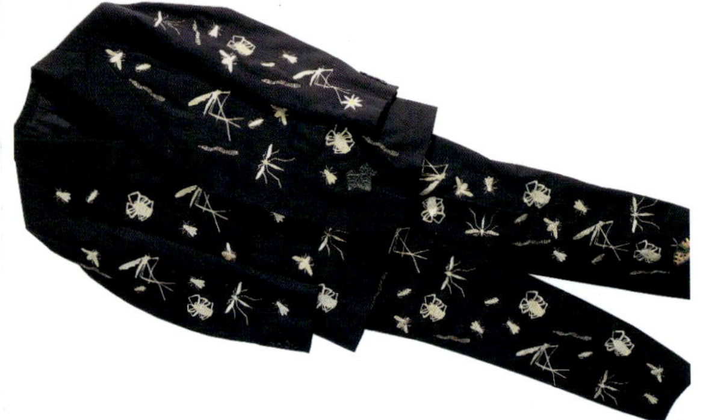

William Wordsworth's Suit, 2003
Colored and gold machine embroidery on wool suit
24 x 60 inches (61 x 152.4 cm)
Photo: Alex Black
Courtesy The Wordworth Trust

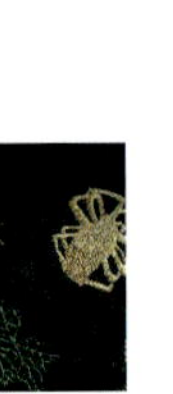

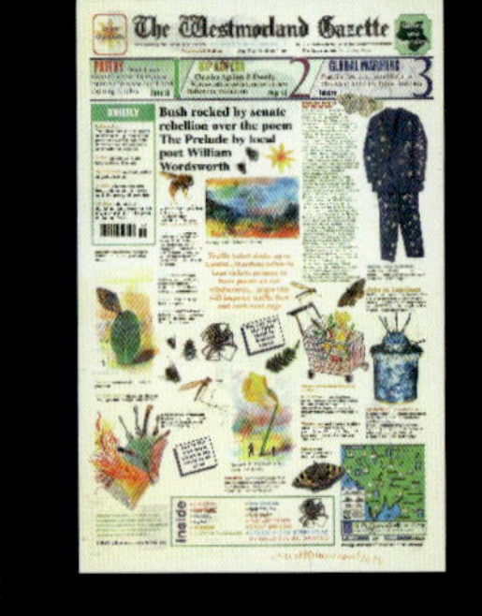

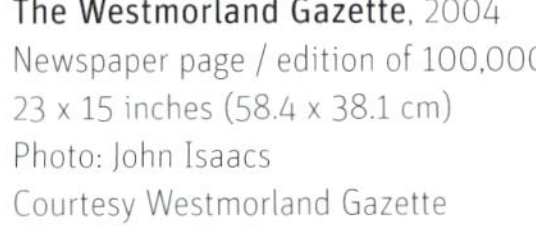

William Wordsworth's Suit, 2003
(detail)
Colored and gold machine embroidery on wool suit
24 x 60 inches (61 x 152.4 cm)
Photo: Alex Black
Courtesy The Wordworth Trust

The Westmorland Gazette, 2004
Newspaper page / edition of 100,000
23 x 15 inches (58.4 x 38.1 cm)
Photo: John Isaacs
Courtesy Westmorland Gazette

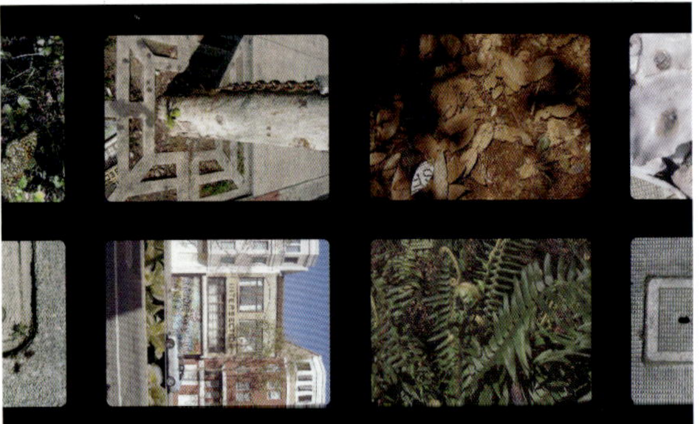

Weeds: Beneath the Street / The Beach, 2005
(section of total work)
Pigment prints
Polyptych: 16 panels, 10 x 17 inches (25.4 x 43.2 cm) each
Photo: Scott Chernis
Courtesy Intersection for the Arts

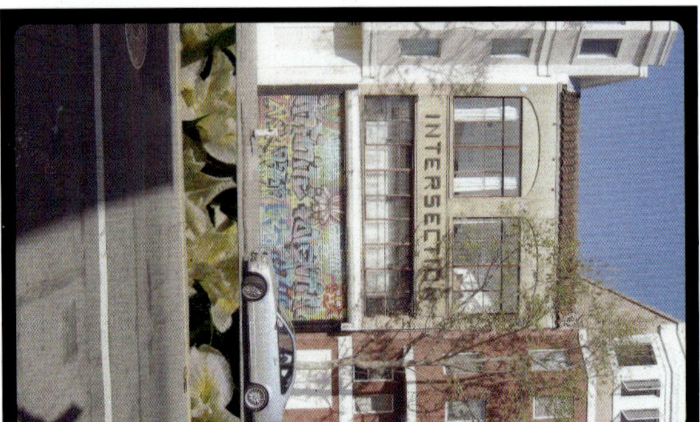

Weeds: Beneath the Paving Stones / The Beach, 2005
(detail)
Pigment prints
Polyptych: 16 panels, 10 x 17 inches (25.4 x 43.2 cm) each
Photo: Scott Chernis
Courtesy Intersection for the Arts